QUANTUM REVOLUTION I

THE BREAKTHROUGH

Vignettes in Physics
A Series by G. Venkataraman

Published
The Many Phases of Matter
Why Are Things the Way They Are?
Bose and His Statistics
Chandrasekhar and His Limit
A Hot Story
At the Speed of Light
The Quantum Revolution (vols.)
1. The Breakthrough
2. QED: The Jewel of Physics
3. What is Reality?
Raman and His Effect
Bhabha and his Magnificent Obsessions
Saha and His Formula

Forthcoming
The Big and The Small

Vignettes in Physics

QUANTUM REVOLUTION . I

THE BREAKTHROUGH

G. Venkataraman

Universities Press

Quantum Revolution 1
UNIVERSITIES PRESS (INDIA) PRIVATE LIMITED

Registered Office
3-6-747/1/A and 3-6-754/1, Himayatnagar,
Hyderabad 500 029 Telangana, India
E-mail: info@universitiespress.com

Distributed by
Orient Blackswan Private Limited

Registered Office
3-6-752, Himayatnagar, Hyderabad 500 029 Telangana, India

Other Offices
Bengaluru, Bhopal, Chennai, Guwahati,
Hyderabad, Jaipur, Kolkata, Lucknow, Mumbai,
New Delhi, Noida, Patna, Visakhapatnam

First Published 1994
Reprinted 1997, 2008, 2010, 2014, 2017, 2020

ISBN: 978 81 7371 002 5

Laser typeset at
Alliance Phototypesetters, Pondicherry – 605 013

501702

Printed at
Graphica Printers & Binders
Hyderabad- 5000 013

Published by
Universities Press (India) Private Limited
3-6-747/1/A and 3-6-754/1, Himayatnagar,
Hyderabad 500 029, Telangana, India

Contents

Preface

To the adult reader

This book and others in this series written by me are inspired by the memory of my son Suresh who left this world soon after completing school. Suresh and I often used to discuss physics. It was then that I introduced him to the celebrated *Feynman Lectures.*

Hans Bethe has described Feynman as the most original scientist of this century. To that perhaps may be added the statement that Feynman was also the most scintillating teacher of physics in this century.

The Feynman Lectures are great but they are at the textbook level and meant for serious reading. Moreover, they are a bit expensive, at least for the average Indian student. It seemed to me that there was scope for small books on diverse topics in physics which would stimulate interest, making at least some of our young students take up later a serious study of physics and reach for the Feynman as well as the Landau classics.

Small books inevitably remind me of Gamow's famous volumes. They were wonderful, and stimulated me to no small extent. Times have changed, physics has grown and we clearly need other books, though written in the same spirit.

In attempting these volumes, I have chosen a style of my own. I have come across many books on popular science where elaborate sentences often tend to obscure the scientific essence. I have therefore opted for simple English, and I don't make any apologies for it. If a simple style was good enough for the great Enrico Fermi, it is also good enough for me. I have also employed at times a chatty style. This is deliberate. Feynman uses this with consummate skill, and I have decided to follow in his footsteps (whether I have succeeded or not, is for readers to say). This book is meant to be read for fun and excitement. It is a book you can even lie down in bed and read. Without going to sleep I hope!

Naturally I have some basic objectives, the most important of which is to stimulate the curiosity of the reader. Here and there the reader may fail to grasp some details, and in fact I have deliberately pitched things a bit high on occasions. But if the reader is able to experience at least in some small measure the *excitement* of science, then my purpose would have been achieved. Apart from excitement, I have also tried to convey that although we might draw boundaries and try to compartmentalise Nature into different subjects, she herself knows no such boundaries. So we can always start anywhere, take a random walk and catch a good glimpse of Nature's glory. Where she is concerned, all topics are 'fashionable'. There is today an unnecessary polarisation of the young towards subjects that are supposed to be fashionable. To my mind this is unhealthy, and I have tried to counter it.

This series is essentially meant for the curious. With humility, I would like to regard it as some sort of a 'Junior Feynman Series', if one might call it that. With much love, and sadness, it is dedicated to the memory of Suresh who inspired it.

To the young reader

Among the living species man is the newest, having made his appearance less than a million years ago. By sheer intelligence he has established his supremacy here on Earth, and is all set to venture to the planets beyond.

The ascent of man is a stirring saga, with many exciting landmarks en route. Man discovered fire, invented the wheel, mastered agriculture, developed languages (and used them to create literature), discovered art and also learnt to probe Nature. In addition he pondered deeply forming notions of space, time, reality, and "the world out there". But all this accumulated knowledge was of little avail when in the early part of this century he began probing inside the atom. For a couple of decades there was a heavy cloud of confusion and mystery until a few daring young men came along and swept it all away by stunning discoveries. There was a sigh of relief when this happened but soon it was realised that the new mechanics, quantum mechanics as it came to be called, was bewildering in its philosophical implications. So far-reaching are they that the discovery of quantum mechanics is often hailed as the greatest revolution in human thought. This volume, the first in a series of three, seeks to capture the drama of this supreme achievement.

The breakthrough referred to above occurred in a short span of five to six years. Thereafter most of the leading personalities turned to an exploration of the new world of subatomic particles (which is an epic story in itself). But in the process, certain crucial issues relating to matter and radiation got sorted out (did they really?); this story will be narrated in Part II (*QED: The Jewel of Physics*).

The dust raised in the twenties at the time of the discovery of quantum mechanics has not completely settled down because profound thinkers, though barely a handful in number, kept going back to the intriguing questions which surfaced at that time. It all boiled down to this: *What exactly is physical reality?* While the final word on this fascinating subject is yet to be said, many subtle aspects not earlier appreciated have come to light. This gripping tale is reserved for Part III (*What is Reality?*).

Quantum mechanics is not exactly an easy subject, especially when it comes to concepts. But modern physics revolves around quantum mechanics, and there is no escape from it. Don't feel disheartened and quit if you find this book a bit tough during the first reading. Try a few times, and the going may get easier. Good luck, and pleasant reading!

Acknowledgements

As earlier, I have received considerable advice and suggestions from Professors V. Balakrishnan and N. Mukunda, to both of whom my grateful thanks. Mr. G. Athithan kindly supplied the computer-generated figures of electron probability density reproduced in the text. Mr. A. Ratnakar has made me even more indebted to him than before by helping me gain access to papers published over half a century ago. Mrs. G. Naga Nirmala had a difficult job this time in preparing the manuscript, having to contend with more than the usual crop of equations. But she rose to the occasion admirably. The Publisher has been particularly patient this time, allowing me generously to exceed the usual page limit.

G.VENKATARAMAN

1 *The Only Mystery*

> Historically, the electron was thought to behave like a particle and then it was found that in many respects it behaved like a wave. So it really behaves like neither. Now we have given up. We say: It is like neither.
>
> *Feynman*

I am going to tell you the story of quantum mechanics by using what in movies is referred to as the flashback technique. In other words, I shall first tell you what QM is all about, how it works and so forth, and then take you back to the early part of this century, to unfold the events as they occurred.

The best way of introducing QM is via what Feynman calls the "only mystery". As he so aptly puts it, "We cannot make the mystery go away by 'explaining' how it works." All that can be done is to tell you how it works; that is the way QM is!

The mystery is best appreciated by considering three experiments similar in concept but different in details. When we compare the outcomes of the three experiments we will get a feel for the stunning difference between classical mechanics (CM) and quantum mechanics (QM).

1.1 An experiment with a machine gun

We start with a machine gun that sprays bullets; but being of poor quality, the gun fires the bullets over a range of angles. The bullets are aimed at a target screen placed some distance away, and on arrival get embedded (without breaking into fragments) into a soft board. Though our gun is erratic as far as direction is concerned, it maintains a steady firing rate.

There is no great fun in simply firing bullets at a screen and so let us try to do something interesting. We place in the path of the bullets an aperture screen with two holes as shown in Fig. 1.1. Now we are all set. We first close hole 2 and fire for five minutes. We then stop, replace the target screen with a fresh one, open hole 2 and close hole 1. We fire

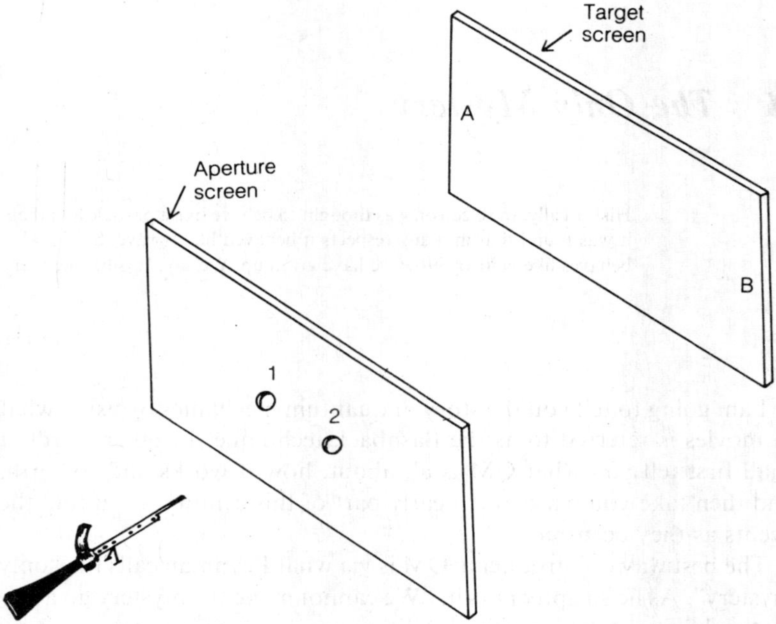

Fig. 1.1 Schematic drawing illustrating the machine gun experiment.

again for five minutes and stop. Once more we replace the bullet-ridden screen with a fresh one and get ready to fire; but this time we leave both the holes open. The firing begins and is kept up for five minutes. We are now ready to take a break and mull over the results.

Figure 1.2 shows how the three target screens would appear. There is nothing tremendously exciting, the pattern on screen 3 simply being a superposition of screens 1 and 2. To make the whole thing a bit more quantitative, we consider slices as shown in the figure and measure the distribution of bullets along the equatorial strips—see also Box 1.1. We then comprehensively represent the results as in Fig. 1.3; this is a signature pattern that we will use to visualise the results of all the experiments.

Our next experiment is again with our erratic machine gun, but this time we put vertical slits in the aperture screen instead of circular holes. This is merely to keep the experiment closely in line with others to be tried later. To get back to the present experiment with bullets and

Box 1.1 Here is a primer on probability distributions, at least to the extent needed for this chapter. We start with figure (a) which shows a schematic of bullet marks. We then mark a strip as shown, and then subdivide the strip into cells. Counting the number of bullet marks in the various cells, we then plot a histogram as in (b). The area under the histogram corresponds to the total number of bullet marks in the strip. If the number of such marks is sufficiently large, one can choose finer cells, as in (c), for plotting the histogram. In the limit, when the cell size is infinitesimally small, the histogram goes over into a smooth curve as in (d). If the area under this smooth curve is unity, then the curve represents a probability distribution.

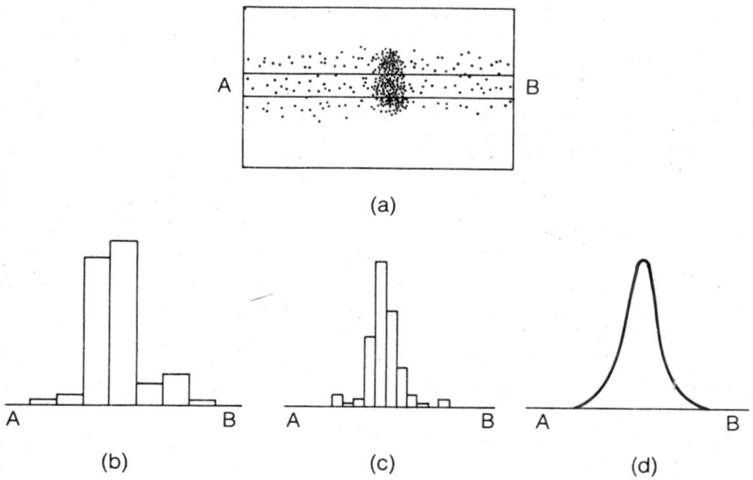

vertical slits, the results are identical to those shown in Fig. 1.3, which of course is to be expected.

1.2 An experiment with light

We now switch to a light source, and the experimental arrangement used is shown in Fig. 1.4. Instead of a target screen, we have a photographic film. As before, we make three tries; first we expose a film with only slit 1 open, then with only slit 2 open and finally with both the slits open. The developed films show the illuminated regions and would present the appearances shown in Fig. 1.5. There are instruments to measure the intensity of the light received in the different regions of the film, and using these we obtain results as in Fig. 1.6.

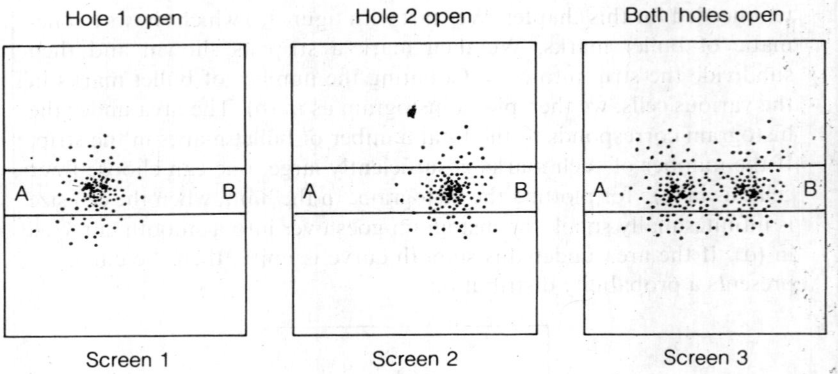

Fig. 1.2 Appearance of the target screen showing the spray of bullets in the case of the three experiments discussed in the text.

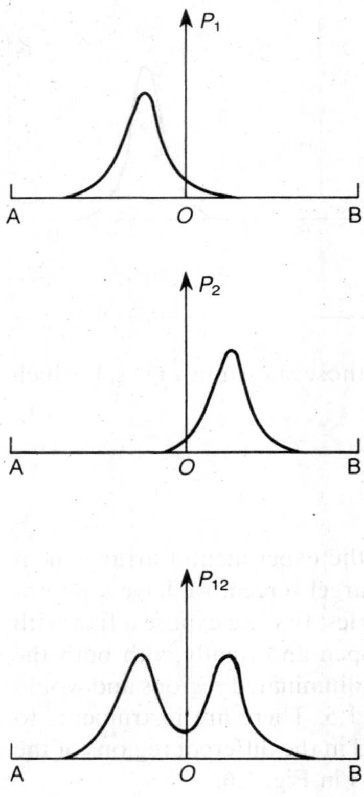

Fig. 1.3 Plotted here are the bullet distributions observed along the equatorial line AB (see Fig. 1.2) in the three cases. Observe $P_{12} = (P_1 + P_2)$.

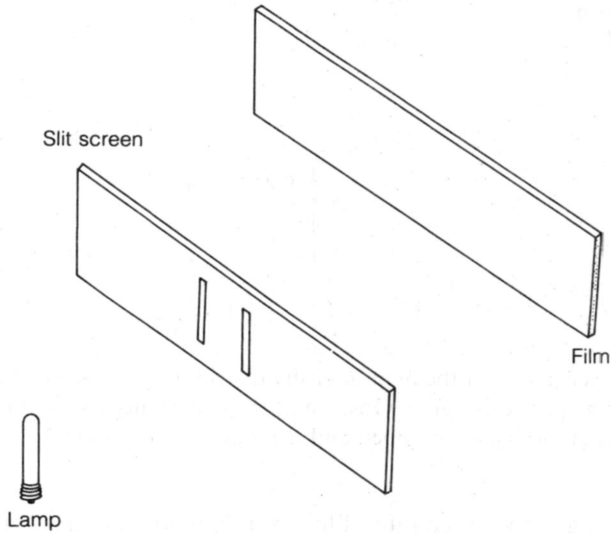

Fig. 1.4 A schematic of the standard experimental arrangement used for demonstrating the interference of light caused by a double slit.

The results of Figs. 1.5 and 1.6 are quite familiar. When only one slit is open there is no interference but when both are open, there is a characteristic interference pattern with several maxima and minima. That interference is possible with light beams has been known for centuries, and in fact it was due to this that Newton's corpuscular

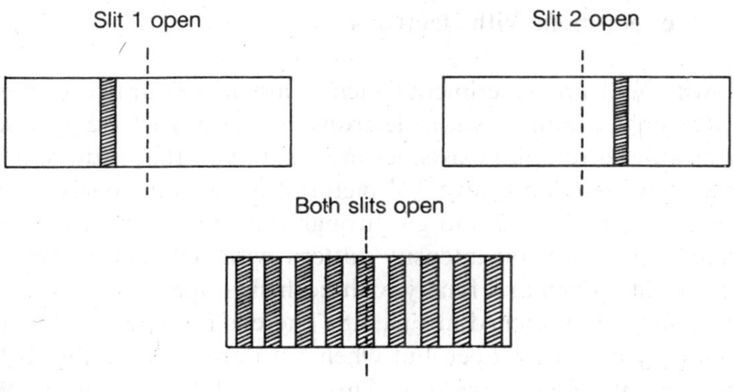

Fig. 1.5 Appearance of the photographic plates in the optical experiment, corresponding to the three cases mentioned in the text.

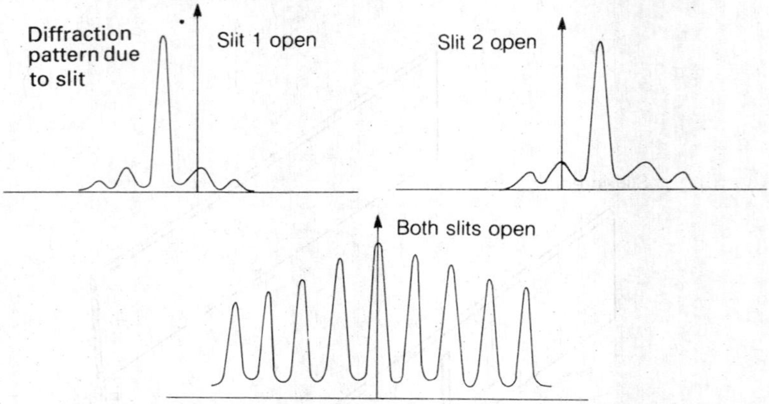

Fig. 1.6 Schematic of the light intensity distribution across the films illustrated in the previous figure. Observe (i) the occurrence of the interference pattern when both slits are open and (ii) that $I_{12} \neq (I_1 + I_2)$.

theory of light had to go into oblivion. In passing, observe the following: If the light intensities (see Fig. 1.6) are given by I_1, I_2, and I_{12} in the three cases respectively, then I_{12} is not equal to $(I_1 + I_2)$. This of course is characteristic of interference patterns.

All that I have said so far is quite familiar. The bullet experiment and the light beam experiment yield quite different results, though performed in a somewhat similar manner. But then, bullets are particles and light is made up of waves; and one knows that interference is possible only with waves. Well, get set for a jolt!

1.3 An experiment with electrons

On now to our third experiment which is rather like our first one except that we replace bullets with electrons. In case you are wondering whether an electron gun exists, let me assure you that it does; in fact, without it we wouldn't have TV pictures! So we put together an arrangement as in Fig. 1.7 and go through our familiar routine, i.e., we first record the electron intensity pattern with only slit 1 open, then with only slit 2 open and finally with both slits open.

The results are sketched in Fig. 1.8. There is nothing striking about it when only one slit is open but when both are open, lo and behold, we get an interference pattern! This is absolutely stunning. When J.J. Thomson discovered the electron in 1897, everyone thought it was a particle. In fact J.J. made electrons fly like bullets, got them moving

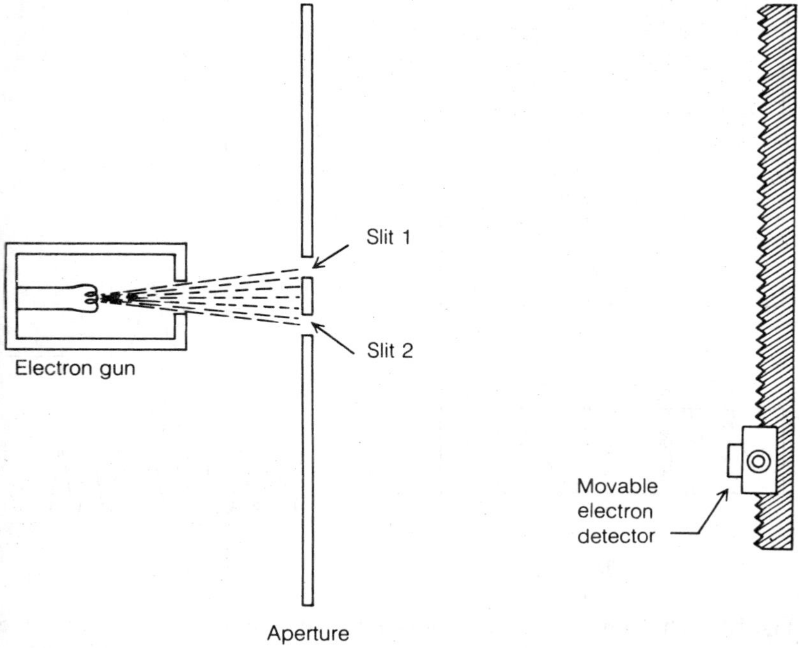

Fig. 1.7 Schematic of the electron gun experiment. In principle, the arrangement is quite similar to that in Fig. 1.1 except for the target screen which is replaced with a more sophisticated arrangement. The latter could be anything from a photographic film to an electronic detector array. For our purpose, these details are not important.

on curved paths and so forth. How come now the electron behaves sometimes like a wave and sometimes like a particle? That matter can behave both like particles as well as waves was first suggested by de Broglie in 1924. More about de Broglie waves later, but let us get back to Fig. 1.8 where we find the electron to behave like a particle when only one slit is open and to behave like a wave when both the slits are open. How does it know when to do what?

1.4 Enter spies

Our curiosity aroused, we probe this business a bit further. This time we are smart and employ secret agents to tell us which way the electrons are going. Interference occurs in the case of light because the same wave

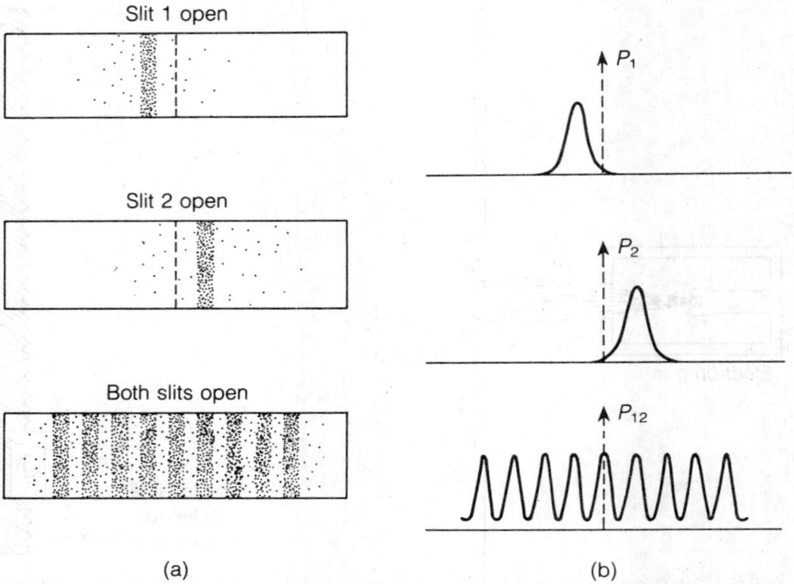

Fig. 1.8 This summarises the results obtained with the electron gun in the three different cases. (a) shows the corresponding spray patterns of the electrons while (b) shows the distribution curves. The striking feature is the interference pattern produced when both slits are open.

goes through both the slits. Interference also occurs in the case of electrons. Does it mean the same electron goes through both the slits? How is that possible? Does the electron secretly break up and then reassemble once it is past the slits? Questions, questions, questions! Let us see if our secret agents can help in finding the answers.

We have two sleuths A and B who take up positions near slits 1 and 2; the third one C is near the detector array—see Fig. 1.9. They all have walkie-talkies (hand-held transmitter-receivers). The electron gun fires at a rather slow (but steady) rate enabling observations to be made conveniently. The conversation between the agents proceeds as follows:

Agent A: Alpha to Charlie, Alpha to Charlie. An electron has just passed slit 1 and is headed your way. Over.

Agent C: Charlie to Alpha. Electron just arrived here at the detector array and has been registered in detector number 12. Over.

Agent B: Beta to Charlie, Beta to Charlie. An electron just slipped through slit 2. Over.

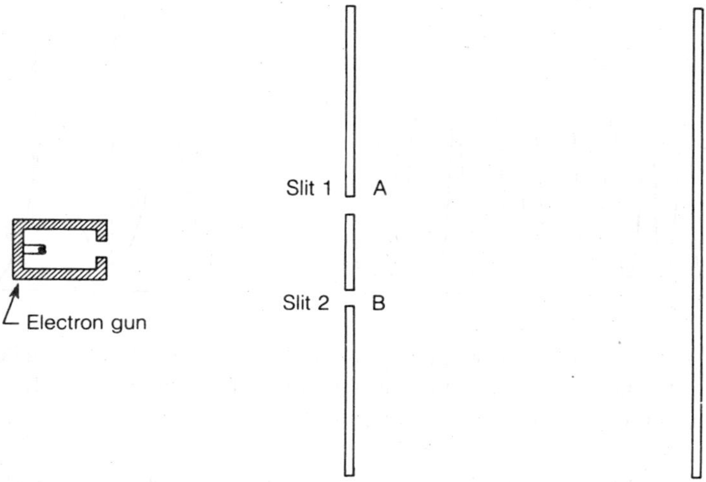

Fig. 1.9 This shows a schematic of the electron diffraction experiment, with observers present near the slits to spot the electrons as they go through. This of course is a rather figurative way of presenting the whole thing. What one really has in mind are observers looking through illuminated microscopes of the type to be described in Fig. 1.11.

Agent C: Charlie to Beta. The electron you spotted has just arrived at detector 7. Over.

This goes on for some time till the agents think they have sufficient data. They then meet, pool information and plot graphs. They find the results as in Fig. 1.10.

The results are strange. Both slits are open and therefore as per Fig. 1.8 one expects the detector array to show an interference pattern. But, instead, one has a result similar to the bullet case. Does this mean we goofed earlier? Let us repeat the experiment, i.e., we keep both slits open and record the pattern, but without any observers. We get back the old interference pattern (Fig. 1.8), which means we did not do anything wrong then. Maybe our agents were unreliable; so let us change the entire gang, introducing new spies say D, E, and F. Once again, when the observers are present the interference pattern is washed out. No matter how many times we repeat the experiment, we get consistent results—*interference if there are NO observers, and NO interference pattern if there are observers. This is confirmed.*

Never in human history had such a thing been encountered before. I mean who ever heard of Nature behaving one way when you are looking

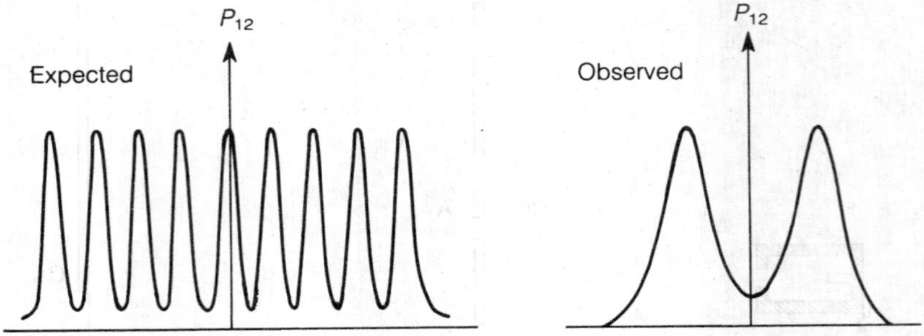

Fig. 1.10 Plotted here schematically are the expected and the observed curves for P_{12} in the experiment corresponding to Fig. 1.9. The interference pattern is washed out, even though both the slits are open.

and in a completely different way when you are not looking? And yet that is precisely what happens, at least in the world of electrons. It seems that when we observe we disturb whatever it is that we are trying to observe.

As Heisenberg once commented about the two-slit experiment:

> This is a very strange result, since it seems to indicate that the observation plays a decisive role in the event and that reality varies, depending upon whether we observe it or not.

1.5 The uncertainty principle

Heisenberg whom I have just been quoting was the first to call attention to the fact that measurements can disturb. He arrived at this conclusion by trying to imagine how one would observe the position of an electron. Since the electron is very tiny, clearly a microscope is necessary to see it. Of course such a microscope that would enable us to see the electron directly does not exist even today, but back in 1926 when Heisenberg first thought about the problem he simply asked: What happens when one looks through a hypothetical microscope in order to measure the position of an electron?

Let us now closely examine this measurement process. Say a particle is placed under a microscope as in Fig. 1.11(a). In the eyepiece there is a graduated screen—see Fig. 1.11(b)—and using this, one can say where the particle is. The closer the grid lines on the graduated screen, the more accurately one can read off the position of the particle. We assume there is no limit to the accuracy with which we can read off

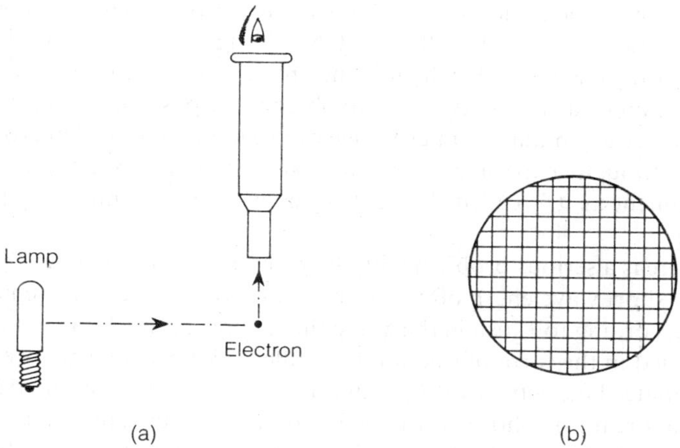

Fig. 1.11 Observation of the position of an electron using a microscope. (a) shows a schematic of the arrangement. To see the electron through the eyepiece, illumination is necessary. In the eyepiece (b), there is a graduated grid which may be used to read off the position of the electron. The grid can be made as accurate as one wants. However, the act of illumination disturbs the electron. As a result, what we actually see is not what we set out to see.

from this graduated screen. But other errors in determining the position are possible, and they arise on account of the very nature of light itself.

When we look through the eyepiece, we will see the particle only if it is illuminated. The light falling on the particle bounces off, and when it reaches our eye an image is formed. It is from this image we get an idea of where exactly the particle is. Now light is made up of waves and if we use light of wavelength λ, then, using classical optics, it can be shown that there is an unavoidable fuzziness in the image. Consequently, there would be an error, of the order λ, in determining the position of the particle. If we denote this positional error by Δx, then all I am saying is that $\Delta x \sim \lambda$($\sim$ means *of the order of*).

There is nothing mysterious about this fuzziness or error Δx. Suppose we have a metre scale graduated in centimetres. Then clearly, the length can be measured accurately only to about 5 mm or so. If the scale is graduated in millimetres, the accuracy of measurement can be improved to about 0.5 mm. A similar limitation of accuracy is well-known in optics and is called the *optical resolution*. To accurately determine the position of the electron, we obviously want as high a resolution as possible, which means λ should be as small as possible. For visible radiation, $\lambda \sim 5000$ Å (1 Å = 1 angstrom = 10^{-8} cm) but for gamma rays, $\lambda \sim 0.1$ Å, which being small can lead to good accuracy in position measurements. Thus, to observe the position of electrons we should use a gamma-ray microscope rather than an optical microscope. In his thought experiment or *gedanken* (German word for thought) experiment as it is called, Heisenberg considered a gamma-ray microscope.

There is a serious problem with the gamma-ray microscope. True the use of short wavelength offers better resolution but we must remember that according to Einstein (he made this discovery in 1905) light energy is carried in the form of quanta now called *photons*. So when we try to illuminate the electron with gamma rays, we are really bombarding it with a stream of photons. In 1923, Compton discovered that when a photon collides with an electron, it imparts momentum besides disturbing the position. Thus to see and measure the position of the electron we must illuminate it; but the moment we shine light on the electron it is disturbed and moves away from the position it was originally in and whose coordinates we are trying to measure.

What it all boils down to is that the moment we employ agents A and B to see which slit the electron sneaks through, we are dealing with an entirely different situation where the *very act of seeing disturbs.* So we reconclle ourselves, perhaps reluctantly, to the following: If we try to watch the electrons going through the slits we get one result but if we don't spy on them, we get another result. *This is a law of Nature, and there is nothing we can do about it.*

A few more words about Heisenberg's gedanken experiment before we get back to the mainstream. As a result of his analysis, Heisenberg came to the conclusion that *one cannot simultaneously measure with infinite precision, both the position and the momentum of a particle.* Nature demands that if Δx is the error in the coordinate measurement and Δp the error in the momentum measurement, then the best we can do is to go by the rule

$$\Delta x \cdot \Delta p \sim \hbar \tag{1.1}$$

where $\hbar = (h/2\pi)$, h being the Planck's constant. What (1.1) implies is that if we try to make $\Delta x = 0$ (i.e., try to measure the position with infinite accuracy) we would make an infinite error in the momentum measurement and vice versa. Rule (1.1) is referred to as the *Heisenberg uncertainty principle*; and please note that it has nothing to do with the practical, experimental accuracy of measurement. Rather, rule (1.1) is a law of Nature; it is at the very heart of QM.

1.6 Mathematics of the mystery

Let us collect together the results of our various experiments and see if we can tie them up. In every case, we shall talk of either the intensity or better, the probability of the outcome.

Bullet experiment:

$$P_{12} = P_1 + P_2 \tag{1.2}$$

Light experiment:

$$P_{12} \neq P_1 + P_2 \tag{1.3}$$

where the symbol $\neq$ means *not equal to*. There is of course a simple way of understanding the result (1.3). One knows that probability is proportional to the intensity measured and that the intensity of a light beam is the square of the amplitude. To represent the amplitude of a light beam we need a complex number (see Box 1.2) and if ϕ denotes the complex number, then the square we are talking about is given by $\phi\phi^* = |\phi|^2$. Thus

$$P_1 = |\phi_1|^2 \qquad \text{and} \qquad P_2 = |\phi_2|^2, \tag{1.4}$$

whereas P_{12} is given by

$$P_{12} = |\phi_1 + \phi_2|^2 = |\phi_1|^2 + |\phi_2|^2 + 2|\phi_1|\,|\phi_2| \cos \delta \tag{1.5}$$

where δ is the phase difference between ϕ_1 and ϕ_2. Clearly P_{12} is different from $(P_1 + P_2)$.

Electron experiment (without spies):

$$P_{12} \neq P_1 + P_2. \tag{1.6}$$

Electron experiment (with spies):

$$P_{12} = P_1 + P_2. \tag{1.7}$$

So here is a quantification of the mystery. We keep experimenting with electrons; under certain conditions an electron behaves like light and at other times it behaves like a particle. From (1.6) it is clear that complex quantities must enter the picture. By analogy with optics, let us introduce a *probability amplitude* ψ which is like ϕ in (1.4) and (1.5). We can now write

$$P_1 = |\psi_1|^2, \quad P_2 = |\psi_2|^2$$

$$P_{12} = |\psi_1 + \psi_2|^2 \neq |\psi_1|^2 + |\psi_2|^2. \tag{1.8}$$

Box 1.2 I am sure you are already aware of complex numbers. Nevertheless, it seems worthwhile drawing your attention to some of its features.

The numbers we first learn are the real numbers. We start with integers, then move on to rational numbers (i.e., those which can be expressed as (n_1/n_2), where n_1 and n_2 are both integers, for example, a number like 2.5 = 5/2). Then come irrational numbers like π, e and so forth, which cannot be expressed in the form (n_1/n_2). Arithmetic gives us various rules for manipulating these numbers.

One of the arithmetical operations is that of taking roots. If I wish to know $\sqrt{36}$, I simply ask: What is that number which when multiplied by itself gives 36? There are rules for finding the solution, and the answer in such cases turns out to be some real number — it could be an integer, a rational number or even an irrational number. However, when we ask for $\sqrt{-1}$, we are stymied. As Feynman puts it: "The square of no rational, no irrational, of *nothing* that we have discovered so far [the reference is to real numbers], is equal to – 1."

There is a way out, which is to extend the concept of numbers by introducing a new number i such that $i^2 = -1$. The number i is called the *unit imaginary* number. With this, the extension to complex numbers is as follows: If p and q are real numbers, then $(p + iq)$ is called a *complex* number. A number such as (iq) is referred to as *pure imaginary*. The number $(p - iq)$ is said to be the *complex conjugate* of $(p + iq)$. If we write $z = (p + iq)$, then $(p - iq)$ is denoted by z^*. Obviously, $zz^* = z^*z = p^2 + q^2$.

In physics and electrical engineering one makes extensive use of complex numbers, especially when dealing with periodic or wave-like phenomena. This is because of the formula

$$e^{i\theta} = \cos\theta + i\sin\theta$$

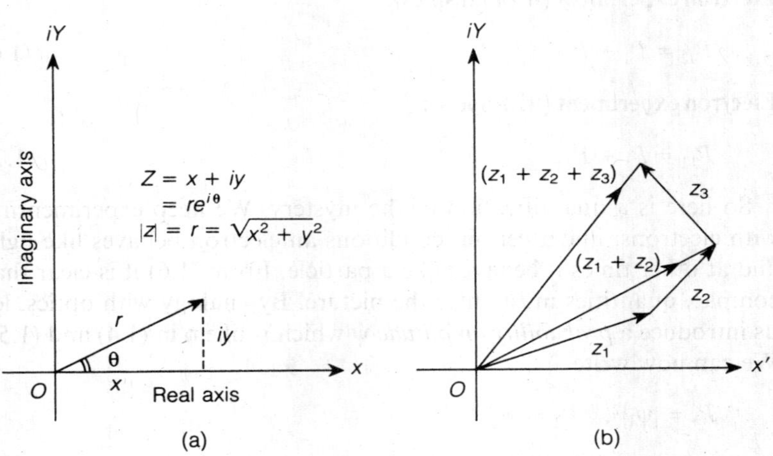

which Feynman refers to as a "jewel". There is a graphical representation for complex numbers which is shown in figure (a). The number $(p + iq)$ is also represented in the form $re^{i\theta}$ in figure (a). This, says Feynman, is one aspect of the "unification of algebra and geometry." The angle θ is called the phase angle.

In optics, the wave amplitude is generally a complex number. Likewise, in QM the wave function or the probability amplitude is a complex number. Figure (b) shows how one adds such numbers graphically. Observe how the resultant changes.

Thus without spies, $P_{12} = |\psi_1 + \psi_2|^2$. However with spies, P_{12} changes to $|\psi_1|^2 + |\psi_2|^2$.

Together, (1.6) and (1.7) imply that electrons behave like waves and interfere when we don't watch them. But when we spy on them, they behave like particles! At this stage let me quote Feynman who says:

> We would like to emphasise a very important difference between classical and quantum mechanics. We have been talking about the probability that an electron will arrive in a given circumstance. We have implied that in our experimental arrangement (even the best possible one) it would be impossible to predict exactly, what would happen. We can predict only the odds! ... Physics has given up on the problem of trying to predict exactly what will happen in a definite circumstance. Yes! physics has given up . . . It may be a backward step, but no one has seen a way to avoid it.
>
> No one can "explain" any more than we have just "explained". No one will give you any deeper representation of the situation. We have no ideas about a more basic mechanism from which these results can be deduced.

I am sure you are mystified by the quantity ψ I have quietly smuggled in. Don't worry, I would have a lot to say about it later.

1.7 Why are bullets different from electrons?

Let us go back again to the results of our various experiments and ask one question we have not asked ourselves so far. Why do bullets behave differently from electrons? After all if bullets are particles, then so are electrons. Why then the difference in behaviour? The answer is now known and can be stated in two slightly different ways. One way is to say: "Look, all this business about disturbing electrons applies because the act of observing administers a whacking big kick to the electron (remember the gamma-ray microscope?). Bullets are far more massive than the electron; you can observe them as much as you like but it would not make any difference to them." This is certainly one way of explaining things. A second way is to argue: "Who says that there are

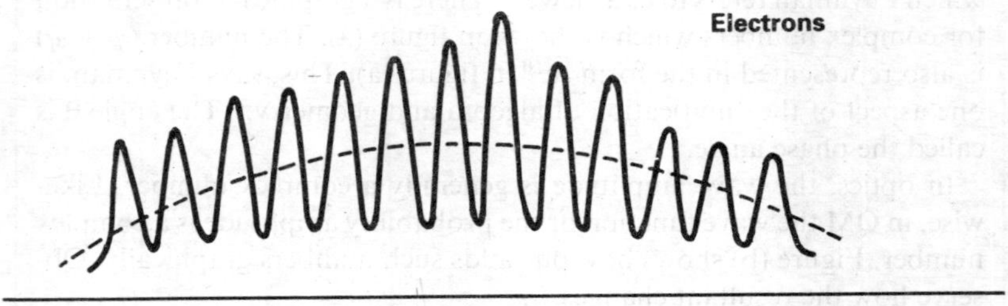

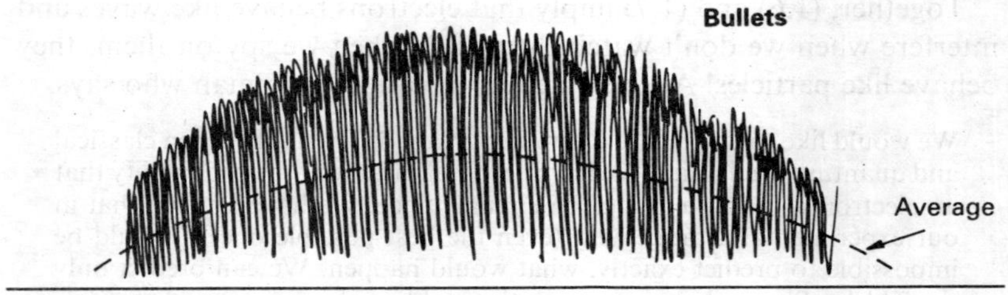

Fig. 1.12 Schematics of the interference patterns obtained with electrons and with bullets. In the case of the electrons, the maxima and minima are well separated, i.e., resolved, and therefore clearly seen. In the bullet case too there are, in principle, such maxima and minima but they are so very crowded that it is impossible to distinguish them. All one can (and does) see is the *average* distribution. Not surprisingly, this smeared out average curve is what we expect from CM.

no interference wiggles in the case of the bullets? They are certainly there, but the wiggles are so very crowded that it is physically impossible to resolve them; one merely sees an average behaviour and so we think we are getting something different"—see Fig. 1.12. This explanation also is OK and, in a manner of speaking, is related to the earlier one. But there is more to this business than these "explanations" suggest.

1.8 QM — its philosophical implications

Four important facts emerge from the experiments discussed above:

1. Classical mechanics (which works for bullets) does not work for electrons.

2. Electrons can behave like both, particles and waves. So also does light. Commenting on it, Feynman once observed:

> You had to know which experiments you were analysing in order to tell if light was waves or particles ... it was jokingly said by someone that light was waves on Mondays, Wednesdays and Fridays; it was particles on Tuesdays, Thursdays and Saturdays, and on Sundays we think about it!

3. The act of observation can disturb; so what you get need not be what you wanted to see.
4. To describe the electron experiment, it is necessary to associate a complex (probability) amplitude.

What neatly ties all these together is quantum mechanics. It has been with us for nearly three quarters of a century and has proved extremely reliable. Its basic rules have never failed. It is possible that in particular situations all the answers sought for are not available, but that is not the fault of quantum mechanics. Rather, it is mostly due to the lack of sufficient information about the physics of the system. In short, QM is a very good cookbook or algorithm, whichever you prefer. The recipe works like a charm, provided one knows how to handle it. Most physicists are quite content to operate at that level, rather like garage mechanics who are not bothered about thermodynamics while repairing car engines!

However, the more philosophically-inclined physicists have not taken such a casual attitude. From day one they have been concerned about the philosophical implications of the new discoveries. After all, it is intriguing that Nature behaves one way when we are looking and another way when we are not. Naturally, opinion was divided about all this, particularly in the early days. The arguments were animated; they haven't died down as yet, and the debate continues. But of this continuing debate, round one is perhaps the most exciting. For a blow-by-blow account of that, you would have to wait until Chapter 8.

The discovery of QM is an exciting drama, but the subject itself is not all that easy. So don't get unduly worried if, in the first reading, you do not understand all that I say. Keep going and come back again for a second, maybe even a third look, to get a better feel for the structure of the subject, what it means and so forth.

2 *What QM Is All About*

2.1 Introduction

If the last chapter was mystifying, this one might appear somewhat dry and abstract. But don't get put off because all this "dry stuff" is needed to appreciate the historical development of quantum mechanics.

As you know, our Universe basically consists of matter and radiation. In the last century, matter was described in terms of classical mechanics and radiation in terms of classical electrodynamics. Each was a great triumph in itself, but at the level of atoms both these pillars of classical physics failed completely. While groping with the problem of the atom, it was realised that:

1. there was a quantum aspect to the atomic world;
2. radiation behaved both like particles as well as waves; and
3. matter itself had a dual character.

Events soon moved rapidly and a new mechanics, i.e., QM was discovered which replaced CM. Shortly thereafter, a link was established between a quantum mechanical description of matter and a similar description of radiation. At this stage it was more or less all over, barring the shouting—or so it seemed.

In this chapter I shall give you a broad qualitative overview of both CM and QM such as we need for our later purposes. It is difficult to deal with these topics without bringing in a certain amount of mathematics. However, I have packaged most of the maths into the next chapter so that we may presently concentrate on obtaining a rapid overview of the basic facts without worrying too much about the details. I know Pundits would sternly disapprove but perhaps you might not!

2.2 A fleeting glimpse of CM

CM got off to a start with Isaac Newton. Thanks to his equations of motion, one could calculate how stones fell when dropped, how cannon balls moved when fired and so forth. In simple problems like these one deals with the motion of just a few particles but frequently one has to deal with the simultaneous motion of many particles or bodies, as in the case of the Solar system. Or else, one might have to deal with constrained motion like that of a roller coaster or of a ball moving on an undulating surface. In these situations, solving Newton's equations becomes a messy affair. This led eighteenth century stalwarts like Euler, Lagrange and Hamilton to develop mathematical methods and equations better suited for such difficult cases.

The beacon that guided these giants was an important law of Nature. There are two or three equivalent versions, so to speak, of this fundamental principle (see Box 2.1) but here I shall make a reference only to one of these called the *Principle of Least Action*. Simply put it says: Nature is lazy! That of course is oversimplifying things somewhat. So let me make amends by quoting Feynman:

> When I was in high school, my physics teacher ... called me down one day after physics class and said, "You look bored; I want to tell you something interesting." He told me the following: Suppose you have a particle (in a gravitational field, for instance) which starts somewhere and moves to some other point by free motion—you throw, and it goes up and comes down [see Fig. 2.1]. It goes from the original place to the final place in a certain amount of time. Now you try a different motion. Suppose that to get from here to there, it went like this [see Fig. 2.2] but got there in just the same amount of time. Then he said this: If you calculate the kinetic energy at every moment on the path, take away the potential energy, and integrate it over the time during the whole path, you'll find that the number you'll get is bigger than that for the actual motion.

What Feynman's teacher told him can be put neatly in mathematical language as follows: Define a quantity S called action. It is the kinetic energy (KE) minus the potential energy (PE) integrated over time, i.e.,

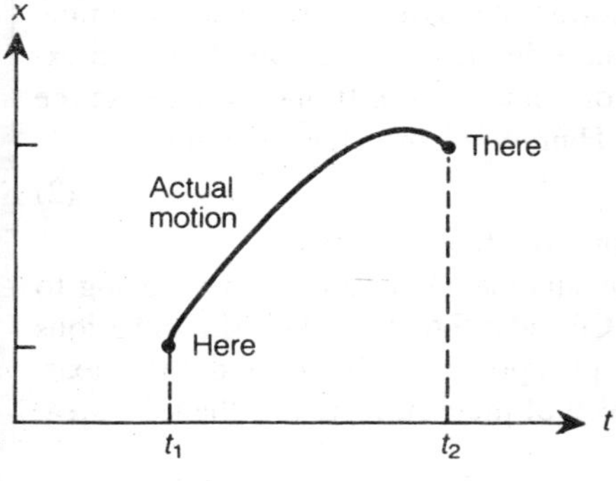

Fig. 2.1 This and the next figure are related to the quote from Feynman. In the *Feynman lectures* (vol. II) from where the quotation is taken, you will see photographs of the curves drawn by Feynman on the classroom blackboard. Here I present sketches of those. This figure shows the schematic of an actual trajectory traced by a particle during its motion from time t_1 to time t_2.

Box 2.1 The principle of least action is an example of what may be called the *minimum* or rather the *extremum* principle. Such an idea was first suggested in 1625 by the French mathematician Fermat who postulated that light rays follow that path for which the travel time is the least. You will hear more about Fermat's principle in Chapter 7.

The next step was taken by the French mathematician Maupertuis who in 1744 declared that Nature always acts in such a way as to keep a certain quantity, which he called "action", a minimum. Maupertuis' definition of action was rather obscure but nevertheless he firmly believed in the principle because according to him, Nature always acts in the simplest possible fashion. In those days, there was frequently an effort to relate science and theology, and Maupertuis was attempting to show that a perfect Supreme Being cannot but have a law of utter simplicity and minimum action—whatever the latter meant!

The minimum principle was stated in a precise form for the first time by Euler, curiously enough in the same year Maupertuis made his pronouncement. But unlike Maupertuis, Euler did not link his statement to God. He merely stated that when a particle travels between fixed points P and Q under the action of forces, it follows that path for which the integral $I = \int_P^Q v ds$ is a minimum, v being the velocity and the integration being over the path. Closer examination shows that the path chosen is not exactly that for which I is a minimum. Rather, if I is the value of the integral for the favoured path and I' that for a neighbouring path that is infinitesimally close, then the difference $\delta I = (I - I')$ is ~ 0. One thus states Euler's condition as

$$\delta \int_P^Q v ds = 0. \tag{1}$$

A statement like this is called a *variational principle*, and presently I shall have more to say about it. A few years later, Lagrange extended Euler's work to a general system of particles which interacted with each other via forces.

In this book we would be interested in a minimum principle stated by Hamilton. According to it, the motion of a dynamical system from time t_1 to time t_2 is such that the action S defined in equation (2.1) is an extremum, (i.e., either a minimum or a maximum). If one were to use the language employed in (1) above, Hamilton's principle demands

$$\delta S = 0. \tag{2}$$

This principle is the gateway to the equations of motion.

A few words now about statements like (1) and (2). They belong to the realm of *variational calculus*. Consider figure (a). This shows various surfaces generated by rotating appropriate curves around the z-axis. The question now arises as to which of these surfaces has the least area.

Variational calculus provides the answer. Perhaps you can now appreciate how and why variational calculus enters mechanics.

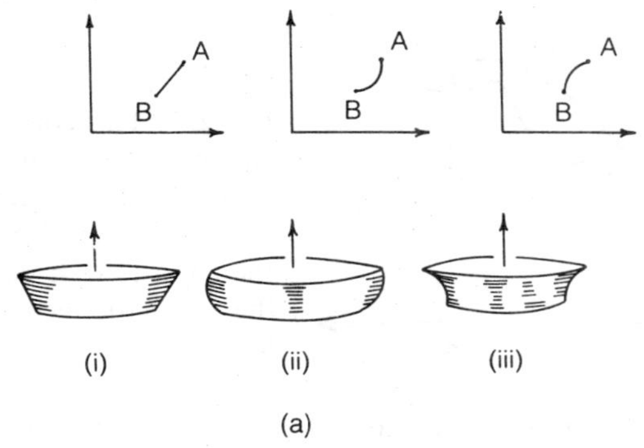

$$\text{Action} = S = \int_{t_1}^{t_2} (\text{KE} - \text{PE})\,dt. \tag{2.1}$$

Remember that both KE and PE vary from instant to instant, i.e., they are functions of time. For every path between two given points, there is a corresponding value of the action S. The "laziness principle" says: Of all the possible paths, the particle would choose that for which the *action is the least*—see Fig. 2.3.

OK, so we have this principle. What does one do with it? I shall tell you a bit more about it in the next chapter but just take it that it is a pathway to the equations of motion. In classical mechanics, one comes across equations of motion due to Lagrange and due to Hamilton. We shall be mainly interested in the latter because of their linkage with QM. Hamilton gave these equations in a rather general form but when tackling any given physical problem, one must first adapt them to the

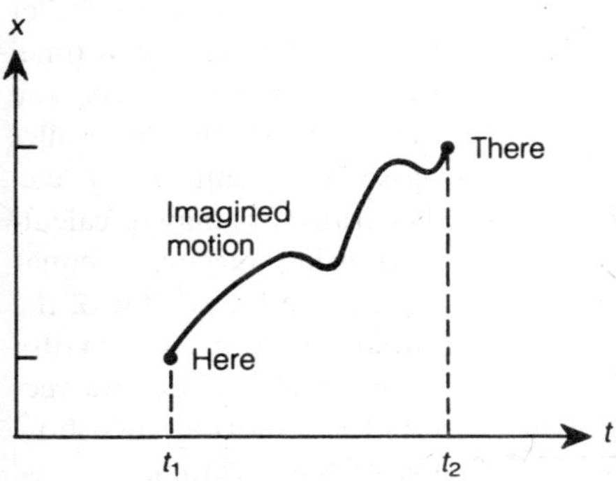

Fig. 2.2 Here is an alternate, imagined trajectory. The path is different from that in the previous figure but the time $(t_2 - t_1)$ taken for the travel remains the same.

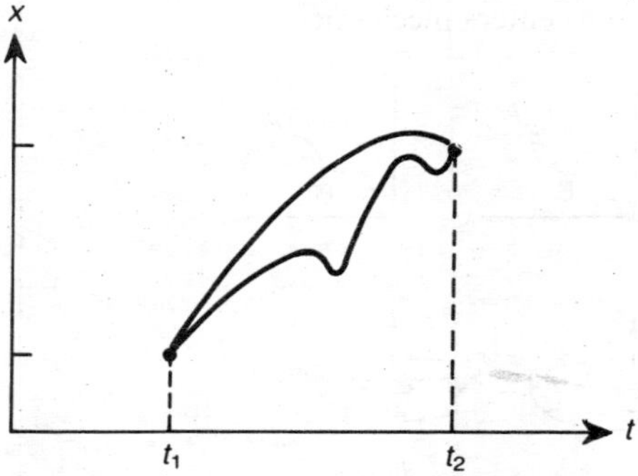

Fig. 2.3 This combines the curves of the previous two figures. When Nature is presented with various alternatives like these, she chooses that path for which the action (defined in (2.1)) is the least.

specific problem on hand. All this might sound rather vague but I shall make amends in the next chapter. For the present, I would like to discuss what is called the *state* of the system.

Suppose a bullet is fired. This is a standard tutorial problem in elementary dynamics and is particularly simple because we have only one particle. Here the bullet constitutes the entire system. As it flies it traces a trajectory (see Fig. 2.4) and one is interested in the latter. If the trajectory is known, the problem is essentially solved. The solution is obtained via Newton's equation but this alone is not sufficient because we must also give the *initial conditions*, i.e., the initial position of the

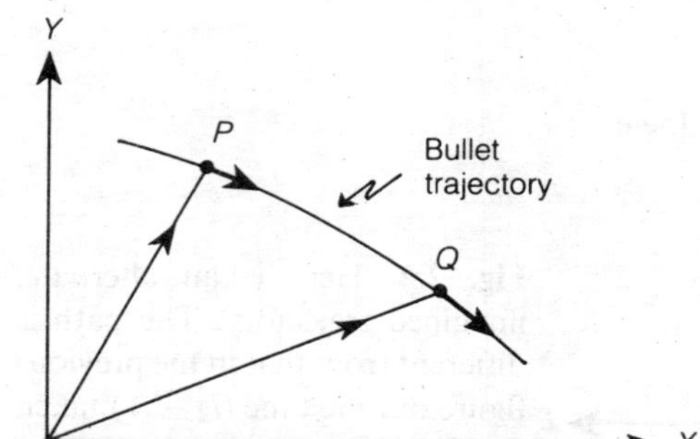

Fig. 2.4 Schematic of the bullet trajectory and how it is characterised. To draw the trajectory we need only the information about vectors like *OP*, *OQ*, etc. If we are also interested in how the bullet traces the trajectory in time, then we must specify the times at which the bullet passes the points *P*, *Q*, etc. The trajectory may be calculated using Newton's equation, and a knowledge of the initial conditions ($\mathbf{r}(0)$, $\mathbf{v}(0)$). [Bold quantities denote vectors.] The short arrows show the velocity vectors.

bullet and its initial velocity. Let us count time from the instant the bullet is fired, i.e., we regard that instant of time as $t = 0$. Given the initial conditions $\mathbf{r}(0)$ and $\mathbf{v}(0)$, we can use Newton's equations to find the position $\mathbf{r}(t)$, and the velocity $\mathbf{v}(t)$ at a later instant t. The combination $\{\mathbf{r}(t), \mathbf{v}(t)\}$ describes the state of the system at time t. Thus finding the trajectory of the bullet boils down to finding the successive states or how the state evolves in time.

Hamilton did not restrict himself to simple systems like a bullet. Instead he considered problems with large numbers of degrees of freedom. To each of these degrees of freedom he assigned a coordinate, labelling them $q_1, q_2, \ldots$ The q's are referred to as *generalised coordinates*. For the bullet they would reduce to x, y, z. Obviously these generalised coordinates would depend on time, and so we would have to write $q_1(t), q_2(t)$, etc. Going back to the bullet for a moment, it not only has a position coordinate but also a momentum ($= m\mathbf{v}(t)$). Analogously, we associate with the coordinates above the *generalised momenta* $p_1(t), p_2(t), \ldots$ The momentum $p_1(t)$ is said to be *conjugate* to the coordinate $q_1(t)$. In this notation, the state of the system is described by the set$(q_1(t), q_2(t), \ldots, p_1(t), p_2(t), \ldots)$, compactly written (q, p). The quantities q and p are also referred to as the dynamical characteristics of the system.

Hamilton obtained equations for the q's and the p's. These are called *Hamilton's equations* . They express the same physics as do Newton's equations of motion, but in more flexible form.To solve these, one must, as in the bullet problem, know the initial conditions $(q(0), p(0))$. Solving means being able to specify $(q(t), p(t))$ for all values of $t > 0$.

The solution of Hamilton's equations can often be quite elusive. One trick for solving them is to convert q and p to new coordinates Q and new momenta P such that the *form* of Hamilton's equations is preserved but the new equations themselves (in terms of Q and P) are easier to solve. The transformation

$$(q, p) \to (Q, P)$$

which does this job is referred to as a *canonical* transformation.

Upto this point, I have been implicitly assuming that the system under consideration has discrete degrees of freedom. There are, however, systems with continuous degrees of freedom, like a vibrating string for example —see Fig. 2.5. The methods developed for dealing with discrete systems have been suitably modified to go over smoothly to the continuous case. The beauty of these mathematical methods is that they apply not only to real mechanical systems like a vibrating string but also to classical fields like electromagnetic fields.

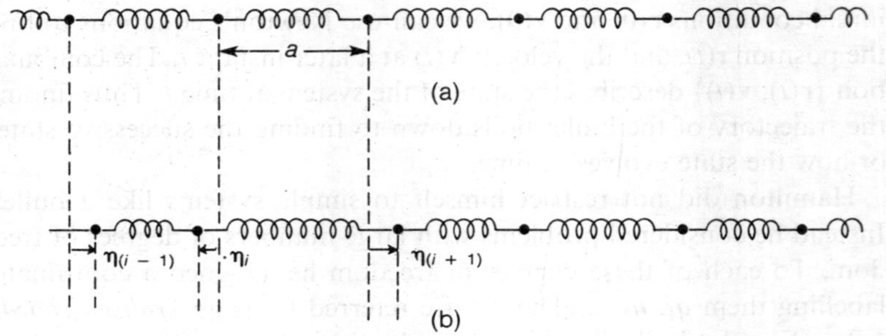

Fig. 2.5 This figure illustrates the transition from discrete to continuous systems. (a) shows a set of coupled oscillators, consisting of equal mass points connected by springs. The equilibrium spacing between adjacent masses is a. (b) shows the masses in displaced positions, η_i denoting the displacement of the ith mass from its equilibrium position. Thus at any given instant t, the configuration of the chain can be given by the set $(\eta_1(t), \eta_2(t), \dots \eta_i(t), \dots)$. The usual mechanics provides a means of calculating how the η_i's vary in time. When a approaches zero, the discrete variable η_i goes over into the continuous variable $\eta(x)$.

I have dwelt on Hamilton's contributions to classical mechanics because in a sense his methods have been borrowed over into QM, with appropriate modifications of course. Further, the methods of CM as applied to classical fields also have been borrowed over for describing fields in QM. All this eventually facilitated the integration of a quantum description of matter with a quantum description of radiation, leading to a comprehensive quantum theory of electrodynamics or *quantum electrodynamics* as it is usually called.

Hamilton's name is well known not only in mechanics but also in optics. In fact Hamilton was very much fascinated by the similarity of the mathematical methods used in these two subjects which clearly deal with very different phenomena. Almost a century later, Schroedinger discovered that there is much more to this similarity than Hamilton himself had realised; this story comes later.

2.3 QM: Some preliminary remarks

QM must be used if one deals with the microscopic world; by that I mean tiny objects like atoms, electrons, etc. This does not imply that

QM is not required in the macroscopic world. Indeed it is required for macroscopic systems also if one wants to explain everything in terms of atoms. For example, superconductivity is a bulk phenomenon, meaning that I can make a piece of lead, 1 kg in mass, become superconducting. But there is no way I can explain superconductivity using classical physics because the phenomenon owes its origin to the peculiar behaviour of electrons under certain circumstances. On the other hand, if there is a steel or wooden beam and I wish to calculate how much it would bend under a given load, then nineteenth century physics is good enough.

The topics in QM that are of common concern at the practical level are (i) states, (ii) wave functions, (iii) calculation of properties, and (iv) the effect of perturbations. Let us slowly get introduced to these.

2.4 Quantum mechanical states

Earlier I told you what is meant by the state of a system in CM. Similar ideas can be carried over into QM but with due caution. To make life simple, consider a system with just one degree of freedom, e.g., a one-dimensional harmonic oscillator (see Fig. 2.6). In CM both q and p can be determined simultaneously with infinite accuracy but thanks to the Heisenberg uncertainty principle (recall section 1.5) in QM this is not possible. This is a great handicap. If for a moment we go back to the bullet problem, the uncertainty principle implies that we cannot specify accurately the position and the momentum of the bullet at start. Let us return to the oscillator. Owing to the fuzziness of the initial condition, we cannot make precise statements about the subsequent evolution of the oscillator state; instead we can talk only in terms of probabilities, as I shall explain later. This is an important point: The specification of a state in terms of coordinates and momenta is less

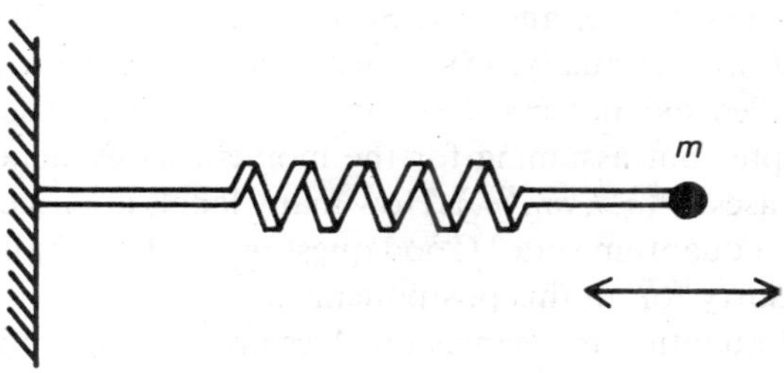

Fig. 2.6 Schematic of a one-dimentional oscillator. It consists of a point mass tied to a spring as shown and capable of motion along only one direction.

complete in QM than in CM; and due to incomplete information, one has to settle for probabilistic predictions.

The state of a quantum mechanical system does not always have to be specified in terms of position coordinates and momenta. There could be other ways of describing it; in fact in some situations, the position coordinate might not even be relevant (as we shall see later in the ammonia problem).

Perhaps an example might be useful to show how states could sometimes be labelled without explicitly bringing in coordinates and momenta. Figure 2.7 shows the energy levels of a hydrogen atom. Associated with each of these levels are one or more states of the hydrogen atom. How does one describe these states? I could call the lowest energy state as the ground state (rather like the ground floor), the next higher energy state as the first excited state and so forth. Loose descriptions like this are sometimes used. Can one do better? Yes, by attaching physically significant labels to these levels. What labels? Well, for a start one could use the *principal* quantum number n first introduced by Bohr. Is this enough? Not quite, because a careful analysis of the hydrogen atom problem shows that the Bohr spectrum (see Fig. 2.7) hides many details.

To cut a long story short, we need to use not only n but another integer l called the *orbital* quantum number. So we need two labels, n and l. But this is not the end of the story, for closer examination shows that for a given pair of values (n, l), there could be many states. For instance, if $n = 2$ and $l = 1$, then associated with this combination of quantum numbers, there are actually three states. If there is no magnetic field present, all these states would have the same energy but if a magnetic field is present, these three states would have slightly different energies (later I shall illustrate all this with a figure). Clearly one more label is needed to distinguish between the three options possible and that is the *orbital magnetic* quantum number m_l which, for $l = 1$, can take the values $+1$, 0, and -1. So our descriptors now become the triplet (n, l, m_l). Actually, even this is not enough on account of a property called *spin* possessed by the electron. I shall discuss spin later in this chapter but assuming for the moment its existence, our set of labels increases to (n, l, m_l, m_s). How many labels are needed in general to describe a quantum state? Good question, and we shall come to that also later (sorry for all this postponement!).

Much of quantum mechanics revolves around what might be called the algebra of states. In the algebra we are normally used to, we use quantities like x, y, etc. We have here instead the entities *bra* and *ket*, denoted by the symbols $\langle\ |$ and $|\ \rangle$ respectively; this notation was introduced by Dirac. Using this notation, one usually writes the state vector

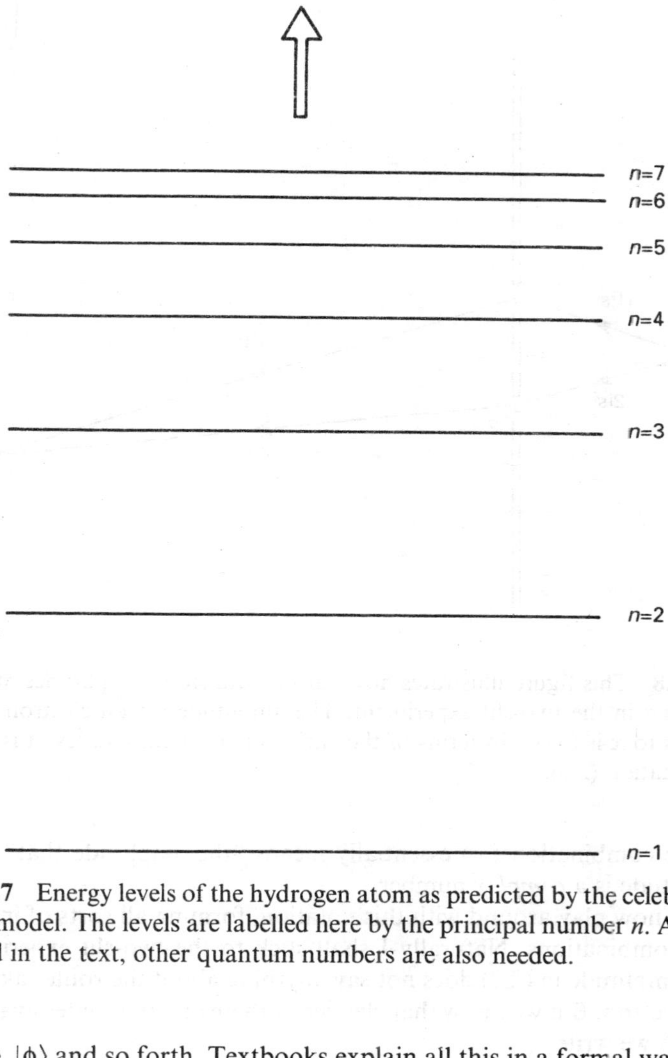

Fig. 2.7 Energy levels of the hydrogen atom as predicted by the celebrated Bohr model. The levels are labelled here by the principal number *n*. As discussed in the text, other quantum numbers are also needed.

as $|\psi\rangle$, $|\phi\rangle$ and so forth. Textbooks explain all this in a formal way but here we shall follow Feynman and pick up greater familiarity with these concepts via the example of the two-slit problem.

Consider the arrangement in Fig. 2.8. Electrons can pass through the slits and arrive at the screen in various ways. Of interest are the (quantum mechanical) amplitudes for various processes. We might, for example, be interested in the amplitude for the electron to go from s to x. We write this as

$$\langle \text{electron arrives at } x | \text{electron leaves } s \rangle; \tag{2.2}$$

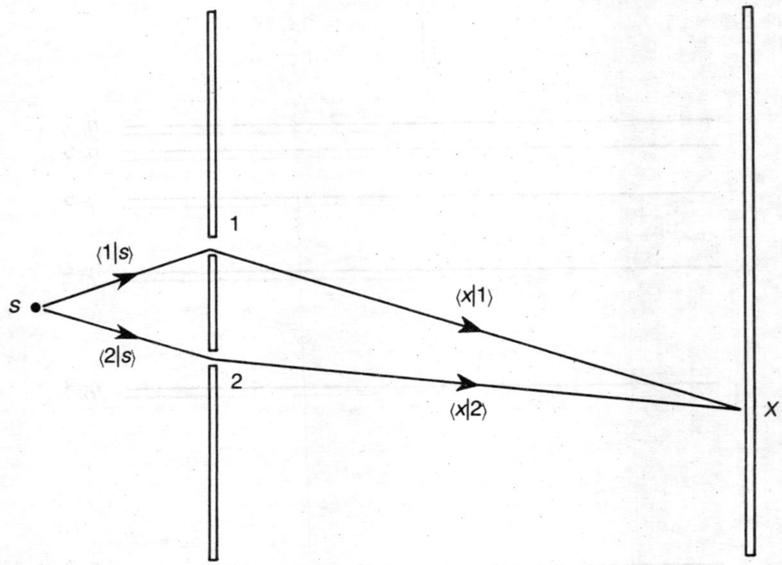

Fig. 2.8 This figure illustrates how various transition amplitudes may be assigned in the two-slit experiment. The amplitude for an electron to go from s to x is $\langle x|s\rangle$. In terms of the various partial amplitudes, it is given by equation (2.5).

so the combination $\langle\ |\ \rangle$ essentially means "the amplitude that". This amplitude is a *complex* number.

We now play around with this notation, forming all sorts of interesting combinations. Naturally I shall stick to the two-slit experiment. The amplitude in (2.2) does not say anything about the route taken by the electron. But we know that classically there are two routes available and so we write

$$\langle x|s\rangle = \langle x|s\rangle_{\text{thru 1}} + \langle x|s\rangle_{\text{thru 2}}. \tag{2.3}$$

We can write $\langle x|s\rangle_{\text{thru 1}}$ itself as

$$\langle x|s\rangle_{\text{thru 1}} = \langle x|1\rangle\langle 1|s\rangle \tag{2.4}$$

where $\langle 1|s\rangle$ is the amplitude for the electron to go from s to slit 1 and $\langle x|1\rangle$ is the amplitude to go from 1 to x. Thus we have

$$\langle x|s\rangle = \langle x|1\rangle\langle 1|s\rangle + \langle x|2\rangle\langle 2|s\rangle. \tag{2.5}$$

If there are many slits, we can generalise the above to

$$\langle x|s\rangle = \sum_i \langle x|i\rangle\langle i|s\rangle \tag{2.6}$$

where $\sum_i$, the sum over i, is over all the slits.

Quantum states are like vectors. Let us therefore brush up a little on vectors. Consider the vector OP in Fig. 2.9(a). This can be resolved into the components $OP_x = a\cdot\mathbf{i}$ and $OP_y = b\cdot\mathbf{j}$ where $\mathbf{i}$ and $\mathbf{j}$ are unit vectors along the x- and the y-axis respectively. We can thus write

$$\text{vector } OP = a\cdot\mathbf{i} + b\cdot\mathbf{j}. \tag{2.7}$$

In the same way, a quantum state $|s\rangle$ can (in general) be written as

$$|s\rangle = C_1|\mathrm{A}\rangle + C_2|\mathrm{B}\rangle + \ldots \tag{2.8}$$

where the "unit" vectors $|\mathrm{A}\rangle$, $|\mathrm{B}\rangle$, ..., etc., are like the unit vectors $\mathbf{i}$ and $\mathbf{j}$ we had before, and the coefficients C_1, C_2, ... are like a and b in (2.7); only, they are now (in general) complex. In a more compact notation,

$$|s\rangle = \sum_i C_i|i\rangle \tag{2.9a}$$

where $|i\rangle$ denotes a unit vector or a *base* vector as it is often called, and the sum is over all the base vectors. Since the vector $|i\rangle$ has "unit" length, it is said to be normalised. Given any *ket* state $|s\rangle$, we can form the corresponding *bra* state via the rule

$$\langle s| = \sum_i C_i^*\, \langle i| \tag{2.9b}$$

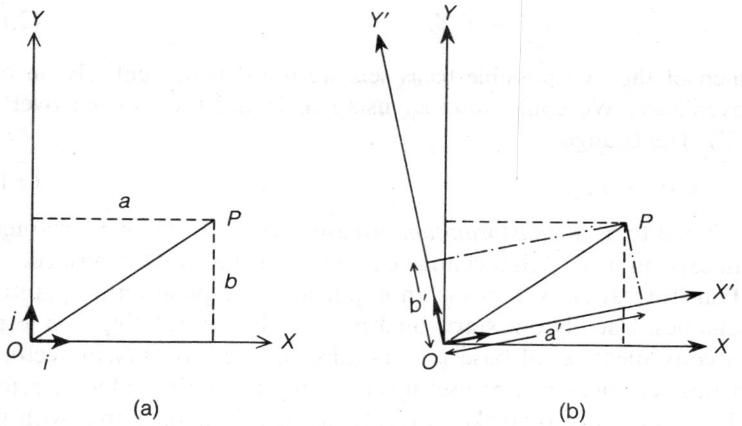

Fig. 2.9 (a) is an illustration of equation (2.7) and shows how a vector OP may be built up from the two base vectors $\mathbf{i}$ and $\mathbf{j}$. (b) illustrates the two options indicated in (2.10).

where C_i^* is the complex conjugate of C_i and $\langle i|$ is the *bra* state corresponding to the *ket* $|i\rangle$.

Going back to Fig. 2.9(a), all vectors in the *x-y* plane can be represented in terms of **i** and **j**. For describing a vector in ordinary three-dimensional space, three base vectors **i**, **j** and **k** are necessary. The number of base vectors needed in quantum mechanics depends on the situation, and at times it could even be infinite.

Possibly this section is a bit difficult to digest. Let me therefore briefly summarise:

- Quantum states can be regarded as vectors.
- Depending on the circumstances, these states are either represented as *bras* ($\langle\ |$) or as *kets* ($|\ \rangle$).
- Of interest generally are the amplitudes for transition from one particular quantum state to another; (2.2) is one example of such an amplitude.

2.5 Quantum states as vectors

Consider now the vector *OP* in Fig. 2.9(b). It can be described either in terms of the basis set (**i**, **j**) or the set (**i′**, **j′**), i.e., we can write

$$\text{vector } OP = a\cdot\mathbf{i} + b\cdot\mathbf{j},$$

or

$$= a'\cdot\mathbf{i}' + b'\cdot\mathbf{j}'. \tag{2.10}$$

Which of the two possible basis sets we use depends entirely on our convenience. We could start by using (**i**, **j**) and then switch over to (**i′**, **j′**). The change

$$(\mathbf{i}, \mathbf{j}) \to (\mathbf{i}', \mathbf{j}') \tag{2.11}$$

is referred to as a *transformation* of base vectors. In the next chapter I shall explain how such a change can be mathematically described.

Transformation of bases is an important manipulation in quantum mechanics. Usually one starts on a problem by formulating it in terms of a convenient set of base vectors (also referred to as *basis* vectors). But this set might not be useful for finding a solution. One therefore makes a switch (rather like in (2.11)) in such a manner that with the new set of base vectors, the problem becomes easier to solve. Discovering such a transformation is thus at the heart of many problems. I am sure you are wondering whether this is similar to the change over

$$(q, p) \rightarrow (Q, P)$$

in CM. Yes of course!

2.6 Measurement in QM

The quantities q and p are referred to as dynamical characteristics of the system. A system could have many other dynamical characteristics. In quantum mechanics, dynamical characteristics can be determined only by measurements. The measurements are made with an apparatus which is "large" compared to the quantum system and is therefore described with sufficient accuracy by classical mechanics. Measurements play an important role in quantum mechanics. Without a measurement, dynamical characteristics have no meaning. You will hear a lot about the "apparatus" in Part III of this trilogy.

2.7 The superposition principle

Quantum states can be superposed; this is an important aspect of quantum mechanics. The idea is very simple: If $|A\rangle$ and $|B\rangle$ are two possible states of a dynamical system, then so is the combination $C_1|A\rangle + C_2|B\rangle$.

There is nothing like the *superposition principle* in classical mechanics. Its physical significance is the following: Consider a dynamical variable and let us say there exists an "apparatus" for measuring the value of this variable. Let $|A\rangle$ and $|B\rangle$ be two states such that when an observation is made on the system in state $|A\rangle$, it is *sure* to lead to the result a; similarly when it is in $|B\rangle$ the result is *certain* to be b. What result will be obtained when the system is in the superposed state $|\psi\rangle = C_1|A\rangle + C_2|B\rangle$? The answer is that the result will sometimes be a and sometimes b. It will never be anything other than both a and b. Also, we can never say when we would get the result a and when we would get b; we can only talk of their probabilities. Once one recognises this basic fact about quantum mechanics, the "mystery" of the two-slit experiment disappears.

2.8 Amplitudes

What good are states for, and what information can one squeeze out of them? The familiar two-slit experiment gives us a clue. Recall that

$\langle x|s\rangle$ describes the amplitude for going from the state $|s\rangle$ to the state $|x\rangle$. *Transition* amplitudes like this are very useful in determining the outcomes of experiments. To appreciate this we write, as in Chapter 1, ψ_1 and ψ_2 for the amplitudes $\langle x|1\rangle\langle 1|s\rangle$ and $\langle x|2\rangle\langle 2|s\rangle$ respectively. Then clearly,

$$\langle x|s\rangle = \psi_1 + \psi_2. \tag{2.12}$$

The superposition principle is used here and we can see this as follows: Observe first that $|1\rangle$ and $|2\rangle$ are our basis vectors. Therefore, using the superposition principle, we can write

$$|x\rangle = a|1\rangle + b|2\rangle.$$

This then implies that

$$\langle x| = a^* \langle 1| + b^* \langle 2|.$$

Therefore,

$$\langle x|s\rangle = a^* \langle 1|s\rangle + b^* \langle 2|s\rangle.$$

Comparing with (2.5), we notice that the coefficients are given by $a^* = \langle x|1\rangle$ and $b^* = \langle x|2\rangle$. So really speaking, the superposition principle is behind (2.5).

Remember the probability P_{12} of Fig. 1.8? Well, P_{12} is nothing but the amplitude squared, i.e.,

$$\begin{aligned} P_{12} &= |\langle x|s\rangle|^2 = |\psi_1 + \psi_2|^2. \\ &= |\psi_1|^2 + |\psi_2|^2 + \psi_1^* \psi_2 + \psi_1 \psi_2^* \end{aligned} \tag{2.13a}$$

whereas

$$P_1 = |\langle x|1\rangle\langle 1|s\rangle|^2 = |\psi_1|^2 \tag{2.13b}$$

and

$$P_2 = |\langle x|2\rangle\langle 2|s\rangle|^2 = |\psi_2|^2. \tag{2.13c}$$

It is useful to review the physics of all that has been said so far. The best way is to quote Feynman who observes:

> If you could, *in principle*, distinguish the alternative final states (even though you do not bother to do so), the total final probability is obtained by calculating the *probability* for each state (not the amplitude) and then adding them together [i.e., $P_{12} = P_1 + P_2$]. If you *cannot* distinguish the final states *even in principle*, then the probability amplitudes must be summed before taking the absolute square to find the actual probability [i.e., $P_{12} = |\psi_1 + \psi_2|^2$].

2.9 Wave-particle duality

It should be clear from Chapter 1 as well as the preceding section that matter can behave both like particles as well as waves. Louis de Broglie was the first to draw attention to this possibility. More specifically, he said that if a particle of mass m moves with a velocity v then it behaves like a wave having a wavelength λ given by

$$\lambda = h/(mv). \tag{2.14}$$

Such a matter wave is sometimes referred to as a de Broglie wave, and λ as the de Broglie wavelength. This discovery of de Broglie was the starting point of what might be called the wave theory of matter which is briefly introduced in the next two sections.

2.10 Wave functions

Let us go back to Fig. 2.7 and the energy levels of the hydrogen atom. The energies corresponding to this level scheme were first computed by Bohr in 1913 using a rather artificial model, but mercifully, modern QM gives the same result (that is, if one ignores some niceties!). You might ask: "OK, QM gives the same level scheme as obtained by Bohr but what does it say about the electron? Bohr had said that the electron in the hydrogen atom moves in privileged or stationary orbits [I shall discuss this in Chapter 5]. What does QM have to say about this?"

The question is fair and needs to be answered. Erwin Schroedinger indicated how this could be done. Basically one introduces a quantity ψ called the *wave function*. For the electron in the hydrogen atom we write it as $\psi(x, y, z)$. Actually this is not enough because the wave function depends on the state of the system which means we must attach to ψ labels such as we had before, i.e., we write $\psi_{n,\, l,\, m_l}(x, y, z)$.

What is this wave function? Perhaps you remember the probability amplitude I talked about in the last chapter. Well, ψ has the meaning of a probability amplitude. To understand this, it is convenient to go back for a moment to the harmonic oscillator of Fig. 2.6. The wave function of the oscillator can be written $\psi(x)$. Any labels? Yes. According to quantum theory, an oscillator of frequency ν can have levels with energies

$$\varepsilon_n = nh\nu \qquad n = 0, 1, 2, \ldots \tag{2.15}$$

where h is the Planck's constant. (QM actually gives the result $(n + 1/2)h\nu$ but for a moment we will ignore this extra (1/2) since it does not affect us.) The label we are looking for is the integer n whence we write $\psi_n(x)$ to denote the oscillator wave function corresponding to the nth state.

The wave function is a complex quantity and cannot be measured in any experiment but we need not lose heart; one can certainly measure $|\psi|^2$ because it has the meaning of a probability. More explicitly, if we consider the (small) interval dx between x and $(x + dx)$, then $|\psi(x)|^2 dx$ is the probability of finding the oscillator between x and $(x + dx)$.

Perhaps I should explain this last remark a little better. For this purpose, consider the simple pendulum in Fig. 2.10. When the amplitude of oscillation is small, the pendulum is a good approximation to the harmonic oscillator. As you know, the pendulum moves very fast past the point O but rather slowly near the end of its range, i.e., near A and B. Suppose we take repeated snapshots of the pendulum with a camera. Clearly, we are more likely to catch the pendulum near A or B rather than near O. If we compile the results from many photographs and construct a probability curve, it would be as in Fig. 2.11(a).

So far, I have implicitly regarded our pendulum as a classical system. What about a quantum mechanical pendulum? This cannot have all possible energies but only a restricted set of energies as in (2.15). Figure 2.11(b) shows the probability density for such a pendulum in one of its quantum states and how it compares with the corresponding result for a classical pendulum. The number of wiggles (in the QM case) depends on n. Clearly when n is very large, the quantum result

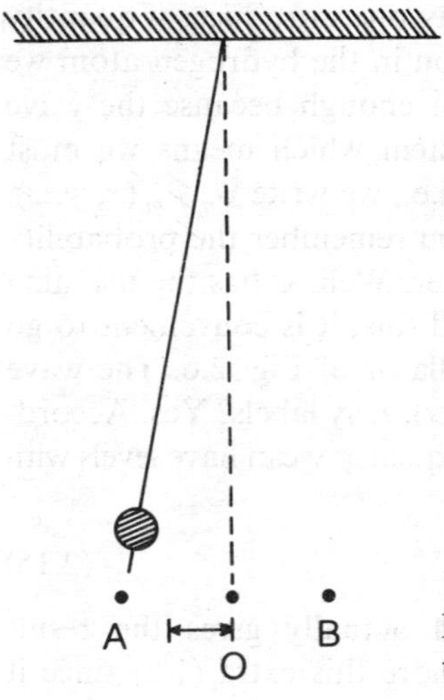

Fig. 2.10 Simple pendulum swinging over the range AB; O is the equilibrium position.

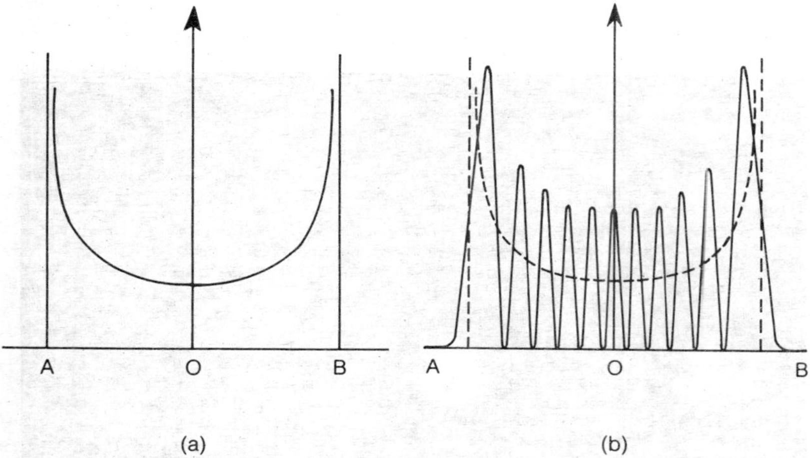

Fig. 2.11 (a) shows the classical probability of finding the pendulum bob with a displacement x (defined in the previous figure). (b) shows quantum mechanical probability when the oscillator is in the state $n = 10$. Observe the wiggles. When n increases, the wiggles come closer and eventually become unresolvable; the pendulum now behaves as if it is a classical object.

becomes indistinguishable from the classical time-averaged result; we see this also in Fig. 1.12.

It is important to digest the significance of all that has just been said. Classically, when we take a photograph of the pendulum, we are sure to find it in some position or the other. In the case of the quantum pendulum also, everytime we try to observe its position we would find it somewhere or the other. However, in contrast to the classical pendulum, there are many positions between A and B where the probability of finding the pendulum dips down to practically zero. Remember, any talk of *probability implies that the experiment is repeated several times*; only then is there any meaning in referring to probabilities.

Decades before QM was discovered, Niels Bohr guessed that the quantum system would behave like a classical system for large values of the quantum number. I have made a brief reference to this earlier; I shall have more to say later about the important role played by this guideline which is referred to as the *correspondence principle*.

Now that we understand what $|\psi|^2$ means, let us go back to the hydrogen atom. Plots of $|\psi_{n,\,l,\,m_l}|^2$ for a few cases are illustrated in Fig. 2.12. It is straightaway clear that the Bohr picture of circular orbits has to be given up (as also the idea of elliptic orbits introduced later by Sommerfeld). Instead, we find that the electron *probability*

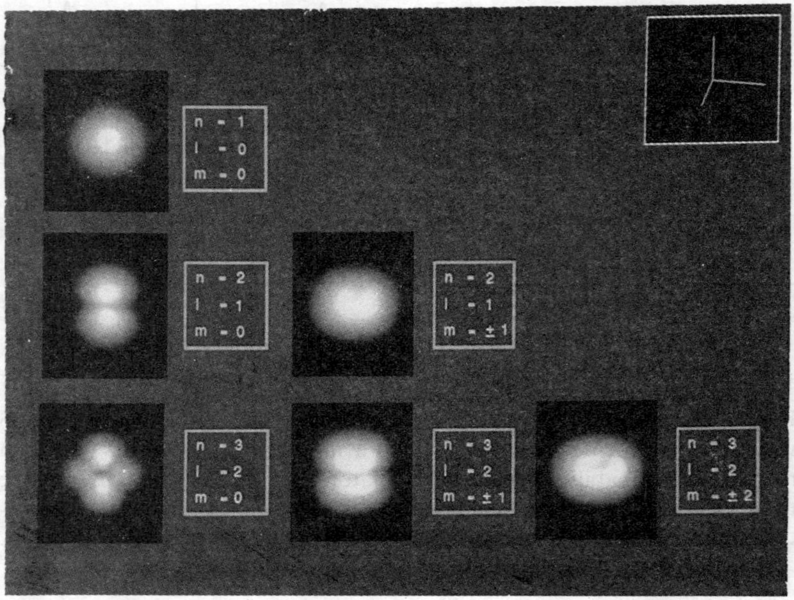

Fig. 2.12 A few plots of $|\psi_{n,\,l,\,m_l}|^2$ for the hydrogen atom.

density cloud forms beautiful and intricate patterns. Depending on the values for n, l and m_l, the probability of finding the electron is more in some directions and less in others, i.e., the distribution is anisotropic. These cloud patterns are also referred to as electron *orbitals*, and form the starting point of modern theories of chemistry.

You might wonder: "Suppose I have a hydrogen atom. In studying it, I am free to choose the x, y, z axes any way I like. And, depending on my choice, the orbitals could be directed differently (as in Fig. 2.13). Which of these different choices is actually selected by the atom?" Good question.

When we actually want to observe the electron, we need to have an apparatus of some sort. Once we have such an apparatus, automatically the coordinate axes get defined and we will observe a $|\psi(x, y, z)|^2$ appropriate to that set of axes. If we rotate the apparatus and repeat the experiments, our new observations would correspond to the new set of axes. A later example would make all this more convincing. Often an

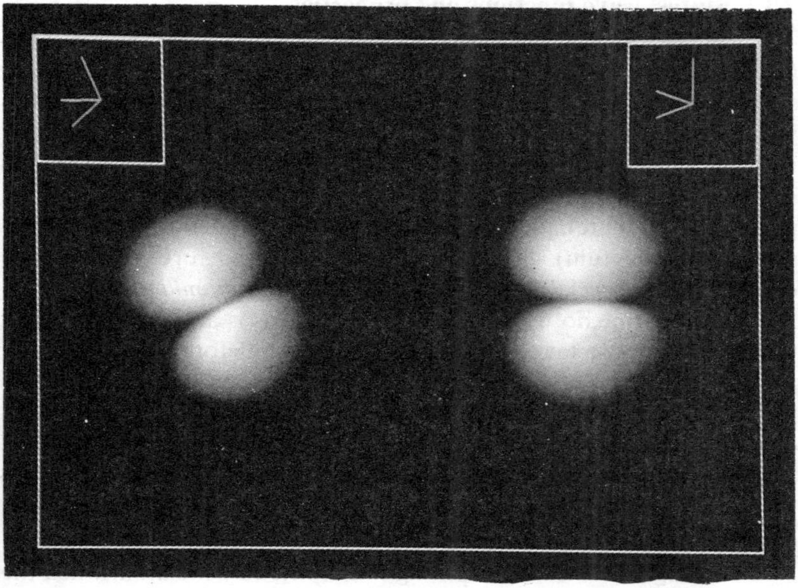

Fig. 2.13 This figure illustrates that the appearance of the orbitals depends on the choice of the reference axes. When external perturbation is present it can and often does provide a natural reference frame.

external magnetic field exists (e.g., the Earth's field). Once this happens, then, no matter how weak the field might be, it automatically provides a reference direction (usually taken as the z-direction). The reference frame could also get defined by the presence of other atoms in the neighbourhood.

2.11 The Schroedinger equation

Wave functions are not obtained by magic! They have to be painstakingly determined by solving an equation called the *Schroedinger equation*. I shall give more details about it in the next chapter but here we shall just take it that finding the wave function ψ by solving the Schroedinger equation is rather like finding the wave amplitude ϕ of an optical wave by solving the wave equation of optics. And just as $|\phi|^2$ denotes optical intensity, $|\psi|^2$denotes probability density. In fact, as hinted earlier, Schroedinger arrived at a wave equation for matter by pushing the analogy due to Hamilton between optics and dynamics.

2.12 States, wave functions and properties

Crudely speaking, QM takes the view that seeing is believing. Stated in somewhat more respectable terms, QM concerns itself with quantities which can be observed (at least in principle) in experiments. Associated with such quantities there are, in the theory, entities called *operators*. Thus one has the position operator (related to the measurement of the position coordinate), the momentum operator (related to the measurement of momentum), the energy operator and so forth. The energy operator has a special name—it is called the *Hamiltonian*.

What does one do with these operators? This is an important question and we must take in the answer slowly. Before we start doing anything with operators, we must somehow find out what the states of the system are—not an easy job generally, but let us say it has been done. We shall learn in Chapter 3 that such states are referred to as *eigenstates* but that is not important for the present. The states $|n, l, m_l, m_s\rangle$ of the hydrogen atom states (see section 2.4) are examples of eigenstates or base states.

According to the Bohr model, light is emitted by the atom when the electron "jumps" from an outer to an inner orbit. Bohr gave an expression for the frequency of the light emitted in terms of the energy difference between the two levels concerned but he could not say what the intensity of the spectral line would be; QM provides the answer to that one. How?

In QM, we don't have orbits like Bohr visualised; we have only states, and instead of a Bohr-type jump between orbits, we have transitions between states. Let $\hat{O}$ be the operator that causes the electron to go from state $|i\rangle$ to another state $|j\rangle$. $\hat{O}$ is called a *dipole* operator but that does not concern us right now. The QM amplitude for the transition $|i\rangle \rightarrow |j\rangle$ is written $\langle j|\hat{O}|i\rangle$ and the intensity of the spectral line ν_{ij} is proportional to $|\langle j|\hat{O}|i\rangle|^2$. Note that whereas $\langle j|\hat{O}|i\rangle$ is a complex number, the observed intensity corresponds to a real, non-negative number as it should. The precise manner in which the complex number $\langle j|\hat{O}|i\rangle$ is "manufactured" out of $|i\rangle$, $\hat{O}$ and $|j\rangle$ will soon be seen.

In a somewhat similar fashion, the energy E_i of the system in the state $|i\rangle$ is given by $\langle i|\hat{H}|i\rangle$ where $\hat{H}$ is the Hamiltonian operator. You would naturally have many doubts about this whole business but hold on. They will (hopefully!) get cleared in the next chapter.

Suppose we have a hydrogen atom. What is the guarantee it is initially in an eigenstate? None at all. Unless special pains are taken, a quantum system would most likely be in some general state $|\psi\rangle$ say, which is a superposition of the eigen or the base states. Thus, we can write

$$|\psi\rangle = C_1|1\rangle + C_2|2\rangle + \ldots + C_i|i\rangle + \ldots \qquad (2.16)$$

Suppose we do an experiment and measure the energy of the system. What answer do you think we would get? Not some average of E_1, E_2, ... but a definite value corresponding to one of the base states; maybe it is E_3. We repeat the experiment under the same initial condition, i.e., we start with the same state $|\psi\rangle$. This time the answer could be different, perhaps E_7. If we keep on making tries, our log book would end up with a string of entries like E_3, E_7, E_1, E_{14}, E_5, ... and so on. Patiently we accumulate a large number N of such readings and then count how many times we hit E_1, how many times we get E_2, etc. Call these numbers n_1, n_2, n_3, ... Obviously we must have

$$N = (n_1 + n_2 + n_3 + \ldots).$$

Are you perturbed that even though the atom is in the general state $|\psi\rangle$ to start with, measurement of the energy forces it to jump to one of the base states? Well, that is what the superposition principle (section 2.7) is all about. In fact, for large enough N we must have

$$(n_1/N) = |C_1|^2, \qquad (n_2/N) = |C_2|^2 \ldots \qquad (2.17)$$

Going back to our log book, let us now use it to calculate the average energy E_{av} according to the formula

$$E_{av} = \frac{n_1 E_1 + n_2 E_2 + \ldots}{n_1 + n_2 + \ldots} = (\sum_i n_i E_i)/N,$$

since $N = (n_1 + n_2 + \ldots)$. When N is large we can use (2.17) and write

$$E_{av} = \sum_i |C_i|^2 E_i.$$

Remembering

$$E_i = \langle i|\hat{H}|i\rangle$$

and (2.16), we then obtain

$$E_{av} = \langle\psi|\hat{H}|\psi\rangle. \qquad (2.18)$$

Sometimes one writes E_{av} as $\langle E\rangle$; you might want to watch out for this alternate notation.

Writing fancy expressions like $\langle j|\hat{O}|i\rangle$ or $\langle i|\hat{H}|i\rangle$ is OK as far as formal algebra is concerned but when it comes to calculating numbers, the wave function is of greater use. In terms of wave functions, these *matrix elements* are given by:

$$\langle j|\hat{O}|i\rangle = \int \psi_j^*(x)\,O(x)\,\psi_i(x)\,dx, \tag{2.19a}$$

$$\langle i|\hat{H}|i\rangle = \int \psi_i^*(x)\,H\psi_i(x)\,dx. \tag{2.19b}$$

If you know calculus you would immediately understand what all these formulae mean but if you don't, let it not bother you. Just tell yourself that the wave function leads to formulae of practical use. You might observe in passing that $\langle j|\hat{O}|i\rangle$ is in general a complex number because the wave functions ψ_i and ψ_j are in general complex.

2.13 Perturbation theory

Very often we would like to find out what happens to the states of a system when it is disturbed or perturbed. Occasionally, even the tiniest perturbation could lead to a drastic change like when a small push given to a stone delicately poised at the edge of a precipice. But more commonly, small disturbances produce only small changes. For example, when a small magnetic field is applied to an atom the levels split (at least some of them) and the splitting increases as the strength of the field is increased. Problems like this are handled by what is called *perturbation theory*. Naturally, when the perturbation is reduced to zero one must recover the original, unperturbed states.

The study of perturbation of quantum systems is a topic of wide interest, and the "technology" for it is well developed.

2.14 Electron spin

I have already narrated the story of electron spin in the companion volume *Bose and His Statistics*. In any case, parts of that story would be repeated in a later chapter. I shall therefore confine myself for the present to explaining what is meant by spin and why it is important.

The notion of electron spin arose out of attempts to understand certain complex features of atomic spectra. Experimentalists had observed that when a magnetic field is applied to a light source, the spectral lines are split. This discovery was made in 1896 by Zeeman of Holland and is referred to as the *Zeeman effect*. Almost immediately, the Dutch physicist Lorentz came up with an explanation—this was nearly fifteen years before the Bohr model. Spectroscopists then discovered that the splitting observed in the case of the prominent "yellow" lines of sodium—which experts call the D_1 and D_2 lines—could not be explained by the theory of Lorentz. So this peculiar case was referred to as the *anomalous Zeeman effect.*

When the Bohr model appeared, people naturally wondered what it had to say about all this. As you know, in the Bohr model, the electron is visualised as going round the nucleus in certain specified orbits. As a result the electron has an orbital angular momentum which modifies the level scheme of Fig. 2.14(a) to that in Fig. 2.14(b). In addition, since the electron carries a charge, it also behaves like a circulating current. Now a circulating current produces a magnetic field rather like a bar magnet does; one can therefore associate an orbital magnetic moment with the electron. To cut a long story short, when a magnetic field is applied, the energy levels of the hydrogen atom get further modified as in Fig. 2.14(c). The staircase of levels is now richer and many more transitions are possible than in the case of the level scheme in Fig. 2.14(a). But all this was not enough to explain the anomalous Zeeman effect, which continued to baffle the best of minds. In 1926, smartly following up on some crucial leads, Uhlenbeck and Goudsmit in Holland came up with the idea of electron *spin.*

To understand their work we need to go back a little. When an energy level scheme as in Fig. 2.14(c) did not work, the first thing that people did was to imagine that while going round the nucleus, the electron was also spinning about an axis, rather like our Earth does while orbiting round the Sun. Spinning introduces an extra degree of freedom into the problem. A point electron has no size. It has only three degrees of freedom, and three coordinates (x, y, z) are sufficient. If the electron has a finite size and also rotates, then additional degrees of freedom are needed for description. Additional degrees of freedom imply a more complicated energy level scheme and therefore possibly also new splittings which people thought would explain the anomalous Zeeman effect. Unfortunately, the idea of a spinning electron did not work.

When Uhlenbeck and Goudsmit analysed the problem, they suspected that though the electron did not physically spin about an axis, it nevertheless possessed a mysterious extra angular momentum of $(\hbar/2)$. Uhlenbeck and Goudsmit then simply *postulated* that the electron possessed an additional degree of freedom (over and above the three associated with position). This extra degree of freedom was peculiar. Consider the spatial degree of freedom, and focus say on the x coordinate of the electron. It is a continuous variable. By contrast, the coordinate associated with the new degree of freedom discovered

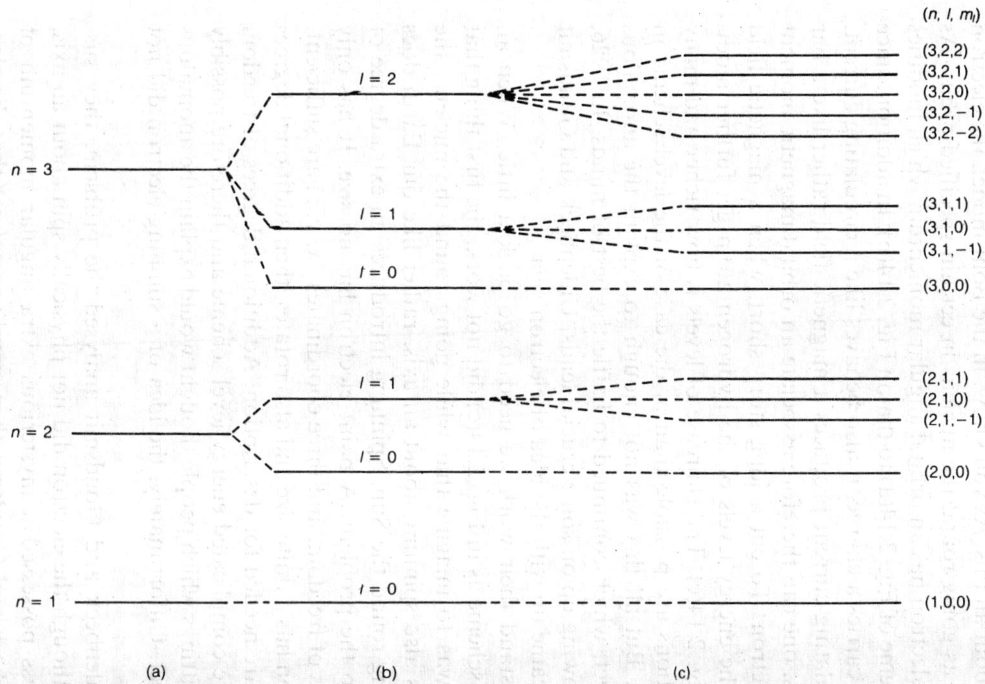

Fig. 2.14 In Fig. 2.7 we saw the energy spectrum of the hydrogen atom as predicted by the Bohr model. Although the levels were shown as single (see (a)), the higher levels really are clusters. If the effect of orbital angular momentum is explicitly included, the scheme of Fig. 2.7 must be labelled as in (b). There are clusters but levels in each cluster are degenerate. When a magnetic field is applied, splitting occurs as in (c).

by Uhlenbeck and Goudsmit can take just two values. Today we understand these things better. Deep analysis shows that this coordinate can only take the values + 1/2 and – 1/2.

Such a *discrete* degree of freedom was totally unknown in classical physics. It is the first "internal" degree of freedom to be discovered in the world of elementary particles. For purely historical reasons Uhlenbeck and Goudsmit referred to it as spin, although it has nothing whatsoever to do with the electron actually spinning about an axis. The word spin for this new degree of freedom is a most unfortunate choice, especially because of the confusion it can (and does) create, but we are stuck with it! Just remember that *electron spin does NOT refer to a spinning electron*. It simply refers to a new, *non-classical* degree of freedom. Earlier, in specifying the coordinates, we had given the value of the space coordinates, now, in addition we must also give the value of the spin coordinate. In other words, instead of x alone as previously, we must now specify (x, σ) where σ is the spin coordinate and can take only one of two possible values.

Once one grants the idea of spin a la Uhlenbeck and Goudsmit, a lot of the previously unexplained facts automatically fall into place, including the anomalous Zeeman effect.

But even after the discovery by Uhlenbeck and Goudsmit, the question remained: Where did this mysterious, non-classical degree of freedom pop up from? That became clear only after Dirac gave his theory of the electron.

2.15 Dirac equation

So far, the theory of relativity has not entered the picture. (For an introduction to relativity, see the companion volume *At the Speed of Light*.) Around 1927, Dirac set about hunting for the relativistic wave equation, and what he found (in January 1928) is referred to as the *Dirac equation*. This is one of the great discoveries of this century, and you will hear more about it later.

Three fall-outs of the Dirac equation must be mentioned. First it removed the mystery of electron spin. In other words, it now became clear that a relativistic electron *must* possess the property of spin which Goudsmit and Uhlenbeck had earlier *postulated*. The second fall-out is the prediction of the *positron* which is the anti-particle of the electron. Finally, the Dirac equation prepared the stage for the unification of the quantum theory of matter and the quantum theory of radiation under one umbrella.

2.16 Collapse of the wave function

I would now like to take you back to section 2.12 wherein I slipped something past you quickly. I said that though the atom was in the state $|\psi\rangle$ to start with, when an observation is made on it in order to determine the energy, the atom jumps to one of the base states. This jump is referred to as the *collapse* of the wave function and is a pretty strange affair. It would concern us quite a bit in Part III. It is something which cannot be mathematically derived but once one grants the collapse of the wave function, many things including the "only mystery" of the previous chapter can be understood. How exactly this is done calls for some technical details which I shall present in the next chapter.

To sum up:

In this chapter I have presented a rapid, qualitative survey of some of the important ideas of CM and QM. The essential points covered are:

- A key concept in the formulation of CM is the *Principle of Least Action.*
- Both in CM and in QM we are interested in the states of the system and how they vary in time.
- Quantum states can be superposed. If $|A\rangle$ and $|B\rangle$ are allowed states of a system, then so is

  $$|\psi\rangle = C_1|A\rangle + C_2|B\rangle$$

  where C_1 and C_2 are complex numbers.
- Practical interest often centres around calculating transition amplitudes.
- Transitions between states are caused by operators.
- An operator is a mathematical tool which represents a physical variable or property that could be measured with a suitable experiment.
- Schroedinger's wave function $\psi(x)$ gives a spatial description of the system corresponding to a given quantum state.
- $|\psi(x)|^2 dx$ represents the probability of finding the system (e.g., a particle) between x and $x + dx$.
- Spin is a quantum mechanical property.
- The Dirac equation is the relativistic analogue of the Schroedinger equation.

- The Dirac equation not only gave a proper place to spin in QM. but also revealed to us the existence of the positron, besides providing a pathway to quantum electrodynamics.

Get ready now for a stiff dose in the next chapter!

3 *A Closer Look*

I am afraid this chapter is going to be a bit mathematical. In physics, mathematics cannot be avoided—at best it can be postponed, which is what I did in the last chapter. Those of you who know calculus may find the going a bit easier but for those who don't, my suggestion is not to worry. Skip portions or equations which you can't quite understand and keep going so as to get at least a broad overview. In any case that is what I am attempting here, particularly because such an overview would help you to appreciate the discoveries on the one hand and the debates on the other. CAUTION: My aim is *not* to teach you QM; that you have to learn from elsewhere. In this book I am merely trying to give you a *feel* for the subject, with a stress on how it all happened.

3.1 Equations of motion in CM

Equations of motion are central to mechanics. Newton developed the subject using the concept of point masses and Cartesian (i.e., x, y, z) coordinates to denote the position of the point. The next step was to consider objects that were not points. Such objects could be thought of as an assembly of a large number of Newtonian points but this was a messy way of dealing with the problem.

Lagrange broke away from the Newtonian tradition by declaring that the dynamics of the system could jolly well be studied by using other types of coordinates. Suppose we have a flywheel that is rotating. Such an object is called a rigid rotator. Let us say one is interested in its rotational dynamics. One could deal with the rotator as if it was made up of zillions of particles but which are tied together—in other words, one would have had to deal with some kind of a complicated, constrained motion. Lagrange (effectively) said: "For me, the rotator is a rigid body and all I am interested in is how its orientation changes with time (see Fig. 3.1). This I describe with an angular coordinate θ and an angular velocity θ (for some notation etc., see Box 3.1). If I can focus just on these, I am on the road to the answer."

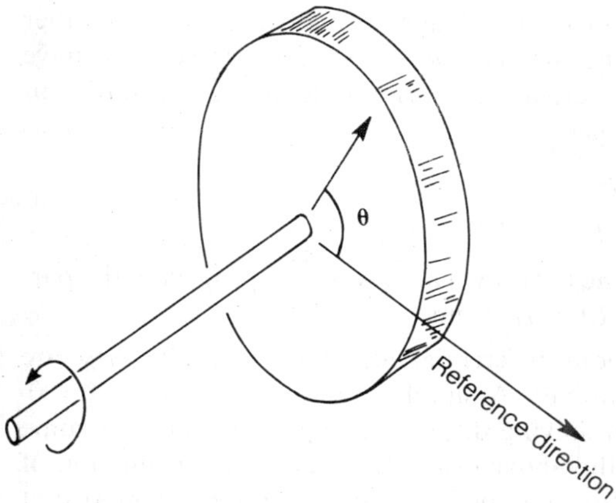

Fig. 3.1 This shows a rigid rotator. Of interest is how the rotation varies as a function of time. This may be studied by locating an arrow and observing the changes in the orientation angle θ (defined with respect to a reference direction).

Box 3.1 This box is meant mainly to explain some notation but maybe I will toss in a bit of calculus as well for those who don't know anything about it. Obviously, this is not the place to teach you the subject but certainly, I can give a flavour of it.

Let us start with figure (a). This shows a plot of a function $y = f(x)$, i.e., y is some function of x. Shown are a few tangents to the curve. The value of the tangent is simply given by tan θ where θ is shown in the figure. Suppose I want to know the value of the tangent without laboriously drawing the curve, drawing the tangent, measuring θ and then looking up the tables for the numerical value of tan θ. Calculus provides rules which bypass such a tedious graphical route. I can't explain the rules here but the tangent or the slope of the curve $y = f(x)$ is written as (dy/dx) or $f'(x)$. Using the rules of calculus, one can write a formula for f' given f. By giving specific values to x (like x_1, x_2, etc.), the corresponding numerical values of f' may be found. The quantity f' is called the *derivative* of f.

Now suppose y is a function of time, i.e., $y = f(t)$. The notation for the *time derivative* (dy/dt) is $\dot{f}$—note the dot on the top.

In the two simple examples considered, y was a function of one variable only; in the first case it was x and in the second it was t. What if y is a function of both x and t? This is possible. In this case, one can have *partial* derivatives, i.e., $(\partial y/\partial x)$ and $(\partial y/\partial t)$. In the former case, the derivative is computed using the usual rules but keeping the value of t fixed at whatever value of t is of interest. Similarly, $(\partial y/\partial t)$ is evaluated by taking the time derivative as usual, but keeping the value of x fixed at the desired value.

Given a function $y = f(x)$, it does not automatically follow that y' can be readily calculated (e.g., without ambiguity). For this, the function must have some desirable properties which normally is the case, in other words, the function is then *differentiable*. Supposing we now have $f'(x)$. Can one again take derivatives? Yes, provided, the standard conditions are met. One then gets

$$f''(x) = \frac{d}{dx}\left(\frac{dy}{dx}\right) = \frac{d^2 y}{dx^2}.$$

In this way one could define $(d^n y/dx^n)$ and, where appropriate, the partial derivatives $(\partial^n y/\partial x^n)$, $(\partial^n y/\partial t^n)$, etc.

Finally, a few words about differential equations. Basically these are equations involving derivatives. A simple example is $(dy/dx) + 4 = 0$. Methods are available for solving differential equations, at least some types. Solving means, in the above example, finding y as a function of x. The Schroedinger equation and the Dirac equations are two important differential equations which occur in QM.

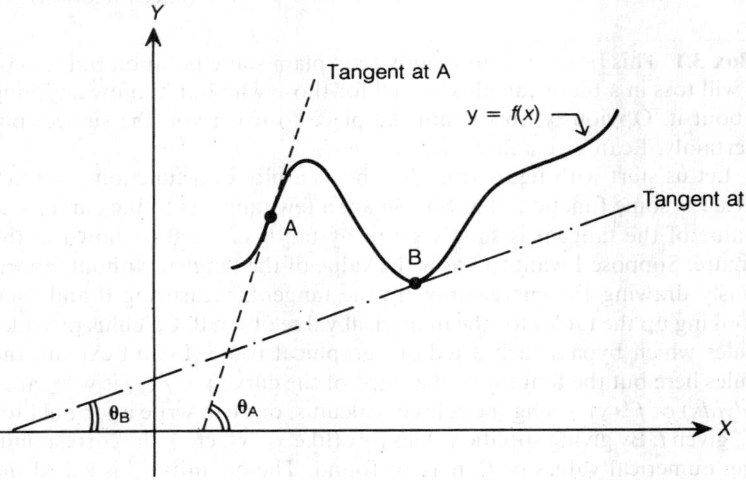

(a)

Coordinates like θ are called *generalised coordinates*, while quantities like $\dot{\theta}$ are referred to as *generalised velocities*. The standard notation for these are $(q_1, q_2, \ldots)$ and $(\dot{q}_1, \dot{q}_2, \ldots)$. The kinetic energy T and the potential energy V would in general depend on these quantities. For example, for the rotator $T = (1/2)\, I\dot{\theta}^2$ where I is the moment of inertia (for a free rotator, $(V = 0)$.

Let us suppose the total energy of the mechanical system is constant. Form the quantity

$$L = T - V. \tag{3.1}$$

L is called the *Lagrangian*, and in terms of it, the equations of motion are given by

$$\frac{d}{dt}\left(\frac{\partial L}{\partial \dot{q}_i}\right) - \frac{\partial L}{\partial q_i} = 0, \qquad i = 1, 2, ..., N \tag{3.2}$$

where N is the number of coordinates. Observe that there is one equation as in (3.2) for each generalised coordinate. For the rotator, it takes the form

$$I\frac{d^2\theta}{dt^2} = 0. \tag{3.3}$$

Equation (3.2) leads to N second-order differential equations. Like I said before, if you don't know calculus, just take it that the set of equations in (3.2) must be solved in order to solve the problem. These equations are called *Lagrange's equations of motion.*

Hamilton had a different version of the equations because instead of generalised velocities $\dot{q}_i$, he had *generalised momenta* p_i defined by

$$p_i = \frac{\partial L}{\partial \dot{q}_i}\,. \tag{3.4}$$

Introduce now

$$H = T + V. \tag{3.5}$$

The quantity H is known as the *Hamiltonian,* and is obviously the total energy of the system. It is a function of all the generalised coordinates and the corresponding momenta and therefore may be written $H(q, p)$. Hamilton's equations of motion are given by

$$\dot{q}_i = \frac{\partial H(q, p)}{\partial p_i}, \qquad \dot{p}_i = -\frac{\partial H(q, p)}{\partial q_i}\,. \tag{3.6}$$

In contrast to Lagrange's equations, there are now $2N$ first-order differential equations. Once again I would like to mention that Lagrange's and Hamilton's equations of motion express the same physics as Newton's laws but in forms better suited for advanced study.

Which is better—the version of Lagrange or that of Hamilton? It turns out that the former is preferable for actually solving problems whereas the latter is more suited for a theoretical study of mechanics. As Hamilton himself wrote, "Among the successors of Galileo, Lagrange has perhaps done more than any other analyst ... the beauty of his method makes his great work a kind of scientific poem."

Without going into technicalities, I should mention that another set of equations called the Hamilton–Jacobi equations are also widely used for solving problems, especially when periodic motion is involved, as in the case of oscillators or planetary motion. In such problems, one uses the *angle* and *action* variables θ and J in place of the usual q and p. In terms of these the equations of motion are:

$$\dot{\theta} = \frac{\partial H}{\partial J}, \qquad \dot{J} = -\frac{\partial H}{\partial \theta}. \tag{3.7}$$

The frequency ω associated with the periodic motion is given by

$$\omega = \dot{\theta}. \tag{3.8}$$

(When describing periodic motion, it is common to use the *angular* frequency $\omega = 2\pi\nu$ in place of ν the frequency; watch out, for there is a factor 2π involved which often gives trouble if one is not careful!) In writing down (3.7) and (3.8) I have supposed that there is only one characteristic frequency ω associated with the system. In general there could be several frequencies, in which case one has to write down such relations for each of these different frequencies.

There is actually more to this Hamilton–Jacobi business and perhaps I should make a brief mention of that. Hamilton was interested in exploring various nuances of mechanics. For this purpose, he introduced two functions $\mathcal{S}$ and W, known as Hamilton's *principal* function and Hamilton's *characteristic* function respectively. The two are related by

$$\mathcal{S} = W - \alpha_1 t \tag{3.9}$$

where α_1 is a constant. The quantity $\mathcal{S}$ above is rather like S defined in (2.1). More explicitly

$$\mathcal{S} = \int L dt + \text{constant}, \tag{3.10}$$

i.e., $\mathcal{S}$ is an indefinite quantity since no start and end times are specified. The $\mathcal{S}$ and W functions are the starting point of one approach to problems in classical mechanics, particularly when periodic motions are involved. The relevant equation, known as Hamilton–Jacobi differential equation, is given by

$$H\left(q, \frac{\partial W}{\partial q}\right) = \alpha_1. \tag{3.11}$$

It is a somewhat long road from (3.11) to the action-angle variables in (3.7), and I am afraid I cannot take you on that. But I should mention that the $\mathscr{S}$ and W functions have a deep significance.

For a given W, $\mathscr{S}$ evolves in time according to (3.9). Geometrically, it can be visualised as an expanding surface in a suitable but rather complicated space called *phase space* (—for an explanation of the phase space concept, see the companion volume *A Hot Story*). Lines that are perpendicular to surfaces of constant $\mathscr{S}$ essentially portray the particle trajectory. In short, Hamilton constructed a description of mechanics that seemed to have, at least from a mathematical point of view, some relation to wave propagation in optics. Hamilton recognised this interesting analogy between mechanics and optics but felt that it was purely formal. As I shall describe in Chapter 7, Schroedinger read more meaning into this connection and thereby discovered wave mechanics.

3.2 Poisson brackets

In the development of classical mechanics, there occurs a quantity known as the *Poisson bracket* (PB). The PB of two dynamical quantities u and v is written $[u, v]_{PB}$ and is defined as

$$[u, v]_{PB} = \sum_i \left(\frac{\partial u}{\partial q_i} \frac{\partial v}{\partial p_i} - \frac{\partial u}{\partial p_i} \frac{\partial v}{\partial q_i} \right). \tag{3.12}$$

We need not bother too much about the above definition but there are two fall-outs we must remember. Firstly, it turns out

$$[p_i, p_j]_{PB} = 0 \qquad \text{for all } i \text{ and } j \tag{3.13a}$$

$$[q_i, q_j]_{PB} = 0 \qquad \text{for all } i \text{ and } j \tag{3.13b}$$

$$[q_i, p_j]_{PB} = 0 \qquad i \neq j \tag{3.13c}$$

$$[q_i, p_i]_{PB} = 1 \qquad \text{for all } i. \tag{3.13d}$$

The last two results are often compressed by writing

$$[q_i, p_j]_{PB} = \delta_{ij}. \tag{3.14}$$

The quantity δ_{ij} is called the *Kronecker delta* and is defined by

$$\begin{aligned} \delta_{ij} &= 0, \; i \neq j \\ &= 1, \; i = j. \end{aligned} \tag{3.15}$$

Shortly we will meet the analogues of (3.14) in QM and see the crucial role they play.

The second important point about the PB is the following:

$$[q_i, H]_{PB} = \frac{\partial H}{\partial p_i},$$

$$[p_i, H]_{PB} = -\frac{\partial H}{\partial q_i}. \tag{3.16}$$

Recalling Hamilton's equations of motion (3.6), we can now write

$$\dot{q}_i = [q_i, H]_{PB},$$

$$\dot{p}_i = [p_i, H]_{PB}. \tag{3.17}$$

In other words, the equations of motion involve the Poisson brackets. This also has echoes in QM.

3.3 Transformation of basis sets in QM

Enough has been said about CM; now for a quick brush up of the more technical aspects of QM. I have already told you (in section 2.5) that quantum states can be regarded as vectors which can be described using different basis sets as in equation (2.10). In fact if we take the help of Fig. 2.9, it is easy to show

$$\mathbf{i}' = \mathbf{i}\cos\theta + \mathbf{j}\sin\theta$$

$$\mathbf{j}' = -\mathbf{i}\sin\theta + \mathbf{j}\cos\theta. \tag{3.18}$$

In matrix notation (see Appendix) this becomes

$$\begin{pmatrix}\mathbf{i}'\\ \mathbf{j}'\end{pmatrix} = \begin{pmatrix}\cos\theta, & \sin\theta\\ -\sin\theta, & \cos\theta\end{pmatrix}\begin{pmatrix}\mathbf{i}\\ \mathbf{j}\end{pmatrix} \tag{3.19}$$

The 2×2 matrix above describes the transformation from the basis set (**i**, **j**) to (**i**′, **j**′).

Transformation of basis vectors is an important manipulation in QM. Recall that in CM one usually formulates the problem using some convenient set of variables (q, p) for a start, but then seeks to discover other variables (Q, P) which make the problem easier to solve. Similar thing here; one formulates the problem using some convenient basis set but then tries to switch over to another which is an easy pathway to the solution. An example to follow should put you at ease!

3.4 Fun with S –G machines

To make some of the above concepts more meaningful, let us do some playing around like Feynman does in volume III of his famous lecture series. We shall follow with interest the progress of a beam of spin 1 particles through an apparatus of the type first used decades ago by Stern and Gerlach in a classic experiment.

In Chapter 2, I introduced you to the spin of the electron and remarked that it (i.e., the electron) behaves as if it had (a spin) angular momentum of ($\hbar/2$). One also describes this using a *spin quantum number s* which, for the electron, takes the value 1/2. In general, s could assume the half integral values 1/2, 3/2, 5/2, ... or the integer values 0, 1, 2, ... Just as the spin of an electron can have two orientations with respect to a reference direction, a particle of spin s can have $(2s + 1)$ orientations corresponding to the magnetic quantum number m_s taking the values $s, s - 1, ... 0, ..., - s$. The spin 1 particle thus has three orientations and we label the corresponding states as $|+1\rangle$, $|0\rangle$ and $|-1\rangle$—see Fig. 3.2. When a beam of spin 1 particles is let in at one end of a Stern–Gerlach apparatus, it comes out separated into the various possible states at the other end, as shown in Fig. 3.3.

We will do our experiments with a slightly modified form of the Stern–Gerlach apparatus which recombines the split beams at the exit

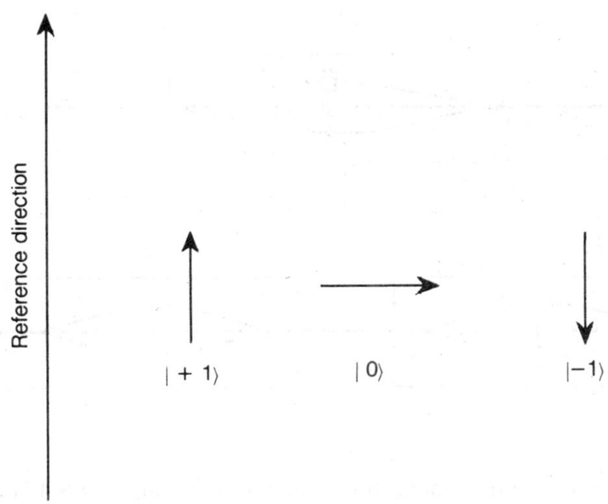

Fig. 3.2 With respect to a given reference direction, a particle of spin 1 can have three states $|+1\rangle$, $|0\rangle$ and $|-1\rangle$. These are customarily depicted by drawing arrows as above.

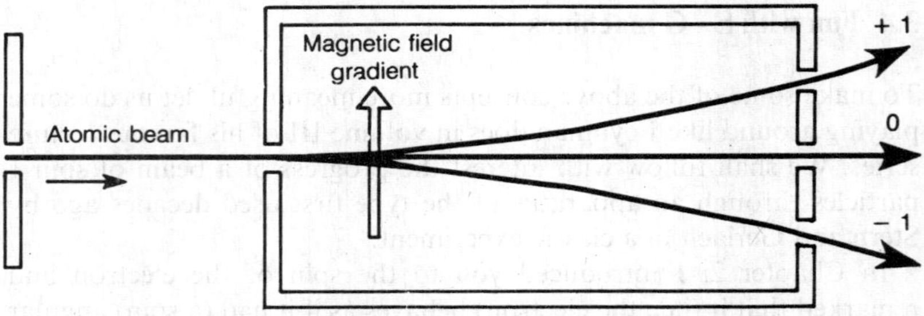

Fig. 3.3 A Stern–Gerlach apparatus essentially consists of an oven which shoots a beam of particles into a chamber in which acts a non-uniform magnetic field. When the beam consists of atoms of spin 1, three separated beams are produced.

end as shown in Fig. 3.4(a). Next we shall introduce stoppers as illustrated in Fig. 3.4(b) so that at the output end we get a *filtered* beam. We now get hold of a second apparatus like the first one, and feed the

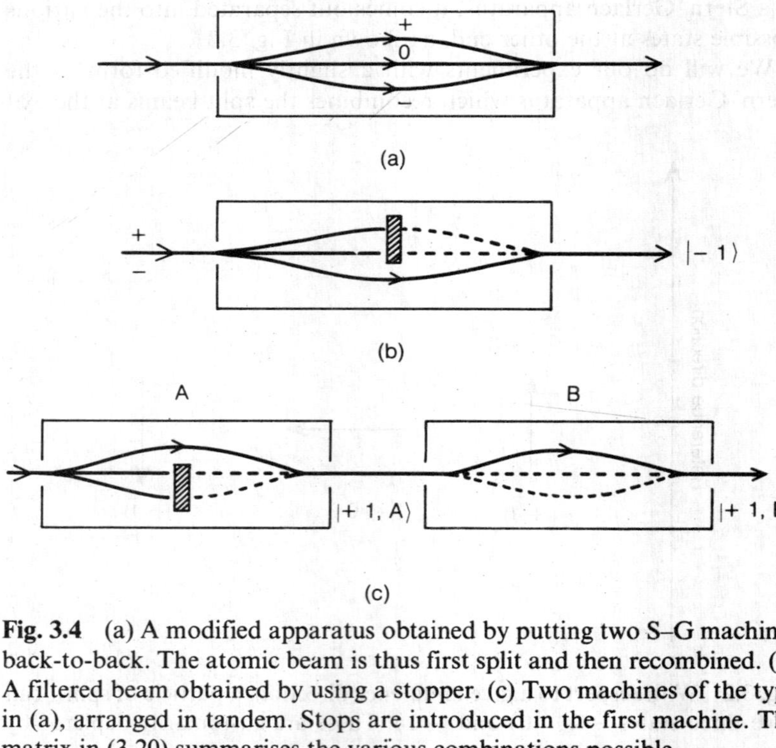

Fig. 3.4 (a) A modified apparatus obtained by putting two S–G machines back-to-back. The atomic beam is thus first split and then recombined. (b) A filtered beam obtained by using a stopper. (c) Two machines of the type in (a), arranged in tandem. Stops are introduced in the first machine. The matrix in (3.20) summarises the various combinations possible.

output beam of the first into the second—see Fig. 3.4(c). The question is: What comes out of the second apparatus when various kinds of stops are put on the way? A little thinking would show that 9 combinations are possible. For each combination we can write an amplitude like, $\langle B, +1|-1, A\rangle$, etc. By introducing filters as in Fig. 3.4(b), we are essentially making A give out a filtered beam, i.e., we are preparing the system (of particles) in a *base* state before feeding it to apparatus B. The 9 possible transition amplitudes $\langle B, j|i, A\rangle$ ($i = +1, 0, -1$, $j = +1, 0, -1$) can obviously be arranged into a 3×3 matrix as below:

To: \ From:	$\|+1, A\rangle$	$\|0, A\rangle$	$\|-1, A\rangle$
$\|+1, B\rangle$	1	0	0
$\|0, B\rangle$	0	1	0
$\|-1, B\rangle$	0	0	1

(3.20)

The example just studied is rather trivial. So let us complicate matters by tilting the second apparatus slightly with respect to the first—see Fig. 3.5. In this case, the matrix analogous to (3.20) has the following appearance:

To: \ From:	$\|+1, A\rangle$	$\|0, A\rangle$	$\|-1, A\rangle$
$\|+1, B\rangle$	$(1/2)(1+\cos\alpha)$	$(1/\sqrt{2})\sin\alpha$	$(1/2)(1-\cos\alpha)$
$\|0, B\rangle$	$-(1/\sqrt{2})\sin\alpha$	$\cos\alpha$	$(1/\sqrt{2})\sin\alpha$
$\|-1, B\rangle$	$(1/2)(1-\cos\alpha)$	$(-1\sqrt{2})\sin\alpha$	$(1/2)(1+\cos\alpha)$

(3.21)

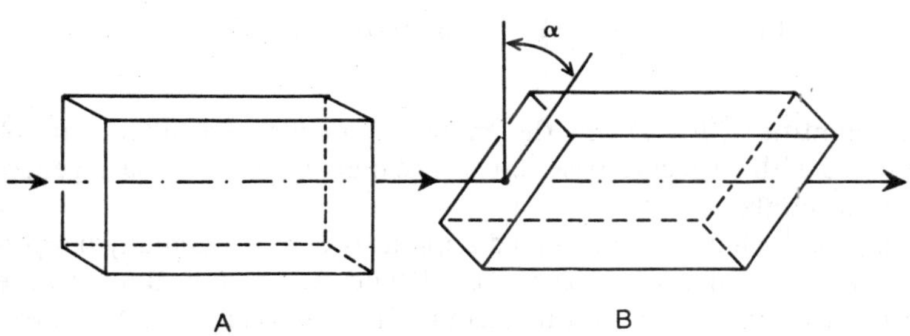

Fig. 3.5 Two S–G filters in series, with the second one tilted by an angle α.

What we have achieved by all this is the illustration of an important principle in QM, namely that any atomic system can be separated by a filtering process into a set of pure or base states. Apparatus A gives us access to the states $|+1, A\rangle$, $|0, A\rangle$ and $|-1, A\rangle$ while B leads us to $|+1, B\rangle$, $|0, B\rangle$ and $|-1, B\rangle$. Depending on the value of α, there are any number of possibilities, each as good as the other. The matrix (3.21) essentially describes the transformation from the A to the B bases.

We continue our exercise and this time we have no hangups about filtered beams. We start with a beam in the state $|\phi\rangle$ and after the measurement it is in the state $|\chi\rangle$ say. The apparatus used for the measurement is some complicated affair but we don't care; we simply denote it by the symbol $\hat{A}$. [I have added a hat on top of A for a reason which would become clear shortly.] In short, we "look" at the system through $\hat{A}$ when it (the system) is in the state $|\phi\rangle$, and as a result of this "looking" the system goes to the state $|\chi\rangle$. We write the transition amplitude as $\langle\chi|\hat{A}|\phi\rangle$. We are interested in this amplitude because its square would give us a probability, which is what we are after.

Now there are many choices for $|\phi\rangle$ and also for $|\chi\rangle$ which means that there are innumerable possibilities for the amplitude mentioned above. How then can one give a concise description of the apparatus $\hat{A}$? The trick is to see how $\hat{A}$ "operates" when used with pure states. For a system made up of spin 1 particles, the base states are $|+1\rangle$, $|0\rangle$ and $|-1\rangle$. So $\hat{A}$ is compactly described by the following matrix:

$$
\text{To: }\left\{\begin{array}{l} |+1\rangle \\ |0\rangle \\ |-1\rangle \end{array}\right.
\overbrace{\begin{array}{lll} |+1\rangle & |0\rangle & |-1\rangle \\ \langle +1|\hat{A}|+1\rangle & \langle +1|\hat{A}|0\rangle & \langle +1|\hat{A}|-1\rangle \\ \langle 0|\hat{A}|+1\rangle & \langle 0|\hat{A}|0\rangle & \langle 0|\hat{A}|-1\rangle \\ \langle +1|\hat{A}|+1\rangle & \langle +1|\hat{A}|0\rangle & \langle +1|\hat{A}|-1\rangle \end{array}}^{\text{From:}}
\tag{3.22}
$$

The quantities $\langle j|\hat{A}|i\rangle$ are the matrix elements associated with $\hat{A}$, evaluated with respect to base states. The matrix elements are in general complex numbers.

Suppose we have a complicated apparatus $\hat{C}$ which actually happens to be made up of two simpler pieces $\hat{B}$ and $\hat{A}$, i.e., $\hat{C} = \hat{B}\hat{A}$. In other words, observing with $\hat{C}$ is equivalent to first observing with $\hat{A}$ and then with $\hat{B}$—note the order. So the matrix for $\hat{C}$ would just be a product of the matrices for $\hat{B}$ and $\hat{A}$, i.e.,

$$\langle j|\hat{C}|i\rangle = \sum_k \langle j|\hat{B}|k\rangle\langle k|\hat{A}|i\rangle, \tag{3.23a}$$

$$\langle \chi|\hat{C}|\phi\rangle = \sum_k \langle \phi|\hat{B}|k\rangle\langle k|\hat{A}|\phi\rangle. \tag{3.23b}$$

Here $|k\rangle$ refers to an intermediate state. It is important that we arrive at the result for $\hat{C}$ via the product $\hat{B}\hat{A}$ and *NOT* $\hat{A}\hat{B}$ because $\hat{B}\hat{A}$ and $\hat{A}\hat{B}$ are not necessarily equal.

The mathematics of quantum mechanics is so interesting that it is easy to get lost in it, especially because it is so vast. I cannot afford that because curious readers might already be wondering: "What has all this algebra got to do with physics?" Patience, we are getting there!

3.5 Ordinary vectors versus quantum state vectors

I have already compared the quantum mechanical state vector to the ordinary vector. Let us follow this up a bit more.

	Ordinary vector	QM vector
(a)	$\mathbf{r} = a\cdot\mathbf{i} + b\cdot\mathbf{j}$	$|\phi\rangle = \sum_i C_i|i\rangle$
(b)	$\mathbf{i}\cdot\mathbf{j} = 0$	$\langle i|j\rangle = 0$
	$\mathbf{i}\cdot\mathbf{i} = \mathbf{j}\cdot\mathbf{j} = 1$	$\langle i|i\rangle = \langle j|j\rangle = 1$
(c)	$\mathbf{A}\cdot\mathbf{B} = \mathbf{B}\cdot\mathbf{A}$	$\langle\chi|\phi\rangle = \langle\chi|\phi\rangle^*$
(d)	$\mathbf{A} = a_1\mathbf{i} + b_1\mathbf{j}$	$|\phi\rangle = \sum_i C_i|i\rangle$
	$\mathbf{B} = a_2\mathbf{i} + b_2\mathbf{j}$	$|\chi\rangle = \sum_i D_i|i\rangle$
	$\mathbf{A}\cdot\mathbf{B} = a_1b_1 + a_2b_2$	$\langle\chi|\phi\rangle = \sum_i C_iD_i^*$
(e)	$\mathbf{r}\cdot\mathbf{i} = a, \mathbf{r}\cdot\mathbf{j} = b$	
	$\mathbf{r} = \mathbf{i}(\mathbf{r}\cdot\mathbf{i}) + \mathbf{j}(\mathbf{r}\cdot\mathbf{j})$	$|\phi\rangle = \sum_i |i\rangle\langle i|\phi\rangle$

Comments:

1. Relation (b) is referred to as the *orthonormality* relation. Essentially it says that the different base vectors are all of "unit" length and "perpendicular" to each other.
2. Relation (b) is often written as:

   $\langle i|j\rangle = \delta_{ij}$

   where δ_{ij} is the Kronecker delta—see (3.15).

3. Result (c) is true for all $|\phi\rangle$. So why not drop ϕ and write

$$| = \sum_i |i\rangle\langle i| ? \qquad (3.24)$$

On the left side is the bar (|) which occurs in *bra* and in *ket*. While doing manipulations, experts often replace the bar by what occurs on the right-hand side. Sometimes, unity is replaced similarly. (I know I am taking unforgivable liberties but otherwise I would be bogged down in explaining intricate technicalities.) Shortly we shall encounter some examples.

3.6 A few tricks

I cannot resist the temptation of giving you a glimpse into a few tricks of the trade even though it would detain us somewhat. Suppose a system is in the state $|\phi\rangle$ and we use the apparatus $\hat{A}$ to see if the system is in the state $|\chi\rangle$. As you know, the amplitude for this is given by $\langle\chi|\hat{A}|\phi\rangle$. There are two bars here which we can replace using rule (3.24), i.e., we write

$$\langle\chi| \text{ as } \sum_i \langle\chi|i\rangle\langle i|, \qquad (3.25a)$$

$$\text{and} \quad |\phi\rangle \quad \text{as} \quad \sum_j |j\rangle\langle j|\phi\rangle. \qquad (3.25b)$$

Are you worried that in (a) I have a sum over *i* whereas in (b) the sum is over *j*? It does not matter what symbol I use since I am summing over all the intermediate (pure) states. Pundits would say there is no problem because *i* and *j* are dummy indices. So we finally get

$$\langle\chi|\hat{A}|\phi\rangle = \sum_i\sum_j \langle\chi|i\rangle\langle i|\hat{A}|j\rangle\langle j|\phi\rangle. \qquad (3.26)$$

Consider now Fig. 3.6. This shows the vector *OP* being changed in two different ways, once by rotation and once by stretching. In other words, we do some operation on *OP* to produce a new vector *OQ*. Similar operations are carried out on quantum vectors using what are called *operators*. Thus

$$|\chi\rangle = \hat{A}|\phi\rangle \qquad (3.27)$$

means that operating on the state $|\phi\rangle$ leads to the state $|\psi\rangle$. A hat (^) is added to A to explicitly indicate that we are dealing with an operator.

Let us now use our old trick. We first write $\hat{A}$ as

$$\hat{A} = 1.\hat{A}.1$$

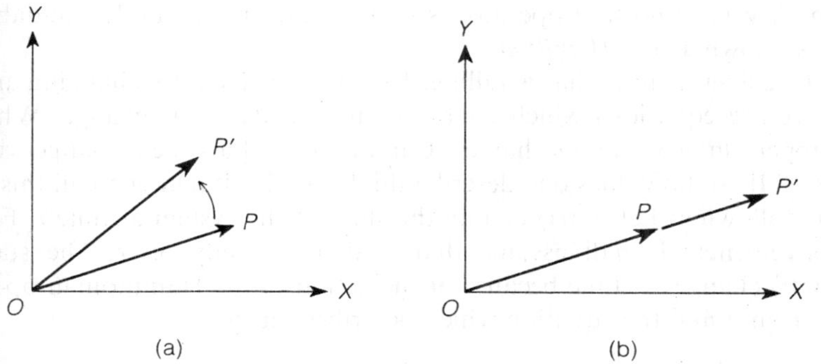

Fig. 3.6 Changes effected on vector OP by (a) rotation and (b) stretching.

and then replace the ones as usual. This gives us

$$\hat{A} = (\sum_i |i\rangle\langle i|)\hat{A}(\sum_j |j\rangle\langle j|). \tag{3.28}$$

Therefore

$$\hat{A}|\phi\rangle = \sum_i\sum_j |i\rangle\langle i|\hat{A}|j\rangle\langle j|\phi\rangle, \tag{3.29}$$

which then leads to

$$\langle\chi|\hat{A}|\phi\rangle = \sum_i\sum_j \langle\chi|i\rangle\langle i|\hat{A}|j\rangle\langle j|\phi\rangle,$$

which is our old result (3.26) again. In view of (3.27), we also have

$$\langle\chi|\psi\rangle = \langle\chi|\hat{A}|\phi\rangle. \tag{3.30}$$

The effect of an operator on a system is described by the matrix of amplitudes $\langle i|\hat{A}|j\rangle$ where $|i\rangle$ and $|j\rangle$ denote the basis vectors needed for describing the states of the system under consideration. Often the matrix element $\langle i|\hat{A}|j\rangle$ is simply written as A_{ij}.

3.7 The Hamiltonian

Time to say something more about operators. For all practical purposes, an operator is a tool that enables us to make a measurement. The apparatuses we have been playing with in the last section are all operators. Similarly, one has a position operator to measure the position coordinate, a momentum operator to measure momentum and so on. A very important operator is that for the energy; understandably it is known as the *Hamiltonian*.

Consider a stone that is falling. Its state is constantly changing and there are equations which enable us to calculate this change. What happens in quantum mechanics? Can the state of a system change with time? If so, how does one describe this? The short answer to all this is the following: Let $|\psi(t)\rangle$ denote the state of the system at time t. For convenience, I shall assume that ψ depends only on t. The state $|\psi(t)\rangle$ changes in time because of the action of the Hamiltonian operator on it and the equation which describes this is

$$i\hbar \frac{d|\psi(t)\rangle}{dt} = \hat{H}|\psi(t)\rangle. \tag{3.31}$$

(I can take the liberty of using the total derivative (d/dt) because ψ depends on t alone.) If we write $|\psi(t)\rangle$ as

$$|\psi(t)\rangle = \sum_i C_i(t)|i\rangle, \tag{3.32}$$

then (3.31) can be rewritten as

$$i\hbar \frac{dC_i(t)}{dt} = \sum_j H_{ij} C_j(t) \tag{3.33}$$

where $H_{ij}(t)$ stands for $\langle i|\hat{H}|j\rangle$. Once one knows the form of the Hamiltonian operator and therefore the matrix elements H_{ij}, one has merely to solve for the coefficients in the above equation, i.e., how they vary in time. From equation (3.32) we then know the state vector $|\psi(t)\rangle$.

We will come back to (3.31) shortly but meanwhile one comment is necessary. As it stands, it is difficult to see why $\hat{H}$ should at all be connected with the energy of the system. As Dirac says one assumes this is so, primarily by certain analogies with classical mechanics. There are a couple of other reasons too, but they are rather technical.

3.8 Ammonia molecule

Finding $|\psi(t)\rangle$ from (3.31) is not always easy but perhaps an example would help in getting the flavour of the whole business. Continuing to follow in Feynman's footsteps, I choose the ammonia molecule as my example of a quantum system. Figure 3.7 shows the molecule. As you can see there are two equivalent geometric arrangements possible, and we adopt these as the base states $|1\rangle$ and $|2\rangle$. The actual state $|\psi\rangle$ of the molecule would be some superposition of these base states:

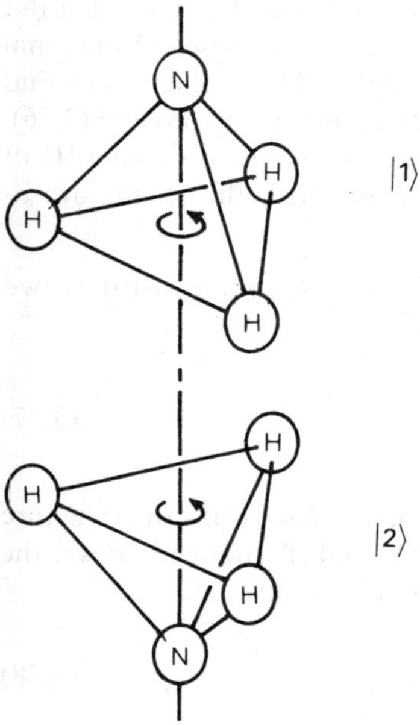

Fig. 3.7 Two equivalent geometric arrangements of the ammonia molecule.

$$|\psi\rangle = C_1|1\rangle + C_2|2\rangle. \tag{3.34}$$

If we want to know how the state of the molecule changes with time, then we have to find out what happens to the coefficients C_1 and C_2. For that we have to deal with (3.33) as applied to this problem which reads

$$\begin{aligned} i\hbar\frac{dC_1}{dt} &= H_{11}C_1 + H_{12}C_2 \\ i\hbar\frac{dC_2}{dt} &= H_{21}C_1 + H_{22}C_2. \end{aligned} \tag{3.35}$$

The Hamiltonian matrix is given by:

$$\begin{pmatrix} H_{11} & H_{12} \\ H_{21} & H_{22} \end{pmatrix} = \begin{pmatrix} E_0 & -A \\ -A & E_0 \end{pmatrix} \tag{3.36}$$

A couple of quick comments for otherwise you would be mystified. If the off-diagonal elements H_{12} and H_{21} were equal to zero, then the ammonia molecule would have only one energy state, the corresponding energy being E_0. But the off-diagonal elements of the Hamiltonian matrix are not zero. By symmetry they are equal, and we have simply set their value equal to $-A$. As yet we do not know the value of A but that does not matter. Thanks to the presence of these off-diagonal terms, the molecule now has two energy states. The problem is to find these energies and the corresponding state vectors via (3.35) and (3.36). I can't go into all the details here (they are available in volume III of the famous Feynman Lectures) but in a nutshell, the results are as follows:

1. From the original base vectors $|1\rangle$ and $|2\rangle$, one constructs two new base vectors $|\mathrm{I}\rangle$ and $|\mathrm{II}\rangle$ given by

$$|\mathrm{I}\rangle = (1/\sqrt{2})\{|1\rangle - |2\rangle\}$$
$$|\mathrm{II}\rangle = (1/\sqrt{2})\{|1\rangle + |2\rangle\} \tag{3.37}$$

In terms of $|1\rangle$ and $|2\rangle$ the Hamiltonian matrix has the structure in (3.36) but in terms of the states $|\mathrm{I}\rangle$ and $|\mathrm{II}\rangle$ defined above, the Hamiltonian matrix assumes the simpler form

$$\begin{pmatrix} E_0 + A & 0 \\ 0 & E_0 - A \end{pmatrix}. \tag{3.38}$$

This sort of a change will be discussed further in section 3.13 but for the present we note that the energies of the two levels of the molecule are given by $(E_0 + A)$ and $(E_0 - A)$.

2. From these new base vectors, one then constructs two state vectors $|\psi_{\mathrm{I}}(t)\rangle$ and $|\psi_{\mathrm{II}}(t)\rangle$ given by

$$|\psi_{\mathrm{I}}(t)\rangle = C_{\mathrm{I}}(t)|\mathrm{I}\rangle$$
$$|\psi_{\mathrm{II}}(t)\rangle = C_{\mathrm{II}}(t)|\mathrm{II}\rangle \tag{3.39}$$

where

$$C_{\mathrm{I}}(t) = e^{-(i/\hbar)(E_0 + A)t}$$
$$C_{\mathrm{II}}(t) = e^{-(i/\hbar)(E_0 - A)t}. \tag{3.40}$$

The states I and II are referred to as *stationary states*, $|\psi_{\mathrm{I}}\rangle$ and $|\psi_{\mathrm{II}}\rangle$ being the corresponding state vectors. Perhaps you are aware of the Bohr atom model and its stationary states (I shall discuss them later); same sort of thing here. If the molecule is in state I, it stays put there unless disturbed; same with state II. The energies of these two states are given by $(E_0 + A)$ and $(E_0 - A)$.

Let us now disturb the molecule and see what happens. How does one disturb the ammonia molecule? This is easy. Now the electrons in

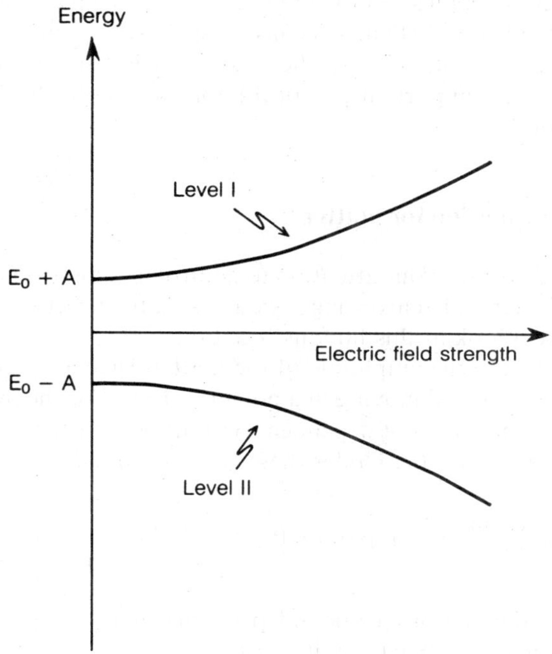

Fig. 3.8 Energy levels of the ammonia molecule in an electric field.

the ammonia molecule are so organised that the molecule as a whole behaves like an *electric dipole*. A simple way of visualising a dipole is to think of a dumb-bell and imagine that one of the balls has positive charge and the other has negative charge. Dipoles get disturbed when an electric field is applied. This gives us a hint about how to perturb our molecule—we should apply an electric field.

Assume a d.c. electric field is applied. The variation it produces on the energy levels is sketched in Fig. 3.8. An interesting thing happens

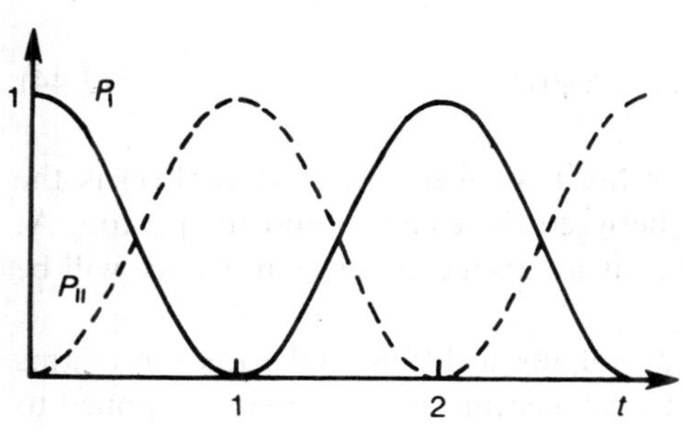

Fig. 3.9 Time variation of the probabilities of the two states, when an a.c. electric field of the correct frequency is applied.

if an a.c. field is applied and if the frequency ν is equal to the energy difference divided by h (Planck's constant). The probability for finding the molecule in the two states then oscillates in time as sketched in Fig. 3.9. This has important practical implications; maybe you should try to find out!

3.9 A wave equation for matter

I have already drawn your attention to de Broglie's discovery about the duality of matter and Schroedinger's wave equation (section 2.9 – 2.11). Time to take a look at this famous equation.

Let $\psi(r)$ denote the amplitude of the matter wave associated with a particle of mass m and moving in a potential $V(r)$. For the moment, we are assuming that ψ is not dependent on time. We further suppose the system is non-relativistic. Under these circumstances,

$$\nabla^2\psi(r) + \frac{8\pi^2 m}{h^2}(E - V)\psi(r) = 0, \quad \nabla^2 = \left(\frac{\partial^2}{\partial x^2} + \frac{\partial^2}{\partial y^2} + \frac{\partial^2}{\partial z^2}\right). \quad (3.41)$$

There it is, the famous (time-independent) Schroedinger equation. Sometimes this is compactly written as

$$H\psi = E\psi \quad (3.42)$$

where H is the Hamiltonian. For the problem considered above, clearly

$$H = \left\{-\frac{\hbar^2\nabla^2}{2m} + V\right\}. \quad (3.43)$$

The exciting story of how such a wave equation was arrived at by stretching the analogy between optics and mechanics is reserved for a later chapter.

What exactly does one do with the Schroedinger equation? To answer this, consider

$$-\frac{\hbar^2}{2m}\nabla^2\psi(r) + V(r)\psi(r) = E\psi(r) \quad (3.44)$$

the Schroedinger equation for the hydrogen atom. Here $V(r)$ is the electrostatic potential energy between the electron and the proton. At present we treat the quantity E as a parameter; its significance will be pointed out shortly.

Mathematical techniques for solving a differential equation of this type have been known from the last century and are readily applied to the problem on hand. When that is done, it turns out that physically reasonable solutions of ψ are possible only for certain values of E, which turn out to be the energies of the various levels of the hydrogen atom. The amplitude ψ is nothing but the wave function I introduced you to in section 2.10. Thus, to each energy level E_i, there is a corresponding wave function $\psi_i(x, y, z)$. I have already explained the physical interpretation of the wave function and presented plots of $|\psi_i|^2$ (see Fig. 2.12).

3.10 Time-dependent Schroedinger equation

The Schroedinger equation is often presented in textbooks in the form

$$H\psi = E\psi.$$

Equation (3.44) is a particular example of the above, as applicable to a particle moving in a potential $V(r)$.

So far there has been no mention of time in the context of the Schroedinger equation. That is because time has not appeared in the Hamiltonian. Even though the Hamiltonian itself is time independent, the wave function can and does depend on time. However, this time dependence has a simple form. If $\psi_i(r)$ denotes a solution of (3.44) corresponding to the state with label i and having energy E_i, then the time dependence of ψ is given by

$$\psi_i(r, t) = \psi_i(r)e^{-(iE_i t)/\hbar}. \tag{3.45}$$

The state i is then said to be a stationary state of the particle since $|\psi|^2$ is constant in time.

Suppose an oscillating electric field is applied to the hydrogen atom. The Hamiltonian in (3.44) must then be suitably altered. As a result, $\psi(r, t)$ can no longer be written down in a simple form as in (3.45). Rather $\psi(r, t)$ has to be patiently obtained by solving the *time-dependent Schroedinger equation.*

$$i\hbar \frac{\partial}{\partial t} \psi(r, t) = H(r, t)\psi(r, t). \tag{3.46}$$

3.11 State vectors and the wave function

You might be wondering what the relationship between the state vector and the wave function is. Let us see. Consider an electron which can wander up and down the x-axis. Its coordinate can therefore be labelled by x: of course, a measurement is necessary to find the coordinate. If the electron is at x we describe the associated state by $|x\rangle$. To start with let us say the electron is in the general state $|\psi\rangle$. The amplitude for finding the electron at x is then given by $\langle x|\psi\rangle$. Corresponding to different points like x_1, x_2, x_3, etc., we would have the amplitudes $\langle x_1|\psi\rangle$, $x_2|\psi\rangle$, etc. Let us change the notation and write these amplitudes as $\psi(x_1)$, $\psi(x_2)$, $\psi(x_3)$, ... The continuous function $\psi(x)$ is nothing but the wave function of Schroedinger.

3.12 More about changes with time

There are two broad approaches available for discussing matters relating to time dependence in QM—one is called the *Schroedinger representation* and the other is called the *Heisenberg representation*. Both are really two avenues to the same result. An analogy may perhaps help you to appreciate how this could come about.

Consider the vector OP in Fig. 3.10. Rotate it by angle α to the position OP' as shown. The result is that the vector now makes an

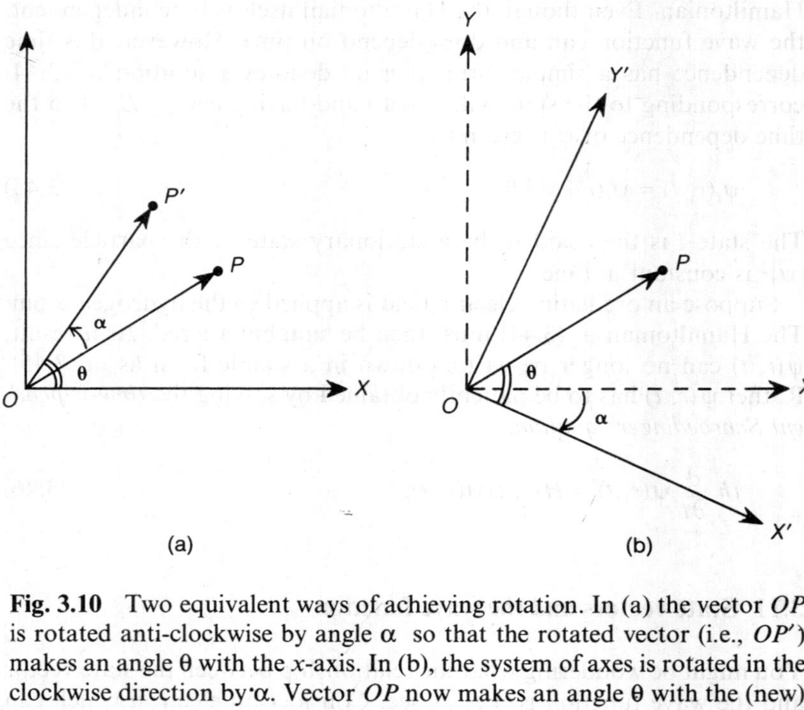

Fig. 3.10 Two equivalent ways of achieving rotation. In (a) the vector OP is rotated anti-clockwise by angle α so that the rotated vector (i.e., OP') makes an angle θ with the x-axis. In (b), the system of axes is rotated in the clockwise direction by α. Vector OP now makes an angle θ with the (new) x-axis.

angle θ with the x-axis. Instead of rotating OP, I could as well have rotated the system of axes itself by the angle α but in the opposite direction—see Fig. 3.10(b). In this case also the vector OP ends up by making an angle θ with the x-axis; the two approaches to the end result are thus equivalent.

In the Schroedinger representation, the state vector $|\psi(t)\rangle$ evolves in time but operators corresponding to dynamical variables do not. In the Heisenberg representation things are the other way about, i.e., $|\psi\rangle$ does not vary with time but operators do. Thus in the former case one deals with quantities like $\langle\psi(t)|\hat{A}|\psi(t)\rangle$ whereas in the latter, one has $\langle\psi|\hat{A}(t)|\psi\rangle$. Both give the same answer. If you wish to dig a bit deeper, see Box 3.2.

Box 3.2 The following is a simple discussion of the equivalence of the points of view involving the Schroedinger representation on the one hand and the Heisenberg representation on the other. In the former picture, the time evolution of the state $|\psi(t)\rangle$ is governed by the equation

$$i\hbar \frac{d}{dt}|\psi(t)\rangle = \hat{H}|\psi(t)\rangle. \qquad (1)$$

This can be integrated to obtain

$$|\psi(t)\rangle = e^{-i\hat{H}t/\hbar}|\psi(0)\rangle. \qquad (2)$$

From this,

$$\langle\psi(t)| = \langle\psi(0)|e^{i\hat{H}t/\hbar}. \qquad (3)$$

Using (2) and (3), we have

$$\langle\psi(t)|\hat{A}|\psi(t)\rangle \qquad (4)$$

$$= \langle\psi(0)|e^{i\hat{H}t/\hbar}\,\hat{A}\,e^{-i\hat{H}t/\hbar}|\psi(0)\rangle \qquad (5)$$

$$= \langle\psi(0)|\hat{A}(t)|\psi(0)\rangle \qquad (6)$$

where

$$\hat{A}(t) \equiv e^{i\hat{H}t/\hbar}\,\hat{A}\,e^{-i\hat{H}t/\hbar}. \qquad (7)$$

Results (4) and (6) express the same result in the two "representations".

In (1) we have an equation for the time dependence of the state vector. In the Heisenberg representation, it is the operator which is time dependent. This time dependence is given by

$$i\hbar \frac{d\hat{A}(t)}{dt} = [\hat{A}(t), \hat{H}], \qquad (8)$$

which is the counterpart of (1).

3.13 A bit more about operators

Prior to section 3.9, I was mainly dealing with operators, their action, etc. A few more remarks have to be added to that discussion.

Operators in quantum mechanics which represent dynamical variables are of a special type. Technically they are said to be linear, self-adjoint operators. Reduced to brass tacks, what these fancy words mean is that if we write down the matrix (using suitable base vectors of course), the matrix elements have the property $A_{ij} = A_{ji}^*$. Such matrices are said to be *Hermitian*.

How would an operator $\hat{A}$ (say) corresponding to some dynamical variable lead us to values which this variable would have when the system is in some quantum state? This is an interesting question and we have to approach the answer step by step. Let us start with A_{ij}. Remember that matrix elements actually stand for

$$\langle \text{some final state} | \hat{A} | \text{some initial state} \rangle. \tag{3.47}$$

What states do we choose in order to work out the matrix element? Answer: Choose a convenient set, the members of which are orthonormal (see section 3.5). In addition, the set of vectors must be complete. What this latter statement means is simply this: Suppose we consider an arbitrary vector **r** in three-dimensional space. To describe it we need the three unit vectors **i**, **j**, **k**; just two alone would not do. So in this case (**i**, **j**, **k**) form a complete set of base vectors for the purpose on hand. Similarly, to describe a general state vector, an appropriate complete set of base vectors is necessary.

In the present case, let the chosen set include the base vectors $|i\rangle$, $|j\rangle$, $|k\rangle$. We can then form matrix elements like $A_{ij} = \langle i|\hat{A}|j\rangle$, $A_{kj} = \langle k|\hat{A}|j\rangle$, etc. For convenience, let us suppose there are N base vectors in the (complete) set. We would then have a $(N \times N)$ matrix as below:

$$\begin{pmatrix} A_{11} & A_{12} & .. & .. & A_{1N} \\ A_{21} & A_{22} & .. & .. & A_{2N} \\ .. & .. & .. & .. & .. \\ .. & .. & .. & .. & .. \\ A_{N1} & .. & .. & .. & A_{NN} \end{pmatrix}. \tag{3.48}$$

This is the form matrices in QM usually have at the start. It is, however, more convenient to have a matrix which is in the diagonal form, i.e., has the appearance

$$\begin{pmatrix} \mathscr{A}_{11} & 0 & 0 & 0 & .. & 0 \\ 0 & \mathscr{A}_{22} & 0 & .. & .. & 0 \\ .. & .. & .. & .. & .. & .. \\ .. & .. & .. & .. & .. & .. \\ .. & .. & .. & .. & .. & .. \\ 0 & 0 & 0 & .. & .. & \mathscr{A}_{NN} \end{pmatrix}. \tag{3.49}$$

What must one do in order to obtain a diagonal form as above, starting with a form as in (3.48)? Remember matrix elements are computed as in (3.47). If we want the off-diagonal elements to vanish, then clearly we have to switch from the basis set which had $|i\rangle$, $|j\rangle$, $|k\rangle$ as representative vectors to a new set in terms of which the off-diagonal elements vanish. Let $|I\rangle$, $|J\rangle$ and $|K\rangle$ be the representative vectors of the new set. The statement just made means that the new set should be so chosen that matrix elements $\mathscr{A}_{IJ} = \langle I|\hat{A}|J\rangle$ are zero for $|I\rangle \neq |J\rangle$.

Going from the original basis set (with $|i\rangle$, $|j\rangle$, etc.) to the new set (with $|I\rangle$, $|J\rangle$, etc.) involves a transformation. Let us formally write the basis transformation as

$$\begin{bmatrix} .. \\ .. \\ .. \\ |I\rangle \\ |J\rangle \\ |K\rangle \\ .. \\ .. \\ .. \end{bmatrix} = \overbrace{\begin{bmatrix} U_{11} & .. & .. & U_{1N} \\ .. & .. & .. & .. \\ .. & .. & .. & .. \\ .. & .. & .. & .. \\ .. & .. & .. & .. \\ .. & .. & .. & .. \\ .. & .. & .. & .. \\ .. & .. & .. & .. \\ U_{N1} & .. & .. & U_{NN} \end{bmatrix}}^{\longleftarrow N \longrightarrow} \begin{bmatrix} .. \\ .. \\ .. \\ |i\rangle \\ |j\rangle \\ |k\rangle \\ .. \\ .. \\ .. \end{bmatrix} \updownarrow N. \tag{3.50}$$

The matrix above is associated with an operator $\hat{U}$ which effects a change of basis. It is like a "rotation" (—recall Fig. 3.10).

What has all this got to do with measurements? Patience! First digest the following:

(i) Initial basis set $\xrightarrow{\text{action of operator } \hat{U}}$ new basis set.

(ii) $\langle$Initial set $|\hat{A}|$ Initial set$\rangle$ $\xrightarrow{\text{leads to}}$ matrix with elements A_{ij}.

As already seen in (3.48), this matrix does not have an elegant, diagonal structure. However,

$$\text{(iii)}\ \langle \text{New set}\,|\hat{A}|\,\text{New set}\rangle \xrightarrow{\text{leads to}} \text{diagonal matrix.}$$

Let us make use of (i) in (iii). Now (schematically),

$$|\text{New set}\rangle = \hat{U}|\text{Initial set}\rangle.$$

We also have

$$\langle \text{New set}| = \langle \text{Initial set}|\,\hat{U}^{\dagger}$$

(don't be scared by the operator $\hat{U}^{\dagger}$ It is just a cousin of $\hat{U}$ and acts on *bras* just as $\hat{U}$ acts on *kets*).
The matrix element in (iii) can therefore be rewritten as

$$\text{(iv)}\ \langle \text{Initial set}|\,\hat{U}^{\dagger}\hat{A}\,\hat{U}|\text{Initial set}\rangle.$$

Define a new operator $\hat{\mathscr{A}}$ given by

$$\text{(v)}\ \hat{\mathscr{A}} = \hat{U}^{\dagger}\hat{A}\,\hat{U}.$$

The matrix (3.49) is just made up of elements of the above operator.

I inflicted all this because the operator $\hat{\mathscr{A}}$ has an interesting property. Suppose we let it act on say $|I\rangle$ (which is a member of the new set). It turns out

$$\hat{\mathscr{A}}|I\rangle = \lambda_I|I\rangle \qquad \text{(for each } |I\rangle), \qquad (3.51)$$

i.e., operator $\hat{\mathscr{A}}$ acting on $|I\rangle$ produces a new vector which is in the same "direction" as $|I\rangle$ but is scaled up by the numerical factor λ_I. This λ_I is a real number (I am here assuming $\hat{A}$ refers to a dynamical variable and has all the required properties).

An equation like (3.51) is referred to as an *eigenvalue* equation; $|I\rangle$ is called the *eigenvector* or *eigenstate* and λ_I the eigenvalue. It should now be obvious that the elements of the array (3.49) are nothing but the eigenvalues of the operator $\hat{\mathscr{A}}$ (which is a transformed version of the operator $\hat{A}$ we started with). At last we are there!

OK, so what it all means is the following:

1. If one can put the system in any one of the states belonging to the new set, say $|I\rangle$, then observation of $\hat{A}$ would lead, with certainty, to the value λ_I. If the system is in $|J\rangle$ one would definitely obtain the result λ_J and so on.

In short, if the system is in an eigenstate of the operator $\hat{A}$, then the result of an experiment in which one attempts to measure the dynamical variable associated with the operator $\hat{A}$ would be the corresponding eigenvalue.

2. If the system is in a general state

$$|\psi\rangle = \sum_I C_I |I\rangle \tag{3.52}$$

and a measurement is made of $\hat{A}$, then the probability of finding the system in state $|I\rangle$ is $|C_I|^2$.

So you see how the superposition principle works in practice. Perhaps you have also noticed that the central problem is to find the eigenvalues and eigenvectors. If we want to find out the energy levels of the hydrogen atom, all we have to do is to diagonalise the Hamiltonian for the hydrogen atom. The eigenvalues so obtained give the energies of the various states. This diagonalisation is achieved once the transformation matrix U_{ij} is known. Although I did not present the details, this is precisely what was done in the ammonia problem too. Using the basis vectors $|1\rangle$ and $|2\rangle$, we first constructed the matrix

$$\begin{pmatrix} H_{11} & H_{12} \\ H_{21} & H_{21} \end{pmatrix} = \begin{pmatrix} E_0 & -A \\ A & E_0 \end{pmatrix}.$$

When diagonalised, this gives

$$\begin{pmatrix} \mathscr{A}_{11} & 0 \\ 0 & \mathscr{A}_{22} \end{pmatrix} = \begin{pmatrix} \lambda_I & 0 \\ 0 & \lambda_{II} \end{pmatrix} = \begin{pmatrix} E_0 + A & 0 \\ 0 & E_0 - A \end{pmatrix}.$$

The change from $\{|1\rangle, |2\rangle\}$ to $\{|I\rangle, |II\rangle\}$ did the trick (recall (3.37)).

One last remark about operators. Formal manipulations in QM are often performed using operators and exploiting their algebra. But when it comes to numerical calculations, one switches to the Schroedinger equation. Two important rules used in such a switch over are:

Replace E by $i\hbar \dfrac{\partial}{\partial t}$, and

replace $\mathbf{p}$ by $-i\hbar\nabla$

where

$$\nabla \equiv \mathbf{i}\frac{\partial}{\partial x} + \mathbf{j}\frac{\partial}{\partial y} + \mathbf{k}\frac{\partial}{\partial z}. \tag{3.53}$$

3.13 What about the uncertainty principle?

Are you wondering where Heisenberg's uncertainty principle comes into all this? Here is the answer. We start with the fact that corresponding to observables, there are appropriate operators. Thus for position and momentum we have $\hat{q}$ and $\hat{p}$ respectively. These form a *conjugate* pair. The uncertainty principle always involves members of a conjugate pair.

The uncertainty principle forbids simultaneous measurements only in certain cases. For instance if there are two electrons and $\hat{q}_1$, $\hat{q}_2$, $\hat{p}_1$, $\hat{p}_2$ denote the corresponding operators, Heisenberg's principle affects us only when we try to measure $\hat{q}_1$ and $\hat{p}_1$ or $\hat{q}_2$ and $\hat{p}_2$ simultaneously. Nothing can prevent us from measuring $\hat{q}_1$ and $\hat{q}_2$ or $\hat{p}_1$ and $\hat{p}_2$ and other such combinations simultaneously.

There is a neat way of stating all this. Let $\hat{A}$ and $\hat{B}$ denote two operators. Form the combination

$$(\hat{A}\hat{B} - \hat{B}\hat{A}).$$

This is called the *commutator* of $\hat{A}$ and $\hat{B}$ and is written $[\hat{A}, \hat{B}]$. In quantum mechanics, either the commutator is zero or it is not. In the former case, simultaneous measurements of $\hat{A}$ and $\hat{B}$ are possible whereas in the latter case they are not. In other words, the uncertainty principle operates whenever the commutator does not vanish.

Go back now to equation (3.14) of CM. Corresponding to that we now have

$$[\hat{q}_i, \hat{p}_j] = i\hbar\delta_{ij}. \tag{3.54}$$

Clearly, the classical Poisson bracket (recall (3.13)) is the "daddy" of the quantum mechanical commutator.

Heavens don't fall if the commutator does not vanish. On the contrary, one can exploit this circumstance. Let $\hat{H}$ denote the Hamiltonian operator for some system and $\hat{A}$ another operator corresponding to some other observable associated with the system. As you already know, $\hat{H}$ allows us to make observations on the energy of the system. Suppose $\hat{A}$ and $\hat{H}$ do not commute, i.e., $[\hat{A}, \hat{H}] = -[\hat{H}, \hat{A}] \neq 0$. This implies that if one tries to measure $\hat{A}$, it would disturb the energy of the system. It turns out that the time rate of change of $\hat{A}$ is given by the equation

$$i\hbar\frac{\partial \hat{A}}{\partial t} = [\hat{A}(t), \hat{H}]. \tag{3.55}$$

Using this, one can track the changes in time of $\hat{A}$. By analogy with (3.17), the above equation is called equation of motion. Taking $\hat{A}$ to be $\hat{q}$ and $\hat{p}$ successively, we obtain

$$\hat{\dot{q}} = (1/i\hbar)[\hat{q}, \hat{H}]$$
$$\hat{\dot{p}} = (1/ih)[\hat{q}, \hat{H}] \tag{3.56}$$

which are to be compared with (3.17). We see that in the transition form CM to QM, the Poisson bracket (of CM) goes over into the commutator (of CM) according to the rule

$$[\mathrm{A}, \mathrm{B}]_{\mathrm{PB}} \rightarrow \frac{1}{i\hbar} [\hat{\mathrm{A}}, \hat{\mathrm{B}}]. \tag{3.57}$$

As an example of (3.55), let us consider the methane molecule (CH_4) which is like a spherical top. The molecule can have angular momentum, to measure which one uses the operator $\hat{J}^2$ ($\hat{J}$ is the angular momentum operator but for technical reasons one must use $\hat{J}^2$ if one wants to make a measurement). It turns out that

$$[\hat{J}^2, \hat{H}] = 0,$$

whence

$$i\hbar \frac{d\hat{J}^2(t)}{dt} = 0$$

which means that $\hat{J}^2$ does not vary in time. In turn this not only implies that one can simultaneously measure the energy of the molecule in a particular quantum state as well as the angular momentum of that same state, but also that the angular momentum remains a constant—it is a *constant of motion.* Incidentally, you might like to take a minute off to wonder what the variables conjugate to $\hat{J}$ and to energy are.

Landau refers to the uncertainty principle as a negative principle in that it simply tells us about something we *cannot* do, in contrast to the rest of quantum mechanics which allows us to calculate, make predictions, etc. Feynman refers to the principle in a different way. According to him, it "protects" quantum mechanics.

3.15 More about commuting variables

Earlier I made the following remarks:

1. Associated with observables are operators.
2. In practical manipulations, operators acquire a matrix form.
3. Matrix multiplication is not commutative.

Taking all these together, you might wonder whether we can at all have commuting variables, and whether we can even measure certain quantities simultaneously without Heisenberg coming in the way? The answer is yes, and to understand it consider the two matrices below;

$$A = \begin{pmatrix} 1 & 0 & 0 \\ 0 & 17 & 0 \\ 0 & 0 & 2 \end{pmatrix}, \qquad B = \begin{pmatrix} 14 & 0 & 0 \\ 0 & 8 & 0 \\ 0 & 0 & -6 \end{pmatrix}.$$

You can easily convince yourself that in this particular case, the order of multiplication is not important, i.e., AB = BA; in other words, the matrices A and B commute. This is true of all diagonal matrices. The message therefore is that if two variables can be simultaneously observed and measured, then it must be possible to choose basis vectors such that with respect to them, both the operators are represented by diagonal matrices, i.e., the matrices are *simultaneously diagonal.*

There is an important significance to this. Recall that I earlier labelled the states of the hydrogen atom in terms of the quantum numbers n, l, m_l and m_s. That was because the energy, orbital and spin angular momentum of the electron could be simultaneously measured. In general, when one tries to study the states of a system one first lists all the dynamical variables which can be simultaneously measured, i.e., one identifies a *complete set of commuting dynamical variables*. One then hunts for basis vectors such that with respect to them, the operators corresponding to the above list are simultaneously diagonal. The eigenvalues of the complete set of commuting variables provide a convenient means of labelling. This is precisely the way in which the hydrogen atom states were labelled.

I have earlier drawn attention to operators, matrix elements, etc., on the one hand and the Schroedinger equation and wave function on the other. Historically (as you will learn in Chapters 6 and 7), these were the outcomes of two independent lines of thought. But Schroedinger discovered that the two approaches are in fact related. Thus, in some textbooks you would find references to wave functions and matrix elements in the context of the same problem. A glimpse into the relationship between matrix elements and wave functions has already been given in (2.19).

3.16 Topics not mentioned so far

Obviously, in a hurried overview such as I am giving, many things have to be left out. There are, however, a few topics which need at least a passing mention.

Scattering problem

The harmonic oscillator and the hydrogen atom are classic problems, and practically every elementary text on QM starts with a study of these. Both in the oscillator and the hydrogen atom, the particle is "bound" to a centre of force. A characteristic feature of bound-state problems is that the energy levels are discrete. People often erroneously assume that energy levels of a quantum system are always discrete; not true! Discrete energy eigenvalues are characteristic of bound states. In the case of unbound states, the energy eigenvalues are continuous even in QM. Examples of such states are to be found in scattering problems, for instance.

Normalisation

Let $\psi(x)$ be the wave function obtained in the case of a (one-dimensional) problem by solving the appropriate Schroedinger equation. Then $A\psi(x)$ where A is a constant is an equally good and acceptable solution. Thus by varying A, one can obtain any number of solutions. In practice, the constant A is chosen in a particular way—the details are a bit technical and I shall not go into that. I just want to mention that when A is so fixed, the wave function is said to be *normalised.* The main objective of normalisation is to get the probabilities correct. Recall section 2.10 where I discussed the one-dimensional oscillator wave function $\psi(x)$. If $\psi(x)$ is properly normalised, then $|\psi(x)|^2$ when integrated from $x = -\infty$ to $x = +\infty$ ensures that there is a probability equal to 1 that the particle would be found.

Tunnelling

Suppose a tennis ball is thrown at a wall. It would bounce back. There is no chance of the ball emerging on the other side of the wall, with the wall completely intact. This is what common sense tells us, what we see in practice, and also what classical physics predicts. Strangely, in QM there is a probability for the ball to emerge on the other side of the wall. True the probability may be extremely small but the point is it is *not* zero as classical physics would demand.

The emergence of the particle on the other side is referred to as *barrier penetration* or *tunnelling*. While barrier penetration probability might be negligible for a tennis ball, it is quite significant for a tiny particle like an electron, facing a barrier say in a solid. In such cases, tunnelling *is* possible and indeed there are devices known as tunnel diodes based on such a phenomenon. Also there is now a new type of microscope based on tunnelling! It is used for scanning surfaces.

Illustrated in Fig. 3.11 is a problem on tunnelling posed by Enrico Fermi to his students. Fermi was trying to impress on his students that QM applies on all scales although effects like tunnelling are visible only in the atomic world. Once a student went to Prof. Hans Bethe of Cornell with a solution for this famous textbook problem. After showing the answer this student asked, "Sir, will the car really tunnel through?" One can understand the student's sense of doubt. In a special lecture at the Wisconsin University, Prof. J. Van Vleck illustrated tunnelling with Fig. 3.12. Next time you visit the zoo, you had better watch out!

3.17 The Dirac equation

We now come to the Dirac equation which is a major landmark in QM. The Schroedinger equation discussed earlier applies to a non-

Problem: A very slowly moving car 1 ton (kinetic energy considered almost zero) encounters a sinusoidal bump in the road which is 1 ft. high and 100 ft. long. Classically, the car can't get past. However III.2 shows that there actually is a finite probability (w) that the car can overcome the bump.

$$w \sim e^{-2\sqrt{\frac{2y}{\hbar^2}}\int_a^b \sqrt{U(x)}dx}$$

$$U(x) = Mg \times 12 \times 2.54 \sin\frac{\pi(x-a)}{3050}$$

$$\int_a^b \sqrt{U(x)}dx \approx 5.3 \times 10^8$$

$$w \sim e^{-14.3\times 10^{31}}$$

$$w \sim 10^{-6\ 2\times 10^{38}}$$

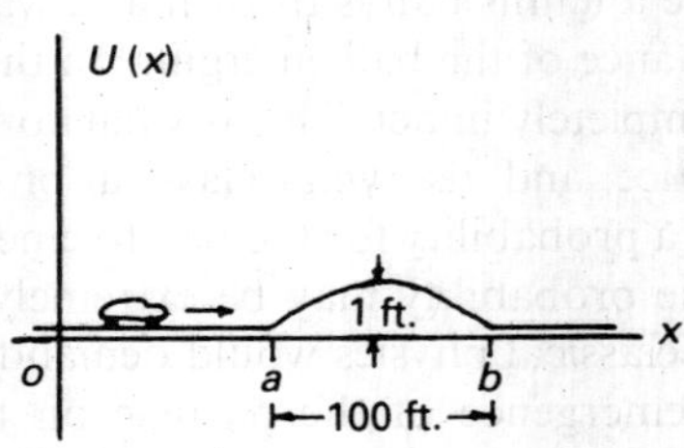

$M = 10^6$ gm

$b - a = 3050$ cm.

Fig. 3.11 A problem from Fermi's book on Nuclear Physics, about a car tunnelling through a bump.

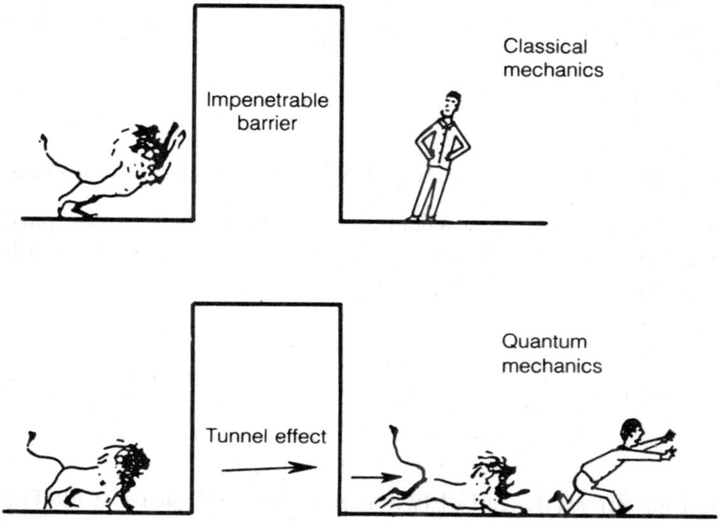

Fig. 3.12 Cartoon used by Prof. Van Vleck to explain tunnelling.

relativistic system. Soon after Schroedinger discovered this equation, there were several attempts to graft special relativity to it but they all failed. Eventually it was an "inspired guess" by Dirac that showed the way. The Dirac equation for a free particle is:

$$i\hbar \frac{\partial}{\partial t} \psi(\mathbf{r}, t) = (i\hbar c\, \alpha \cdot \nabla - \beta mc^2)\psi(\mathbf{r}, t). \tag{3.58}$$

This innocent looking equation hides many important things which I shall shortly comment upon. If you like, the quantity within brackets on the right-hand side is the relativistic Hamiltonian for a free particle. If the particle is subjected to a potential (like the electron is in the hydrogen atom), then the Dirac–Hamiltonian must be suitably modified.

For a minute, let us forget the Dirac equation and ask how we represent the wave function of the electron when we take its spin into account. I have already told you that in this case, the space coordinate **r** alone would not do and that we must consider also the spin coordinate σ which is discrete and can take only one of two values. Correspondingly, the wave function $\psi(\mathbf{r}, \sigma)$ is really made up of two wave functions $\psi_1(\mathbf{r})$ and $\psi_2(\mathbf{r})$, and the pair is written as a column:

$$\psi(\mathbf{r}, \sigma) = \begin{pmatrix} \psi_1(\mathbf{r}) \\ \psi_2(\mathbf{r}) \end{pmatrix}. \tag{3.59}$$

If the behaviour of the spin coordinate is not dependent on **r**, then the column matrix above, sometimes called a *spinor*, could be written

$$\psi(\mathbf{r})\begin{pmatrix} C_1 \\ C_2 \end{pmatrix}. \tag{3.60}$$

The column matrix $\begin{pmatrix} C_1 \\ C_2 \end{pmatrix}$ deals with spin alone and represents the spin part of the wave function where as $\psi(\mathbf{r})$ represents the space part. We now get back to the Dirac equation and note that $\psi(\mathbf{r}, t)$ is really the column matrix

$$\psi(\mathbf{r}, t) = \begin{bmatrix} \psi_1(\mathbf{r}, t) \\ \psi_2(\mathbf{r}, t) \\ \psi_3(\mathbf{r}, t) \\ \psi_4(\mathbf{r}, t) \end{bmatrix}. \tag{3.61}$$

Why four entries instead of two as in (3.59)? Ah, please wait! Turning to the other quantities in the Dirac–Hamiltonian, let us consider first β. This is a matrix having the form

$$\left(\begin{array}{cc|cc} 1 & 0 & 0 & 0 \\ 0 & 1 & 0 & 0 \\ \hline 0 & 0 & -1 & 0 \\ 0 & 0 & 0 & -1 \end{array}\right). \tag{3.62}$$

The product $\alpha \cdot \nabla$ may be expanded as

$$\alpha_x \frac{\partial}{\partial x} + \alpha_y \frac{\partial}{\partial y} + \alpha_z \frac{\partial}{\partial z}$$

where

$$\alpha_x = \left(\begin{array}{cc|cc} 0 & 0 & 0 & 1 \\ 0 & 0 & 1 & 0 \\ \hline 0 & 1 & 0 & 0 \\ 1 & 0 & 0 & 0 \end{array}\right) \quad \alpha_y = \left(\begin{array}{cc|cc} 0 & 0 & 0 & -i \\ 0 & 0 & i & 0 \\ \hline 0 & -i & 0 & 0 \\ i & 0 & 0 & 0 \end{array}\right)$$

$$\alpha_z = \left(\begin{array}{cc|cc} 0 & 0 & 1 & 0 \\ 0 & 0 & 0 & -1 \\ \hline 1 & 0 & 0 & 0 \\ 0 & -1 & 0 & 0 \end{array}\right). \tag{3.63}$$

By introducing the notation

$$\sigma_x = \begin{pmatrix} 0 & 1 \\ 1 & 0 \end{pmatrix} \quad \sigma_y = \begin{pmatrix} 0 & -i \\ i & 0 \end{pmatrix} \quad \sigma_z = \begin{pmatrix} 1 & 0 \\ 0 & -1 \end{pmatrix}, \tag{3.64}$$

the α matrices in (3.63) may be compactly written as

$$\alpha_i = \begin{pmatrix} 0 & \sigma_i \\ \sigma_i & 0 \end{pmatrix} \qquad (i = x, y, z). \tag{3.65}$$

I hope you are not turned off by all these definitions and notations. By the way, the (2×2) matrices defined in (3.64) are referred to as *Pauli matrices*. Theoretical physicists literally worship them! The Pauli matrices come in handy when one wants to deal with problems in a non-relativistic way and yet include the effects of spin. An example is the behaviour of an electron in a magnetic field.

3.18 Spin again

The Dirac equation has spectacular fall-outs, one of these being electron spin. Now (3.58) has been written for a free particle. Dirac examined the case when a magnetic field is present and discovered that in this fancy new description he had, the electron behaved as if it had an intrinsic angular momentum $(\hbar/2)$ and as if it was a magnetic dipole with magnetic moment $(e\hbar/2m_0c)$ where m_0 is the rest mass. These are precisely the facts that Goudsmit and Uhlenbeck had earlier *postulated*. Now it all came out quite naturally.

3.19 Positrons

Perhaps the most spectacular fall-out of the Dirac equation is the positron. It is a particle having the same mass and the same spin as the electron but opposite charge. It is the anti-particle of the electron. While Dirac's theory of the electron predicted the existence of such a particle, the experimental proof that such a particle actually exists was provided by Anderson. That story can be found in Box 3.3.

How did Dirac arrive at the idea of positrons? There is a story behind that also which is narrated in Chapter 7. Here let me discuss some of the related physics. According to special relativity, the expression for the energy of a particle is

$$E^2 = p^2c^2 + m_0^2c^4 \tag{3.66}$$

Box 3.3 The first direct experimental evidence for the existence of the positron was provided by Carl Anderson of the California Institute of Technology in 1931. Anderson was studying cosmic rays using a cloud chamber placed in a magnetic field—see figure (a). When charged particles traverse a cloud chamber, they leave behind a cloudy track, rather like the trails left behind by high-flying jets. The cloud chamber track shows how the particle actually travelled while inside the chamber. If the particle causes a reaction producing other charged particles, their tracks also show up.

Figure (b) is a sketch of the picture that Anderson produced as evidence for the positron (and which earned for him the Nobel Prize!). In the middle of the chamber was a lead plate 5 mm thick, and as one can see the portion of the track below the plate has less curvature than the portion above it. One knows (i) that traversal through the lead plate would reduce the particle energy, and (ii) that the lower the particle energy, the greater would be the curvature of its trajectory. Clearly, in this case the particle came into the chamber from below and travelled upwards. What about the charge of the particle? Using our knowledge of how charged particles deflect in a magnetic field, one can say the particle in this case must have had a positive charge. If the charge had been negative, the curvature would have been opposite as sketched in figure (c).

OK, so the particle had a positive charge. How do we know it was not a proton? From the curvature of the track, Anderson showed that if the particle was a proton, it would have had an energy of about 0.3 MeV

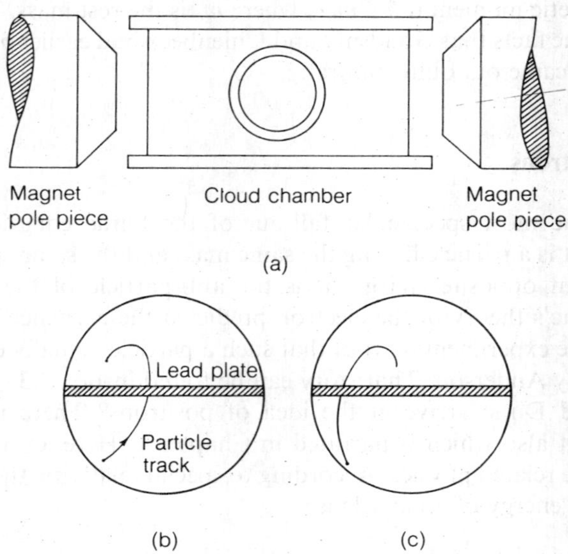

and would have been completely stopped by the lead plate. So clearly the particle in question was *NOT* a proton, though it had the same charge as the proton. Other reasoning showed that it had a mass equal to that of the electron. As Anderson wrote, "It seems necessary to call upon a positively charged particle having a mass comparable with that of an electron." The editor of *Science News Letter* which published Anderson's discovery suggested that the particle be called the *positron*, a name which has stuck. Was Anderson influenced by Dirac's work? Anderson has this to say: "Yes, I knew about Dirac's theory ... But I was not familiar in detail with Dirac's work. I was too busy operating this piece of equipment to have the time to read his papers ... The discovery of the positron was wholly accidental."

where m_0 is the rest mass and p the momentum of the particle. Therefore,

$$E + \pm \sqrt{p^2c^2 + m_0^2c^4}. \tag{3.67}$$

This applies for all particles including a free particle. In the case of the latter, the energy is kinetic, apart of course from the rest energy m_0c^2. Since kinetic energy cannot be negative, in classical physics one always considers only the positive root in (3.67). With the Dirac equation, the story is different.

Figure 3.13 shows the spectrum of the allowed energy levels. From (3.67), we see that the minimum positive energy the particle can have is not zero but m_0c^2. Thus the spectrum of positive energy states starts from m_0c^2 and extends upwards forming a continuum. A similar thing happens on the negative energy side and as a result there is an energy gap of $2m_0c^2$. The negative energy states cannot be excluded for two reasons, (i) physical and (ii) mathematical. As far as the physical part is concerned, Dirac's theory predicts a definite probability for transition from a positive energy state to a negative energy one. So if negative states are summarily excluded, there would be trouble with predictions of the theory. Perhaps the mathematical objection is more serious. Basically it says that without the negative states, the description is incomplete.

One is thus stuck with the negative energy states. So what does one do with them? Dirac solved the problem by declaring that all those states are already filled and therefore transitions to them are not allowed! Filled with what? Electrons of course. Electrons? We started with a theory for a single electron and now an infinite number of them are being smuggled in!!

Yes, that is the price one has to pay, namely allowing for a "Dirac sea of electrons". In postulating such a sea of filled states, Dirac took care to invoke the Pauli exclusion principle according to which each

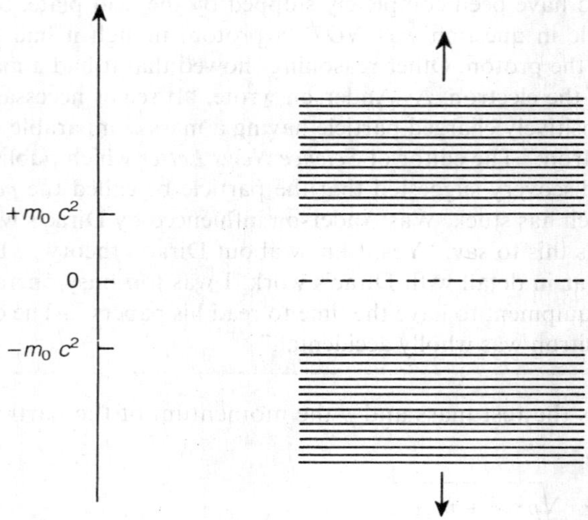

Fig. 3.13 Spectrum of energy levels allowed by the Dirac equation. There are two continuum of levels, one on the positive energy side and another on the negative energy side, with a gap in between.

quantum state can be occupied by only one electron. Otherwise, all the electrons in the sea could crowd into just a few levels or may be even just one, leaving empty negative energy states.

Is it not possible for an electron in the Dirac sea to somehow escape to a state of positive energy? Indeed it is possible and it is the "hole" so created that acts like a positron—see Fig. 3.14. Let me summarise all this in Dirac's own words. He says:

> We are led to infer that negative-energy solutions refer to the motion of a new kind of particle having the mass of an electron and the opposite charge ... We assume that *nearly all the negative energy states are occupied*, with one electron in each state in accordance with the exclusion principle of Pauli. An unoccupied negative-energy state will now appear as something with a positive-energy, since to make it disappear, i.e., to fill it up, we have to add an electron with negative-energy. We assume that *these unoccupied negative-energy states are the positrons.*

3.20 Wave function collapse again

Let us look at wave function collapse again, this time a bit more closely. Say we have a system which can be described by two base vectors $|A\rangle$ and $|B\rangle$, and let the system be in the state

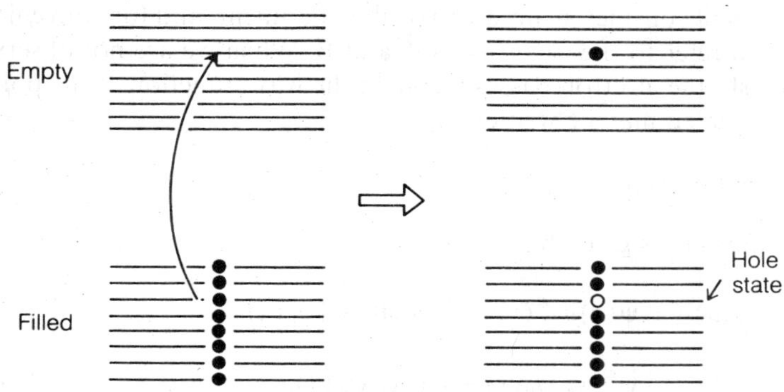

Fig. 3.14 A vacancy or a hole in the "negative energy sea" acts like an electron with a positive charge, i.e., a positron.

$$|\psi\rangle = C_1|A\rangle + C_2|B\rangle.$$

If we leave the system all alone and to itself, $|\psi\rangle$ would evolve smoothly, perhaps as schematically shown in Fig. 3.15(a). This evolution can be described by the time-dependent Schroedinger equation.

Suppose we now try to make an observation. Then $|\psi\rangle$ jumps either to the state $|A\rangle$ or to the state $|B\rangle$. The probability for the former is $|C_1|^2$ while for the latter jump it is $|C_2|^2$. The Schroedinger equation is of *no help* in determining the state to which the jump would take place. Schematically, the jump would be as in Fig. 3.15(b). This is the collapse business to which I made a reference earlier in section 2.

The collapse itself cannot be mathematically described but once one grants it, many things can be explained including the 'Feynman mystery'. Let us briefly see how this is possible.

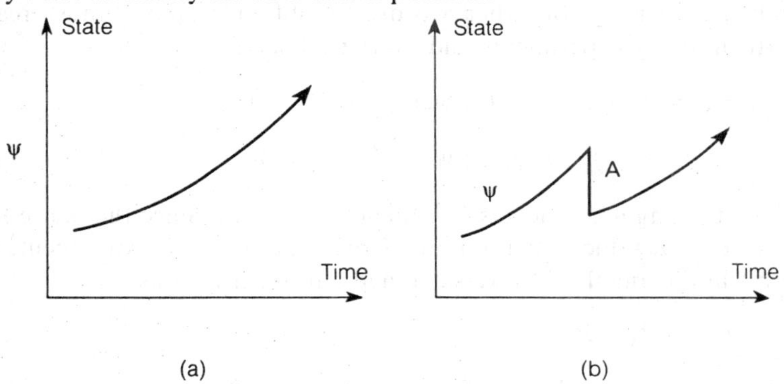

Fig. 3.15 (a) Schematic of the smooth evolution of the wave function. (b) Jump caused by an observation. After the jump, normal evolution resumes, now in the new state.

We shall consider again the two-slit experiment, and for convenience we shall refer to the two-slits as A and B. When we are not observing which slit the electron passes through, the wave function at the point x on the screen may be written

$$\psi(x) = \psi_A(x) + \psi_B(x). \tag{3.68}$$

The intensity is given by

$$|\psi(x)|^2 = \psi(x)\,\psi^*(x) = |\psi_A(x)|^2 + |\psi_B(x)|^2$$

$$+ \psi_A^*(x)\,\psi_B(x) + \psi_A(x)\,\psi_B^*(x). \tag{3.69}$$

The interference terms $(\psi_A^*\,\psi_B + \psi_A\psi_B^*)$ give rise to the maxima and minima

We now spy on the electrons. By the act of observing, we are actually trying to localise the electrons. This disturbs the wave function, adding to it an *unpredictable* and an *uncontrollable* phase factor $e^{i\alpha}$. Thus instead of (3.68), we now have

$$\psi(x) = \psi_A(x)e^{i\alpha_A} + \psi_B(x)e^{i\alpha_B}. \tag{3.70}$$

Therefore,

$$|\psi(x)|^2 = |\psi_A(x)|^2 + |\psi_B(x)|^2 + \psi_A^*(x)\,\psi_B(x)e^{-i(\alpha_A - \alpha_B)}$$

$$+ \psi_A(x)\,\psi_B^*(x)e^{i(\alpha_A - \alpha_B)}. \tag{3.71}$$

Remember that the phase factors $e^{i\alpha_A}$ and $e^{i\alpha_B}$ are determined by Nature in a completely *random* manner and also that $|\psi(x)|^2$ has a probabilistic meaning. In other words, to obtain P_{AB}, we must really perform many experiments and average. Therefore,

$$P_{AB} = P_A + P_B + \psi_A^*(x)\,\psi_B(x)\,\langle\, e^{-i(\alpha_A - \alpha_B)}\rangle$$

$$+ \psi_A(x)\,\psi_B^*(x)\langle e^{i(\alpha_A - \alpha_B)}\rangle \tag{3.72}$$

where the angular brackets $\langle\ldots\rangle$ denote averages. Since the phase factors $(\alpha_A - \alpha_B)$ fluctuate randomly from experiment to experiment, the terms in the angular brackets average out to zero. Thus,

$$P_{AB} = P_A + P_B.$$

In simple terms, the interference pattern is wiped out on account of the wave function collapse that occurs when we try to check whether the electron is in the state ψ_A or the state ψ_B.

3.21 An overview of the chapter

Perhaps you feel I have inflicted a lot of mumbo-jumbo on you in the name of explaining QM. I am sorry about it and as I warned you earlier a certain amount of maths is inevitable, particularly in the case of QM. In any case, do not be perturbed if you can't follow all of it right away. What I would like you to appreciate is that behind all these technicalities lie some serious considerations. Let me try to summarise these for you.

In Chapter 1 we learnt that (i) matter can behave sometimes like a particle and sometimes like waves, and (ii) observation can itself change the very nature of what we are trying to observe. The latter is not a simple thing to comprehend. This question has been taken all the way to philosophy, consciousness and all that as we shall see in Part III. (I might add that Bohr also tried to extend the complementary principle to the problem of life and living organism but here his ideas did not work out.) Even at a lower level we are in trouble. We use the word *particle* often. Do you realise we cannot any longer think of a particle like we used to before? Normally, a particle is something hard and rigid. Can we think of the electron in this manner? As Max Born puts it:

> Can we call something with which the concepts of position and motion cannot be associated in the usual way, a thing, or a particle? And if not, what is the reality which our theory has been invented to describe?

So you see, behind the mumbo-jumbo lie deep questions bordering on philosophy. When it comes to philosophical debates, logic is a must. In the present case, some appeal to mathematical logic becomes inevitable. It is just for that reason I exposed you to some technicalities, and not merely for educating you about the tool kit of the "quantum mechanic". I hope this reassures you. Anyway, there would now be a change of gear and further reading should become more exciting.

Appendix to Chapter 3

This is a crash course on matrices! Basically, a matrix is an array of numbers. We shall be concerned only with square matrices, i.e., arrays of the form

$$\begin{pmatrix} A_{11} & A_{12} & A_{13} & A_{14} \\ A_{21} & A_{22} & A_{23} & A_{24} \\ A_{31} & A_{32} & A_{33} & A_{34} \\ A_{41} & A_{42} & A_{43} & A_{44} \end{pmatrix}. \tag{1}$$

This is an example of a (4×4) matrix. The entries are numbers, which, in QM, are in general complex.

Matrices can be added, subtracted and multiplied. Consider a matrix sum C = A + B as below:

$$\begin{pmatrix} C_{11} & C_{12} & C_{13} & C_{14} \\ C_{21} & C_{22} & C_{23} & C_{24} \\ C_{31} & C_{32} & C_{33} & C_{34} \\ C_{41} & C_{42} & C_{43} & C_{44} \end{pmatrix} = \begin{pmatrix} A_{11} & A_{12} & A_{13} & A_{14} \\ A_{21} & A_{22} & A_{23} & A_{24} \\ A_{31} & A_{32} & A_{33} & A_{34} \\ A_{41} & A_{42} & A_{43} & A_{44} \end{pmatrix} + \begin{pmatrix} B_{11} & B_{12} & B_{13} & B_{14} \\ B_{21} & B_{22} & B_{23} & B_{24} \\ B_{31} & B_{32} & B_{33} & B_{34} \\ B_{41} & B_{42} & B_{43} & B_{44} \end{pmatrix} \tag{2}$$

The rule for addition is

$$C_{ij} = A_{ij} + B_{ij} \qquad (i = 1, 2, 3, 4; \; j = 1, 2, 3, 4). \tag{3}$$

Subtraction follows a similar rule.

Matrix multiplication is slightly more involved. Here we shall consider only square matrices. When a $(N \times N)$ matrix A multiplies a $(N \times N)$ matrix B, the resulting matrix C is another $(N \times N)$ matrix. Consider the matrix product

$$\begin{pmatrix} C_{11} & C_{12} & C_{13} & C_{14} \\ C_{21} & C_{22} & C_{23} & C_{24} \\ C_{31} & C_{32} & C_{33} & C_{34} \\ C_{41} & C_{42} & C_{43} & C_{44} \end{pmatrix} = \begin{pmatrix} A_{11} & A_{12} & A_{13} & A_{14} \\ A_{21} & A_{22} & A_{23} & A_{24} \\ A_{31} & A_{32} & A_{33} & A_{34} \\ A_{41} & A_{42} & A_{43} & A_{44} \end{pmatrix} \times$$

$$\begin{pmatrix} B_{11} & B_{12} & \overset{\downarrow}{B_{13}} & B_{14} \\ B_{21} & B_{22} & B_{23} & B_{24} \\ B_{31} & B_{32} & B_{33} & B_{34} \\ B_{41} & B_{42} & B_{43} & B_{44} \end{pmatrix}. \tag{4}$$

We want, like in (3), the value of an element of C say, the 23rd element, i.e., we wish to know the value of C_{23}. This is given by the following sum:

$$C_{23} = A_{21} \times B_{13} + A_{22} \times B_{23} + A_{23} \times B_{33} + A_{24} \times B_{43}. \tag{5}$$

The general formula for the product is:

$$C_{ij} = \sum_k (A_{ik} \times B_{kj}). \tag{6}$$

You can easily convince yourself that the matrix product A × B is in general *NOT* equal to the product B × A, i.e., the *order* is important unlike when we multiply numbers say 3 and 4.

In QM, one deals with what are called Hermetian matrices. Let A be a matrix with elements A_{ij}. Form now another matrix $A^{\dagger}$ (read A dagger) with elements

$$(A^{\dagger})_{ij} = A^{*}_{ji}, \tag{7}$$

i.e., the (ij)th element of $A^{\dagger}$ is just the complex conjugate of the (ji)th element of A. If $A = A^{\dagger}$, then A is said to be Hermetian.

Can one have a matrix B which is one over another matrix A, i.e., can one have

$$B = 1/A? \tag{8}$$

Yes, provided A is not *singular*. I won't go into the technical details but basically this simply means 1/A, also written as A^{-1}, is not infinite. Assuming A^{-1} exists, it is obvious $AA^{-1} = A^{-1}A = 1$ where 1 is the unit matrix.

4 *Dramatis Personae*

I am sure you must have heard of the founders of QM. Even so, it seems best to unfold the drama by starting with profiles of leading characters. I hope you will not fail to notice that most of them were pretty young when they ushered in the revolutionary changes; and also that they all duly picked up the Nobel Prize!

Quantum mechanics burst on the scene roughly between 1925 and 1930. The spade work was over by 1928, and during the next few years a lot of "cleaning up" went on. It was a most exciting period, and I doubt if physics has witnessed a comparable era either before or since. It was, as someone put it, a period when second-rate people could do first-rate work.

A number of people were associated with the launching of this revolution but of the many, I shall restrict myself to the following: Einstein, Bohr, Born, de Broglie, Heisenberg, Schroedinger and Dirac. Important omissions include Kramers, Pauli, Jordan and Slater.

ALBERT EINSTEIN

We start with Einstein, the senior-most among the players. Einstein did not make any discovery that directly related to quantum mechanics but he was one of those who set the ball rolling. More important, once quantum mechanics came into being he sharply questioned its philosophy, leading subsequently to a dramatic debate with Bohr which I shall discuss in Chapter 8 (and in Part III).

I have covered the biography of Einstein in the companion volume *At the Speed of Light*; hence I shall restrict myself here to a mere outline. Einstein was born in 1879 in a small town named Ulm in Germany. He belonged to the Jewish faith, and this created problems for him later on. As a boy he was not in the best of health. He disliked school, though he did well in mathematics and Latin. His uncle Jakob and his friend Talmud aroused his interest in science and mathematics. In 1896, young Albert joined the polytechnic ETH in Zurich, Switzerland. Four years later he passed out of ETH. Though he got good grades, his hope of getting a job there did not materialise. So he took up a job as a "technical expert, third class" in the Swiss Patent Office.

The job was not demanding and as result Einstein was able to devote much time to his own scientific research.

The year 1905 was a momentous one for him because during that year, he published three landmark papers. First there was a paper on photoelectricity in which Einstein made the daring suggestion that light energy was propagated in the form of quanta or packets, later named as *photons*. This was indeed a revolutionary concept for it revived, in a manner of speaking, the corpuscular theory of light first put forward by Newton but later given up since it could not explain interference and the diffraction of light. Einstein's paper made it clear that while light might appear to be a wave as far as phenomena like diffraction were concerned, there was no way of understanding the photoelectric effect unless one invoked the light quantum (photon) hypothesis.

Einstein's theory was put to careful tests by experimentalists (which included the famous Millikan) and it came out with flying colours; and yet, few would believe in the photon, at least at that time. In 1922, Einstein was awarded the Nobel Prize for his work on the photoelectric effect but of the photon, not a word! The photon concept received universal acceptance only a couple of years later, following the discovery of the Compton effect.

Einstein's discovery of the light quantum did not do away with the wave theory of light; rather, it established that light had a dual aspect—a wave-like one and a particle-like one. Depending on the circumstances, one had to think of light either as a wave or as a particle. (Recall Feynman's remark quoted at the end of Chapter 1.) This later inspired de Broglie to speculate that perhaps matter too had a dual character which then lead to wave mechanics, duality and all that. In a sense therefore Einstein was a forerunner.

To get back to the Einstein story, apart from his monumental work on the photon concept, in 1905 Einstein also did his famous work on Brownian motion and on the *Special Theory of Relativity*. All this research enabled Einstein to obtain the doctorate degree from the University of Zurich in 1907. He then quit his Patent Office job to enter the academic world. After short spells in Zurich and in Prague, he came to Berlin as Professor in 1913. Around this period Einstein was mainly interested in the *General Theory of Relativity*, which he finally published in 1915. It was this theory that later propelled him to incomparable heights of fame, making him perhaps the best known scientist of all time.

After developing the General Theory, Einstein became interested in what is called the *Unified Field Theory*, which sought to link electromagnetism and gravity. Einstein worked on this until his death, but success eluded him.

In a sense, Einstein triggered the development of QM but strangely, he remained aloof thereafter; however, he took a keen interest in what was happening. He was quite unhappy with the philosophy of quantum mechanics and repeatedly raised objections. From anyone of a lesser stature, these objections would have been ignored but since they were from one who had himself given a push to quantum theory in the crucial early days, the objections were listened to with respect and carefully answered. This story I shall narrate in Chapter 8.

In 1918, Germany suffered defeat in the First World War and was subsequently humiliated. Frustrated Germans then began blaming the Jews for all their problems. And so in the twenties, Einstein faced much hatred, notwithstanding his worldwide fame. In the early thirties Adolf Hitler came to power in Germany. Hitler hated the Jews, and things now became very much worse for them. Many leading scientists left Germany to take refuge elsewhere, and this included Einstein who went to America. There Einstein joined the Institute for Advanced Studies in Princeton where he remained till he died.

Always a pacifist at heart, he was deeply disturbed by the Second World War as well as the events leading to it. In later life he became an ardent champion for nuclear disarmament and world peace but the times were such that noble ideas like these were laughed at by many. Nevertheless Einstein remained a towering figure, both in the scientific community and in humanity at large, which saw in him a human *par excellence.*

Einstein died in 1955.

NIELS BOHR

Niels Bohr was like Einstein in that his early work triggered the birth of quantum mechanics. And when the new mechanics was formulated, he became its chief spokesman, interpreter and defender.

Bohr was born in Copenhagen, Denmark, in 1885. His father was a Professor of Physiology and his brother a mathematician (besides being a very good football player). As a young student, Bohr won a science contest organised by the Danish Academy of Sciences. The results were published as an original article in the *Transactions of the Royal Society*.

Bohr went to Cambridge in 1911 with the idea of working under Sir J.J. Thomson, famous for his discovery of the electron. But it did not work out because Bohr did not know English well at that time. He then devoted a lot of time towards improving his English, and Charles Dicken's famous book *The Pickwick Papers* became his constant companion.

In March 1912, Bohr went to Manchester to work in Rutherford's laboratory and it was here in 1913 that he developed his famous model of the atom. The model was daring and successful but clearly it was not the full story of the atom; no one realised this more than Bohr himself. However, the instant success of the model in clearing up several old problems in spectroscopy immediately enabled Bohr to get a lecturer's job in Manchester. Soon after, the Danish Government offered him a Professorship at the Copenhagen University. Three years later the Danish Government created The Institute for Theoretical Physics with Bohr as the Director. Bright young physicists from all over the world flocked there contributing to the invigorating atmosphere. Bohr became the presiding deity, and over the years far-reaching ideas flowed from the Institute.

In 1922, Bohr received the Nobel Prize for his work in atomic physics. The Nobel Prize is often the end of the road for many scientists because after receiving the prize they drift to other things. If they continue to remain in science, as some do, then it is difficult for them to come up again with great contributions. With Bohr it was quite different. Having become a father-figure of sorts, he played a key role in the twenties in the interpretation of quantum mechanics.

In the thirties, his attention turned to nuclear physics and in 1936 he proposed the famous *liquid drop* model of the nucleus, later to prove useful in explaining the phenomenon of *nuclear fission*. When the Nazis occupied Denmark at the beginning of the Second World War, Bohr escaped to Sweden and from there to America where he worked on the atom bomb project. About this escape, George Gamow tells the following story:

> When World War II started, Bohr was in Copenhagen, and he decided to "sit it out" through the Nazi occupation to give as much help as he could to his compatriots. But one day he heard from the Danish underground that he was to be arrested by the Gestapo [German secret police] the next morning. That same night a Danish fisherman rowed him across the Sund to the Swedish shore [Sweden, like Switzerland, was neutral during the war], where he was picked up by a British Mosquito bomber. Mosquito bombers were small, and the only place for Bohr was the vacant seat in the tail of the plane, usually occupied by a tail gunner. He could communicate with the cockpit only by the intercom. Somewhere over the North Sea the pilot wanted to ask how Bohr felt but couldn't get any response. Thoroughly alarmed, the pilot, on landing at the English airstrip, rushed to the tail of the plane and opened the door of the tail gunner's compartment. There was Bohr, quite safe and sleeping quietly!

Like Einstein, Bohr was a pacificist and he really hated nuclear weapons. If at all he worked on them during the Second World War, it was because of his intense dislike of Nazi dictatorship which at that time threatened to overcome the world. Later, he never failed to raise his voice against war mongering.

Bohr received numerous honours. He came to India in 1960 to attend the Indian Science Congress. On that occasion, he visited many places in the country.

He died in 1962.

MAX BORN

Max Born was born in Germany in 1882. He studied in several universities before settling down in Gottingen. Following his father's advice, he kept an open mind and avoided specialising in any one subject. But he was much attracted to mathematics, especially that which involved applications. He followed with great interest the course given by the famous astronomer Karl Schwarzschild but curiously, did not find physics interesting—at least at that time.

After obtaining the doctorate degree (with a thesis in applied mathematics) he became a lecturer at the Gottingen University. Came the First World War in 1914, and like most scientists of the day Born had to serve in the army. His job was to do some calculations on ballistics but since he could finish these off in a jiffy, he and his friend Theodor von Karman (later to become famous in aerodynamics) secretly worked on a theory for the vibration of atoms in a crystal lattice. This theory called the Born–von Karman theory is used even today. (In 1973, I wrote a book on the subject which I dedicated to the memory of Born.)

As far as quantum mechanics is concerned, Born shot into the limelight with his famous probabilistic interpretation. Somehow, at least at that time, he did not receive the credit that was his due. People often thought that the probabilistic interpretation of quantum mechanics was given by Niels Bohr. To make matters worse, Max Born was overlooked when the Nobel awards were made for the discovery of quantum mechanics. Naturally Born was very much upset. When Hitler came to power, Born was one of those who fled Germany. He first went to Cambridge and while there he received an offer from Raman to be a Visiting Professor at the Indian Institute of Science, Bangalore. Raman liked Born so much that he tried to get him a permanent job at Bangalore. This did not work out—a sad tale, but I shall not go into it here.

Born then returned to Europe and settled down in Edinburgh where he went back to his old love namely, lattice dynamics. But this time he gave it a proper structure, based on quantum mechanics. That edifice still stands, and the book he wrote on the subject remains a classic. It is interesting that Raman who once greatly admired Born did not like his theory of lattice dynamics. This led to a controversy; but Born was correct, and Raman rather isolated in his objections.

In 1954, Born was finally awarded the Nobel Prize for his contributions to the development of quantum mechanics. A belated recognition, but Born was happy at last; so were many others. By now the war was slowly being forgotten. So, after retirement, Born went back to Germany to settle down there. This upset Einstein very much because he could never forgive Germany.

Born died in 1970.

LOUIS DE BROGLIE

Louis de Broglie was born in an aristocratic family in France in 1892. After passing out of school in 1909, he first took up a study of history. Finding that he liked science better, he made a switch in the following year and earned a science degree in 1913. During the First World War, young Louis was conscripted by the French army. However, throughout the war, he was posted in Paris and in the famous Eiffel tower! (I don't know why.) Anyway, it gave de Broglie a lot of spare time to study problems in science and engineering.

After the war he resumed his study of physics and began to take particular interest in the research of his brother Maurice. A lot of work in Maurice's lab involved X-rays, and this got young Louis thinking about the dual character of light, i.e., the wave-like character known from the last century and the particle-like aspect discovered by Einstein in 1905. De Broglie began to speculate that matter might behave in a similar fashion, and in 1924 sent several notes to the French Academy outlining his thoughts. Soon he wrote it all up as a thesis for a doctorate degree. Einstein saw the thesis and described it as "the first feeble ray of light" in the darkness that then prevailed.

The bold ideas of de Broglie inspired the birth of wave mechanics. That matter could indeed exhibit wave-like characteristics was demonstrated in 1927, thanks to brilliant experiments by G.P. Thomson in Britain and Davisson and Germer in America. Two years later, de Broglie received the Nobel Prize; Thomson and Davisson received it later.

After the discovery of quantum mechanics, there was much debate about its interpretation. An "official" viewpoint (called the Copenhagen interpretation) finally emerged but de Broglie did not quite agree with it. By now he was a Professor in the Institut Henri Poincaré where he spent time developing his ideas.

De Broglie received many awards, which includes the Kalinga award of the UNESCO, made for contributions to the popularisation of science. By the way, this award was instituted by an Indian. The first award was made in 1956, and it went to de Broglie.

De Broglie died in 1987.

WERNER HEISENBERG

Heisenberg was born in Germany in 1901. His father was a Professor of Greek. Young Werner studied physics at Munich under the famous Arnold Sommerfeld, and his fellow students included Wolfgang Pauli. In 1922, Sommerfeld brought his star pupil to Gottingen to attend a course of lectures being given by Bohr (called the Bohr festival). There Heisenberg promptly came under the notice of both Born and Bohr. For his doctoral dissertation, Heisenberg studied a complicated problem in turbulence and the result pleased Sommerfeld very much. Unfortunately, Wien the examiner (known for his law of radiation) was not so much impressed because Heisenberg failed to answer some simple questions on optics! As a result, Heisenberg did not receive as high marks as he deserved.

After a doctorate, Heisenberg became Born's assistant at Gottingen. A little later he obtained a Rockefeller fellowship which enabled him to work in Bohr's Institute. It was during this period that he made his famous discovery which later earned for him the Nobel Prize.

During the Second World War, Heisenberg stayed back in Germany. Not being a Jew, he escaped persecution from the Nazis. In 1941, he was appointed Professor of Physics at the Univesity of Berlin and Director of the Kaiser Wilhelm Institute for Physics there. During this period Heisenberg became involved with a project to build a nuclear reactor as part of a programme to develop an atomic bomb. But the project did not progress well.

After the war, he and several other German scientists were taken prisoners by American troops. There was a special team of the American army which went hunting for German scientists. Helping this army team was Goudsmit, one of the discoverers of electron spin. Heisenberg was then sent to England for being interned. He was released in 1946 and on his return set about building up physics again in Germany. He started at Gottingen at the Institute for Physics. In 1948 it was renamed the Max Planck Institute for Physics. In 1955 he had the Institute shifted to Munich and expanded its activities to cover astrophysics.

After coming into contact with Bohr, Heisenberg took much interest in the philosophical aspects of quantum theory. At the same time, he also took pains to explain the new discoveries to the layman. He was an accomplished player of the piano and greatly enjoyed table tennis which he played left-handed.

Heisenberg died in 1976.

ERWIN SCHROEDINGER

Erwin Schroedinger was born in Vienna in 1887. He was the only child of his parents. His father owned an oil-cloth factory but he was more interested in botany, chemistry and painting. Young Erwin's early education was by private tuition at home but Schroedinger later recalled that he learnt more from his father than from his tutor. He then entered the Gymnasium where he concentrated on Latin and Greek rather than on science. However, during this period he discovered the pleasures of science and promptly switched to it in the university. He emerged with a doctorate degree in 1910 but had to serve in the army during the First World War. (Have you noticed how many leading scientists of those days were drafted by the army? This was true on both sides; some were even killed during the action.)

After the war, Schroedinger worked for a while in Vienna where he did some experimental work. In 1920 he moved to Zurich in Switzerland to a Professor's post previously held by Einstein. At Zurich, Schroedinger started working in statistical physics, following in the footsteps of the great Austrian physicist Ludwig Boltzmann.

As already mentioned, in 1924 de Broglie proposed the radical idea that matter had a dual aspect. In the same year, Satyen Bose sent a paper on photons to Einstein which Einstein translated into German and got published (for the full story, see the companion volume *Bose and His Statistics*). Shortly aftewards, Einstein wrote a sequel paper introducing the novel idea of *Bose condensation*. In this paper, Einstein called attention to de Broglie's work. When Schroedinger saw this paper, he began thinking. He did not quite like Bose statistics (!) and wanted to understand Einstein's results in a different way. And in the process he discovered what today is referred to as *wave mechanics*.

In 1927, Schroedinger went to Berlin to succeed Max Planck as the Professor in the University there. But life became difficult after 1930 when Hitler came to power and started persecuting Jews (Schroedinger belonged to the Jewish faith). So he left for England in 1933. During this period there was some talk about his coming to India to settle down here like Max Born was trying to do. Schroedinger was attracted to this idea because of his liking for Indian philosophy; but it did not work out. In 1939, he shifted to Ireland. After the Second World War Austria tried very hard to persuade Schroedinger to return to his native country. Even the President of Austria pleaded, but Schroedinger refused since Soviet troops were still in occupation in Austria. Finally, when the Soviet troops left in 1956 Schroedinger returned home.

He was awarded the Nobel Prize in 1933. He died in 1961.

PAUL ADRIAN MAURICE DIRAC

Paul Adrian Maurice Dirac was born in England in 1902. His father was Swiss while his mother was English. Father Dirac worked as a teacher of French in England and so all the children grew up there. However, they were registered as Swiss citizens. Young Paul studied in Bristol. His father was a strict disciplinarian, and the children were required to speak only in grammatically correct French! Later Dirac said that this was responsible for making him a rather silent person.

In school the young lad excelled and it was clear that he had extraordinary abilites in mathematics. After school, Dirac took the B.Sc. degree in engineering but his dream was to study science and mathematics in Cambridge. His family could not afford such an education, but eventually he realised his ambition by winning a scholarship.

In Cambridge Dirac had Fowler as his supervisor (Fowler was also Chandrasekhar's supervisor). Great discoveries were in the air and hearing about some of them Dirac followed up on his own, discovering what later came to be called the *transformation theory*. In 1926 Dirac wrote up his thesis and also gave his first lecture course on quantum mechanics. Later this formed the basis for his famous book on quantum mechanics, often hailed as the book of the century. About Dirac's lectures, one of his students writes:

> There were students from other disciplines, such as, mathematics, biology, chemistry, and even philosophy. When I asked one of them, "Do you understand what Professor Dirac is writing on the blackboard?" his answer was, "No." I said, "Why are you then attending his classes so regularly?" He replied, "I shall be able to say one day that I was among the students sitting in Professor Dirac's class on quantum mechanics."

In 1928, Dirac discovered the *Dirac equation* and roughly four years later he laid the foundation for relativistic field theory. In between, he was appointed Lucasian Professor in Cambridge, a post previously held by Newton. In Cambridge, Dirac became a legendary figure. The Cambridge colloquia for theoretical physics was held in a room adjacent to Dirac's office. There was only one comfortable chair there. It was known as Dirac's chair and no one else would sit in it. He seldom missed a colloquium but he slept through most of them! Despite this, he asked sharp questions at the end which often lead to research papers.

Dirac received many honours, including of course the Nobel Prize. Many universities were keen to award him an honorary doctorate but Dirac refused such offers. He was quiet and soft-spoken in his speech and very clear in his writings. The story is told that after a lecture by

Dirac, one person in the audience made a long remark. No one knew what this person was trying to say and everyone was rather annoyed. Dirac gave the person a patient hearing and at the end simply asked, "Was that a question or a comment?" The audience roared with laughter.

I cannot resist the temptation of slipping in a few more stories. Once again the source is Gamow. As a theoretical physicist, Dirac loved theory so much that he would reduce even ordinary problems of life to the language of a theorist. Once at a party he proposed a theory according to which there is a certain distance at which a woman's face looks its best. His reasoning went as follows: At $d = \infty$ we cannot see anything anyway while at $d = 0$ one cannot take in the whole face. There is thus an optimum distance at which the face looks best!

Once Peter Kapitza (the Russian wizard famous for his work at low temperatures) and Dirac were discussing the well-known Russian novel *Crime and Punishment* by Dostoevski. Kapitza asked Dirac, "How do you like it?" Dirac replied: "It is nice but in one of the chapters the author has made a mistake. He describes the Sun as rising twice on the same day." This was Dirac's only comment!

Another time when he was visiting Kapitza's home, Dirac was watching Mrs. Kapitza knit a sweater even as he and Kapitza were engaged in discussing physics. Suddenly Dirac said to Mrs. Kapitza: "You know, Anya, watching the way you were making this sweater I got interested in the topological aspect of the problem. I found there is another way of doing it and that there are only two possible ways. One is that you are using and the other way is ..." Dirac explained what the other way was. Mrs. Kapitza stared at Dirac and said, "Your other way is well-known to all knitting women. It is called purling." So much for Dirac's great topological discovery in knitting!

In the fifties Dirac toured India and gave lectures on quantum mechanics at the Tata Institute for Fundamental Research, Bombay. I have a copy of the lecture notes which I treasure. Dirac took his lectures very, very seriously. A good friend of mine tells me that during that tour of India, Dirac delivered a lecture in his college. Naturally, the subject was quantum mechanics. A little before the lecture, this friend of mine tried to see Dirac at the hotel where he was staying but Mrs. Dirac (sister of the Nobel Prize winner Wigner) told my friend that Professor would not like to be disturbed as he was busy preparing for his forthcoming lecture! When Dirac visited Calcutta, he called on S.N. Bose the founder of Bose statistics. He was surprised to learn that Bose was not yet a Fellow of the Royal Society. On his return, he proposed the name of Bose for election and soon Bose was duly honoured.

While on a visit to Moscow in 1955 Dirac gave a lecture at the famous university there. During the lecture he wrote on the board:

PHYSICAL LAWS SHOULD HAVE MATHEMATICAL BEAUTY.

Those words are still preserved!

Dirac passed away in 1984.

5 *The Curtain Rises*

The nineteenth century saw classical physics rise to its greatest heights. The mechanics of Newton was consolidated and embellished by Lagrange, Euler and Hamilton. The mystery surrounding heat was stripped and replaced by thermodynamics and statistical mechanics, thanks to the efforts of Carnot, Clausius, Helmholtz, Kelvin, Maxwell, Boltzmann and Gibbs. And finally, Clerk Maxwell added the crowning touch with his equations of electromagnetism which, as Feynman says, will be remembered for a long, long time as the most important event of the last century. A veritable feast had been laid out and so happy did people feel that some even thought that physics had become a closed subject, with hardly any discoveries remaining to be made. But within a few short years, all such astrologers were proved wrong!

In 1897, J.J. Thomson discovered the electron. Around the same time came a host of other stunning discoveries like that of radioactivity, X-rays, etc. It is usual to count the turning point in physics from this period. However, we shall go back a bit further and start with Gustav Kirchhoff, sometimes called the grandfather of the quantum revolution. Kirchhoff died much before the revolution. In fact he was not even aware that he was starting one. The developments triggered by him are shown in Fig. 5.1. In it you will observe two branches—the radiation stream and the matter stream. Kirchhoff was interested in both.

We start with the radiation stream. When you switch on an electric iron for pressing clothes, it becomes hot. If you take your hand near the hot surface, you can *feel* the heat being radiated. Kirchhoff was interested in this radiation. To study it theoretically, he defined what is called a *blackbody* which is essentially a hollow hot-cavity, blackened on the inside. Kirchhoff said that the energy density ρ of the radiation inside the cavity was a universal function of the frequency ν of the radiation and the absolute temperature T of the cavity. Kirchhoff challenged experimentalists to determine by measurements the form of this energy density function $\rho(\nu,T)$.

Experimentalists worked hard during the next few years, and the name of the game now was to come up with theoretical models which agreed with the experimentally observed distribution function

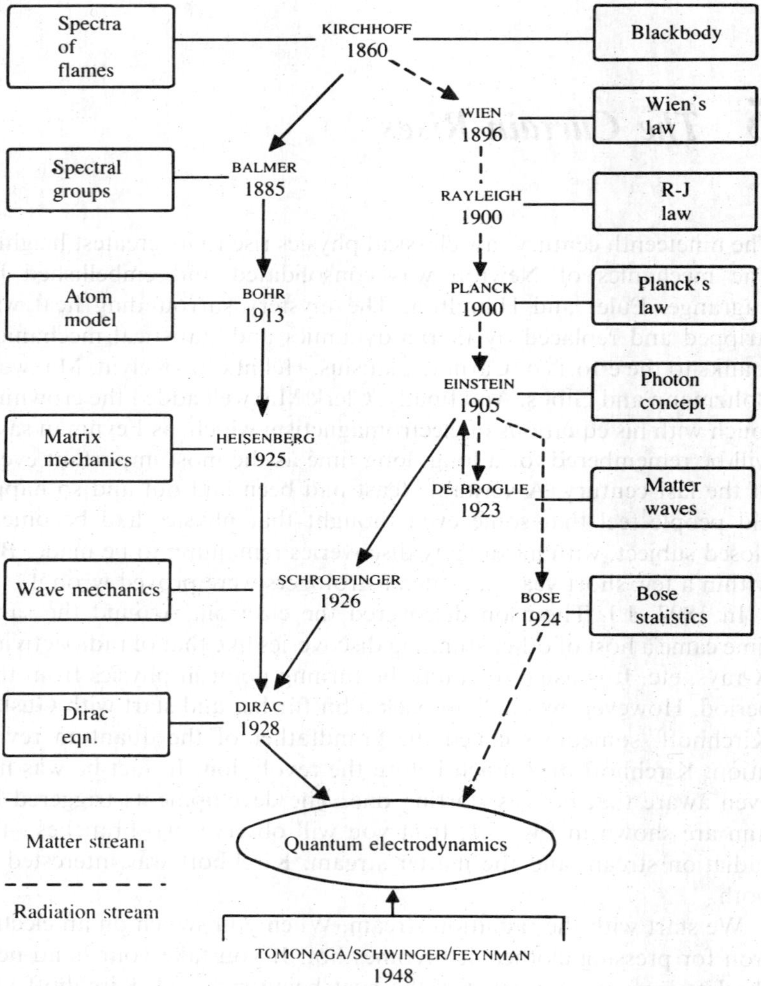

Fig. 5.1 Flow chart giving a broad overview of events (starting with Kirchhoff's studies) and their culmination in the development of quantum mechanics. Observe the two streams which eventually merged.

$\rho(\nu, T)$. (A more detailed account of this can be found in the companion volume *Bose and His Statistics.*) Initially experimental data was available only in the high-frequency region and it was well explained by *Wien's displacement law*. Later Rubens made careful measurements in the low-frequency region and here Wien's law was not so good; the

Rayleigh law as predicted by classical theory seemed to do a much better job. Putting everything together, it seemed as if Nature favoured Wien's law at the high-frequency end of the spectrum and the Rayleigh law at the low-frequency end. What was needed was one universal law which worked for all frequencies. Planck discovered precisely this in December 1900, and it turned out to be a great Christmas present for physics.

Planck's reasoning went roughly as follows: Radiation is emitted by atoms. According to Lorentz, electrons in atoms vibrate, in the process emitting radiation of the same frequency. So the starting point for Planck was the large number of oscillators tucked away in the walls of the hot cavity. Rayleigh had shown how classical theory could be used for describing these oscillators and thence calculating the radiation density $\rho(\nu, T)$. But the Rayleigh law did not work. What could be wrong?

Planck decided to go backwards and check; he could do this because he had already guessed earlier the correct form of the radiation law. And when Planck did this backtracking, he had a stunning surprise. He discovered that contrary to classical theory, the oscillator could not assume all energies but only a discrete set given by the formula

$$\varepsilon_n = nh\nu, \qquad n = 0, 1, 2, 3, \ldots$$

where ε_n is the energy of the nth oscillator level, ν is the frequency and h is a universal constant now known as the Planck's constant.

Towards the end of the nineteenth century, Lord Kelvin delivered a series of lectures at Baltimore during which he spoke of many "dark clouds" hanging over classical physics. The radiation problem was one of them; but now Planck had cleared it up, at least partially. Nevertheless, there were many unanswered questions.

Five years after Planck made his discovery, Einstein began to wonder about some inconsistencies in Planck's quantum theory. According to the latter, the energy of the oscillator was quantised. Oscillators supplied energy to radiation and did so in quanta, but according to Maxwell's theory radiation energy itself was continuous. How could that be? Analysing the problem, Einstein came to the conclusion that light energy must itself be packaged into quanta. Using this idea, he was able to successfully explain the hitherto baffling problem of photoelectricity. All aspects of Einstein's theory of photoelectricity were verified by careful experiments, and there was no doubt about its correctness. It was therefore no surprise that Einstein received the Nobel Prize in 1922 for this important discovery. What is surprising is that inspite of the success of this theory, few were prepared to accept the idea of the light quantum itself. The skeptics included Planck and Bohr; such was the iron grip of classical electromagnetic theory.

In 1923, Arthur Compton of Chicago performed definitive experiments which established the correctness of the light quantum concept. Soon the chemist Gilbert Lewis gave the name *photon* to the light quantum, and one by one the skeptics became converted to the photon idea. So what exactly was light? Was it made up of waves or of particles? It seemed to be both! At times it behaved like waves (as in diffraction) and at other times it displayed particle behaviour (as in photoelectricity). In short, there was a *duality*. This was a stunning revelation. There seemed to be no meaning to the question: "Is light made up of waves or of particles?" Depending upon the situation, it appeared to behave one way or the other.

The discovery of the duality of light was a landmark. Even before its significance began to sink in there was an even more stunning discovery, namely the duality of matter. But that story comes later. Let us leave the radiation stream for a while and go over to the matter stream.

We start again with Kirchhoff who was the first to show that spectral lines could be analysed quantitatively. This inspired Balmer, a Swiss school-teacher, to arrange the spectral lines of hydrogen into groups and write down neat empirical formulae for their frequencies (see Box 5.1).

Box 5.1 In 1885, Balmer discovered that the spectral lines of hydrogen in the visible region could be expressed by the formula

$$\lambda_n = K\frac{n^2}{n^2-4} \qquad n = 3, 4, 5, \ldots \qquad (1)$$

Here λ_n is the wavelength and K is a constant having the numerical value ~ 3646 Å.

The series is generated by giving various values to n as indicated. Using the relation $\nu\lambda = c$, the result in (1) can be rewritten as

$$\nu_n = \frac{4c}{K}\left(\frac{1}{2^2} - \frac{1}{n^2}\right) \qquad (2)$$

It turns out that there are other lines in the spectrum of hydrogen whose frequencies are also expressed by formulae as in (2). These are:

$$\nu_n = \frac{4c}{K}\left(\frac{1}{1^2} - \frac{1}{n^2}\right) \qquad n = 2, 3, \ldots \text{ Lyman series}$$

$$\nu_n = \frac{4c}{K}\left(\frac{1}{3^2} - \frac{1}{n^2}\right) \qquad n = 4, 5, \ldots \text{ Paschen sereis}$$

$$\nu_n = \frac{4c}{K}\left(\frac{1}{4^2} - \frac{1}{n^2}\right) \qquad n = 5, 6, \ldots \text{ Brackett series} \qquad (3)$$

Clearly, the universal formula

$$\nu = R\left(\frac{1}{n_1^2} - \frac{1}{n_2^2}\right) \qquad (4)$$

with $R = (4c/K)$ and the integers n_1 and n_2 suitably chosen can represent all the four series. This formula defied explanation on the basis of classical mechanics and classical electrodynamics. The great triumph of the Bohr model was that it not only enabled formula (4) to be derived but also enabled R to be calculated from the fundamental constants e, h, m and c.

In 1913, Bohr gave his famous atom model in which he made two daring innovations which are explained in Box 5.2. Let us try to understand what it was that made Bohr introduce the idea of stationary orbits. According to classical electromagnetic theory, an orbiting electron would gradually lose all its energy and finally fall into the nucleus, thus annihilating the (hydrogen) atom. Bohr declared that the atom

Box 5.2 This is what Bohr himself says about his postulates: The quantum theory of line-spectra rests upon the following fundamental assumptions:

1. That an atomic system can, and can only, exist permanently in a certain series of states corresponding to a discontinuous series of values for its energy, and that consequently any change of the energy of the system, including emission and absorption of electromagnetic radiation, must take place by a complete transition between two such states. These states will be denoted as the 'stationary states' of the system.
2. That the radiation absorbed or emitted during a transition between two stationary states is 'unifrequentic' and possesses a frequency ν, given by the relation

   $$E' - E'' = h\nu,$$

   where h is Planck's constant and where E' and E'' are the values of the energy in the two states under consideration:

Observe that Bohr's style is a bit involved. Many people including Dirac had trouble in understanding it!

had "privileged" orbits such that if the electron stuck to them, it, i.e., the electron was "safe" meaning that it would not fall into the nucleus. This, according to him, was the reason why the atom was stable. He did not of course explain *why* there should be such stable or stationary orbits. The second important and related idea of Bohr was that the angular momentum of an atom increases or decreases by discrete amounts (related to Planck's constant) when the electron moves from one orbit to another. Bohr was convinced that the quantisation discovered by Planck had something to do with the atoms also. After all, it is the atom which emits radiation, and if the explanation of the radiation distribution required an appeal to the quantum idea, should not the same idea apply to the atom ? This is what induced Bohr to graft quantisation to the atom.

Once one granted the two fundamental assumptions mentioned above, the rest of the theory followed. Radiation was emitted when the electron jumped from a higher energy orbit to a lower energy one—see Fig. 5.2. On the whole, the Bohr model of the atom was a roaring success, at least as far as the hydrogen atom was concerned. Formulae could be derived for the various spectral series, which earlier were mere empirical results.

There is more to the Bohr model than its ability to reproduce empirical formulae for spectral lines which had been guessed earlier. People who had been studying and analysing spectral data earlier had realised that the spectral lines of an element could be represented as the differences of a relatively small number of terms. If the terms are arranged in a linear array T_1, T_2, ... *then the atomic frequencies form a two-dimensional array as below:*

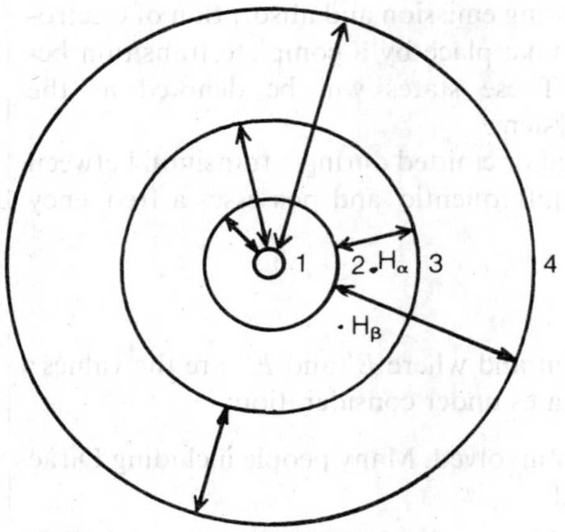

Fig. 5.2 Transitions in the Bohr model. Electron jumps from outer to inner orbits lead to emission of spectral lines while those from inner to outer orbits are associated with absorption.

$$\begin{array}{cccccc} & T_1 & T_2 & T_3 & \ldots \\ T_1 & 0 & \nu(12) & \nu(13) & \ldots \\ T_2 & \nu(21) & 0 & \nu(23) & \ldots \\ T_3 & \nu(31) & \nu(32) & 0 & \ldots \\ \ldots & \ldots & \ldots & \ldots & \ldots \end{array} \tag{5.1a}$$

In short,

$$\nu(nm) = T_n - T_m, \tag{5.1b}$$

i.e., every spectral frequency was linked to *two different* terms. There were no frequencies like $\nu(11)$, $\nu(22)$, ...etc., linking a term to itself. It was also observed that spectral frequencies followed an additive law as follows:

$$\nu(nk) + \nu(km) = \nu(nm). \tag{5.2}$$

This is known as the Rayleigh–Ritz combination principle, and at the time it was discovered nobody knew why there was such a rule in Nature. Bohr's model solved this mystery because according to it frequency is given by

$$\nu(nm) = (E_n - E_m)/h, \tag{5.3}$$

from which the Rayleigh–Ritz principle at once follows. As Bohr himself pointed out later,

> This explanation of the combination principle is seen to differ fundamentally from the usual ideas of electrodynamics, as soon as we consider that there is no simple relation between the motion of the atom and the radiation sent out.

Bohr further emphasized that (5.3) implies that the frequency of the radiation emitted by the atom is determined not only by the motion of the atom at the beginning of the radiation process (i.e., the initial state), but also depends on the state to which the atom goes (i.e., the final state).

It was soon felt that circular stationary orbits such as Bohr had envisaged were rather special and that there could in fact be elliptic orbits as shown in Fig. 5.3. Sommerfeld took things even a bit further by adding a dash of special relativity, which then enabled him to successfully explain the fine structure of hydrogen. Einstein called it a "revelation", while Bohr wrote to Sommerfeld, "I do not believe ever to have read anything with more joy than your beautiful work."

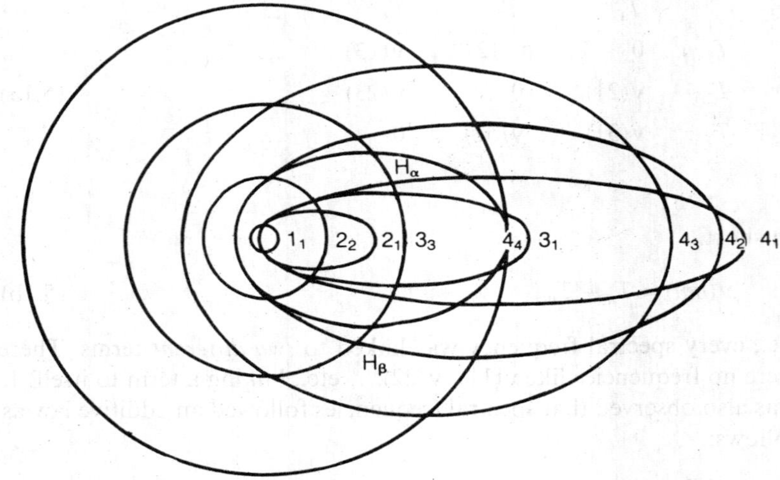

Fig. 5.3 Orbits in Sommerfeld's model which was an extension of Bohr's model.

In spite of its many successes, the Bohr model, even with Sommerfeld's brilliant extensions, had many limitations. For one thing, it could not explain the spectrum of helium. Slowly it became clear that the Bohr model while offering good pointers, was not the whole story. At the same time, no one knew what should be done instead. The stationary states were OK but the jumps could neither be visualised nor described by classical physics. In classical electrodynamics one could describe the emission of radiation in terms of charges accelerating and so forth but now one merely said the electron "jumped"—no description of what precisely was meant by jump and no equations to describe it. All one knew for certain was that *classical dynamics and electrodynamics simply did not work in the world of the atom.* The theory developed upto this stage is commonly referred to as the old quantum theory.

We are now around the years 1923/1924, and let us turn our attention to Louis de Broglie in Paris. As I told you earlier, he had done some work on X-rays along with his brother Maurice and this got him thinking a lot about photons. In October 1924, he wondered: The nineteenth century view was that light is wave-like in nature whereas Einstein regarded radiation as a gas of particles. In short, light had a dual character. Would a similar duality apply to matter? As he himself put it much later,

> After long reflection in solitude and meditation, I suddenly had the idea that the discovery made by Einstein in 1905 should be generalised by extending it to all material particles and notably to electrons.

De Broglie went further and also discussed how the wave-like nature of matter could be experimentally established by experiments involving electrons. Such experiments were performed by G.P. Thomson in England and by Davisson and Germer in America (for which Thomson and Davisson shared the Nobel Prize in 1937). G.P. Thomson was the son of J.J. Thomson who discovered the electron. It is rather interesting that while the father believed that the electron was a particle, the son showed that it had a wave-like aspect to it.

Getting back to Louis de Broglie, he put all his findings into his doctoral thesis. One of his thesis examiners was Langevin who sent a copy to Einstein for his perusal. Einstein heartily approved of the idea of wave-particle duality. In fact he himself had almost worked out the equation obeyed by the matter wave but for some reason stopped short of writing it down. Schroedinger was to achieve that later.

We are now in the year 1924. For a moment let us leave Europe and go to Dacca, then in India and now in Bangladesh. A young Reader of Physics in the Dacca University named Satyen Bose was trying to teach the Planck law of radiation to his students. Many derivations of this formula were available but Bose was not satisfied with any of them. He therefore decided to try out an entirely new derivation, starting with the photon concept just then dramatically confirmed by Compton. To get going, Bose made many daring assumptions the most important of them being that photons were *indistinguishable* particles.

Bose wrote up his derivation in the form of a paper and sent the draft to Einstein in Berlin with a request that if he (Einstein) approved of the manuscript, he may kindly get it translated into German and have it published. Luckily for Bose, Einstein did not dismiss the letter as from a crank (celebrities get a lot of junk mail, and one cannot quite blame them if they toss much of what they receive into the waste basket; incidentally, Srinivasa Ramanujan had a similar lucky break when his letter to G.H. Hardy received attention). Einstein carefully read Bose's manuscript, became convinced that Bose had made an important discovery, translated the paper and then sent it for publication.

A little later Einstein published a paper which was a sequel to Bose's work. In it he discussed what happens to a gas if the atoms are regarded as indistinguishable. He found that the gas underwent a strange change at low temperatures, a transformation now referred to as *Bose condensation.* No one quite understood (at that time) what Bose condensation really meant but it did seem as if particles of matter too could be regarded as indistinguishable, just as photons are. Was there any significance to this? Yes, and we shall come to that shortly.

Around 1924–1925, events began to move rather rapidly. First Heisenberg, then in Bohr's Institute, came up with a radically new method of dealing with quantum jumps which Bohr had introduced in an *ad hoc* manner in his model. Barely a few weeks later, Max Born realised that the "new" method of Heisenberg utilised matrix algebra discovered earlier by mathematicians. As a result, Heisenberg's method came to be known as *matrix mechanics.* At last there was a systematic method available for studying the internal structure of the atom, and

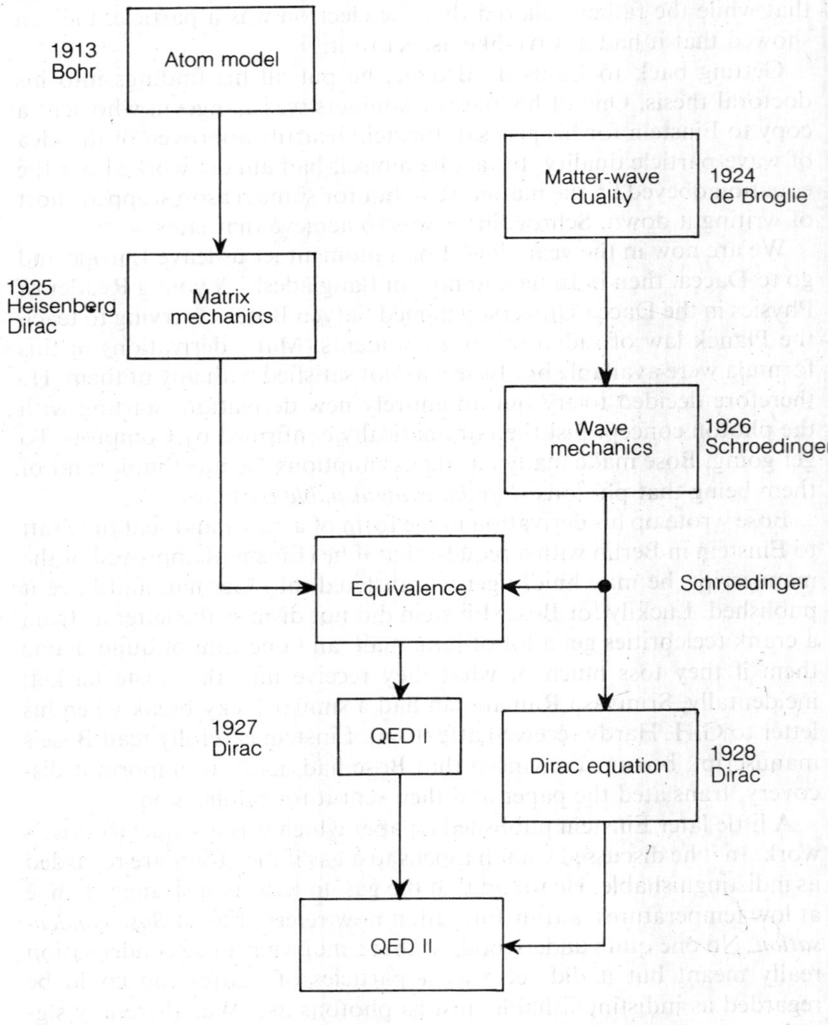

Fig. 5.4 Some important stages in the evolution of QM.

no longer was one worried about the failure of classical mechanics at the atomic level. In other words, there was a new mechanics to replace the old one.

Around this time, Schroedinger read Einstein's paper on Bose condensation. Bose had dealt with the radiation problem by considering photons to be indistinguishable. Einstein followed suit by regarding atoms themselves as indistinguishable, a marked departure from what Boltzmann had done earlier (which was to assume that atoms were *distinguishable*). If light could behave both like waves as well as particles, and if Einstein could apply the same kind of statistics to atoms as one did for photons, why not then go one step further and consider a *wave theory for particles*? After all, de Broglie had already speculated that matter too might have a dual character. Out of this enquiry was born the *Schroedinger wave equation* and *wave mechanics*. Soon followed Born's interpretation of the wave function.

For a while it seemed as if matrix mechanics and wave mechanics were two different solutions to the problems of atomic structure but it was not long before Schroedinger made it clear that they were really two sides of the same coin. Meanwhile, working quietly in Cambridge, Dirac independently rediscovered many of the results obtained by Heisenberg, Born and others in Germany. Dirac further realised that quantum systems could be described in different but equivalent ways and that these different representations could be suitably interrelated. This codification came to be called the *transformation theory*.

At this stage (~ 1927) one had separately, so to speak, some modern concepts about radiation, and a good modern theory for matter. What was needed was a happy blend of the two. This happened in two stages. First there was the extension of the classical theory of fields to the quantum case; this enabled particles—photons and electrons—to be described in terms of suitable fields. (Of course the two fields had very different properties.) Then Dirac tied it all up, giving us for the first time, a quantum theory of electrodynamics. Shortly thereafter, he deftly linked special relativity to the wave equation. Earlier, several others had taken a crack at this problem but Dirac scored. The final touch was added in the early thirties namely, linking Dirac's relativistic theory for the electron with the quantum theory of radiation. The long quest that started with Kirchhoff had finally ended—at least so it seemed.

The following chapters offer a blow-by-blow account of this exciting drama. While going through them, you might like to keep in mind Fig. 5.4 which summarises the various stages through which QM evolved.

6 *Act I Scene I*

> Finally, in 1926, an "uncommon-sensy" theory was developed to explain the "new type of behaviour" of electrons in matter. It looked cock-eyed, but in reality it was not; it was called the theory of quantum mechanics."
>
> *Feynman*

6.1 Introduction

At last we are ready for the history. Maybe we should quickly go over the setting once again. 1900, Planck announces his famous law of radiation. In the process, he discovers that oscillator energy is quantised. Five years later Einstein wonders: How come the energy of the oscillator which pumps energy into radiation is quantised but radiation energy itself is continuous (for that is what Maxwell effectively said, i.e., that radiation energy is continuous)? Einstein then disagrees with the classical electromagnetic theory, declaring that radiation energy also is quantised. (It is a different matter that few took him seriously at that time.)

1913, Bohr presents his atom model which becomes an instant hit. The spectrum of the hydrogen atom which until then had been a baffling mystery now becomes child's play. Others follow adding various touches, prominent among them being Arnold Sommerfeld.

Despite all the jazzing up, the Bohr model faces many problems. It is unable to predict the spectrum of helium, and it has no answer for the anomalous Zeeman effeet. And where radiation is concerned, the model simply sweeps a lot of things under the rug.

6.2 The correspondence principle

Perhaps I should amplify the last remark. Classical mechanics allows us to discuss particle motions. If the particles are charged, we use (Maxwell's) classical electrodynamics which says that radiation is emitted when a charged particle is accelerated. But Bohr discovered that he could make no progress with model building on that basis. So he simply *declared* that when electrons moved in *stationary* orbits, they were not obliged to radiate! Then how come atoms emit light? That, said Bohr, happens when the electron in the atom jumps from one orbit to another.

By jump I really mean transition. How, when and why does an electron make a transition? Nobody knew and Bohr was very much worried, despite the success of his model. Everyone was pretty frustrated at this point because both classical dynamics and classical electromagnetism had failed; and there was no alternative in sight. For about a dozen years or so, people played a guessing game. The feeble light that guided them was Bohr's *correspondence principle*. About this Kramers once said:

> It is difficult to explain what the correspondence principle consists of, because it cannot be expressed in exact quantitative terms, and it is, on this account, also difficult to apply. In Bohr's hands it has been extraordinarily fruitful in most varied fields.

Kramers was no doubt voicing the general opinion but to be fair to Bohr, let me also quote what the latter had to say:

> According to the correspondence principle, the occurrence of transitions between the stationary states accompanied by the emission of radiation is traced back to the harmonic components into which the motion of the atom may be resolved and which, according to the classical theory, determine the properties of the radiation ...

> According to the correspondence principle, it is assumed that every transition process between two stationary states can be co-ordinated with a corresponding harmonic vibration component in such a way that the probability of the occurrence of the transition is dependent on the amplitude of the vibration.

This last remark is crucial, and I shall come back with greater explanations shortly. For the moment, let me mention what people used to do with this famous principle enunciated by Bohr. They would dream up some kind of a model for whatever problem they were tackling, hoping that this was the quantum truth (remember that at that time QM did not exist). How do we know whether the answer so obtained was correct or not? Bohr said that the proposed theory must pass two tests which were based on his principle.

1. If the dynamics of the system under study is periodic, i.e., is characterised by a frequency ν, then in the limit $\nu \to 0$ the results must coincide with whatever classical theory predicts.

2. If n denotes the quantum number of one of the states of the system, then in the limit $n \to \infty$ one must get the same result as in classical physics. (See also Box 6.1.)

So the name of the game was systematic guessing, guided by the above recipe. As Max Born later put it:

> The art of guessing correct formulae, which deviate from classical formulae, yet contain them as a limiting case according to the correspondence principle, was brought to a high degree of perfection.

Eventually the gamble paid off, with Heisenberg hitting the jackpot.

Box 6.1 We can understand this argument roughly as follows: Consider the spectral line emitted as the result of a transition from level n to level m. According to the Bohr model the frequency is given by

$$\nu = R\left(\frac{1}{m^2} - \frac{1}{n^2}\right) \tag{1}$$

where R is the Rydberg constant. Let us rewrite (1) as

$$\nu = \frac{R(n-m)(n+m)}{m^2n^2}. \tag{2}$$

If $n >> 1$ and $(n - m) = 1$, then

$$\nu \sim \frac{2R}{n^3}, \tag{3}$$

i.e., the frequency depends only on the *initial* orbit.

6.3 Dispersion—the classical view

Have you ever wondered how exactly a prism disperses white light into VIBGYOR? For some materials the dispersion is more while for others it is less. Why? Clearly the atoms must have something to do with it but in what manner?

Usually we think of the refractive index n as being a constant quantity. Actually it varies with the frequency of light, the variation typically being as sketched in Fig. 6.1. An empirical formula which explains such a behaviour is

$$n^2 = (1 + 4\pi N\alpha), \qquad \alpha = \left(\frac{e^2}{4\pi^2 m}\right)\cdot\frac{f}{\nu_0^2 - \nu^2}. \tag{6.1}$$

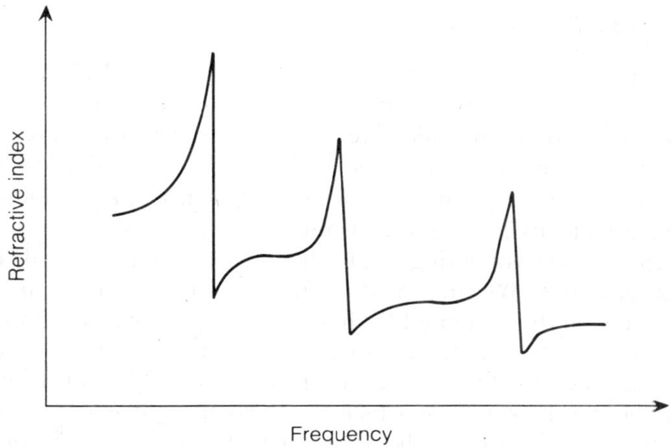

Fig. 6.1 Variations (schematic) of the refractive index n with frequency. The resonances are related to the absorption frequencies of the atom. Strictly speaking, the refractive index is a complex quantity but to keep things simple, we ignore this (important) aspect.

Here N is the number of atoms per unit volume and ν_0 is a characteristic frequency associated with the atom. α is called the *polarisability* of the atom. This leaves the quantity f about which I shall comment shortly.

A word now about the frequency ν_0. Experimentally, this corresponds to the frequency of a spectral line. As far as theorists were concerned, in those days many of them used to lean on a model due to Lorentz. Soon after J.J. Thomson discovered the electron, Lorentz said that an atom could be pictured as if it was an oscillator, i.e., it had inside it an electron that vibrated back and forth. And when the electron vibrates it emits radiation of the same frequency as that of the oscillations. When Planck gave his law of radiation, he had such oscillators in mind.

Consider a Lorentz oscillator on which is acting an (oscillating) electric field $E = E_0\cos(2\pi\nu t)$. The oscillator would now be forced to oscillate at the applied frequency ν instead of its natural frequency ν_0. No doubt the amplitude of the forced oscillations would depend upon E_0 but the closer the applied frequency ν is to the natural frequency ν_0, the greater would be the response. Glossing over some technicalities, a simple classical calculation shows that the response may be expressed by the formula

$$\alpha = \left(\frac{e^2}{4\pi^2 m}\right) \cdot \frac{1}{(\nu_0^2 - \nu^2)} \tag{6.2}$$

which is essentially the same as that given for α in (6.1), barring the quantity *f*. The latter was interpreted as the *number of dispersion electrons per atom*. An atom could surely have more than one electron, but not all of them might be involved with the polarisation and dispersion—that was the basis for introducing *f*. Remember (6.1) comes from experiment while (6.2) is a product of classical theory.

Perhaps you are wondering what is the physics behind formula (6.2). The answer is this. We first divide refraction into a two-step process: (i) Light falls on the atom and (ii) light is re- emitted by the atom—see Fig. 6.2. The incident light has associated with it an oscillating electric field and this applied field excites the atomic oscillator—this is part of step (i) above. The extent to which the incident light is able to tickle the atom is determined by the value of α. Once the oscillations get going, the atom radiates (at the oscillating frequency which is the same as the applied frequency, i.e., the frequency of the incident light). The radiation emerging from the atom is the dispersed light. The coherent action of the dispersed light from a large number of atoms leads to the refracted ray in optics. Thus the polarisability α is the crucial quantity in determining dispersion.

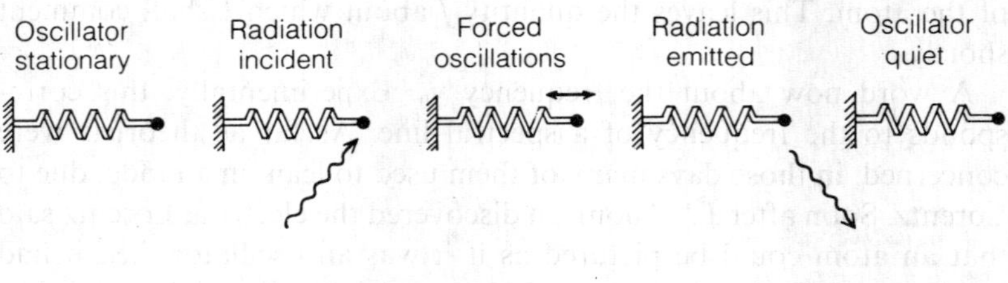

Fig. 6.2 Stages involved in the classical picture of scattering of light by electrons in an atom. The electron is visualised as an oscillator, and the scattering to be via a two-step process—first absorption and then re-emission.

6.4 Dispersion and absorption—a bridge between the two

Once the Bohr model appeared, the oscillator model received a jolt for it now became clear that spectral lines were not emitted the way Lorentz said they were. Immediately there were all sorts of problems. To start with there was a question about the derivation of Planck's law itself. Planck had assumed that atoms behaved like oscillators but from Bohr's work it seemed that they behaved quite differently. Could the Planck law be derived using the Bohr model?

Einstein tackled that question in 1916–1917 and showed that indeed such a derivation could be made. (This is discussed in the companion volume *Bose and His Statistics*.) But then there was something mysterious about this oscillator business. If it was all that wrong, how come Planck arrived at the correct answer for the radiation law? And it was based on Planck's quantisation idea, that Bohr was able to make progress. To add to the mystery, the oscillator model seemed to be quite OK for discussing dispersion.

In 1921, Ladenberg decided to do a bit of "tying up", that is, he wanted to establish links between absorption and emission as discussed by Einstein in his 1916 paper and the traditional Lorentz formula for the polarizability α. He was convinced that some such connection must exist because the formula for dispersion involves a spectral frequency. Notice that Ladenberg was trying to build a bridge between a *classical* approach to the dispersion of radiation and the (old) *quantum* theory approach to the emission and the absorption of radiation (as proposed by Einstein).

In his paper (of 1916), Einstein introduced two transition probabilities now called the Einstein A and B coefficients whose meaning is explained in Fig. 6.3. Ladenberg showed that A could be written as

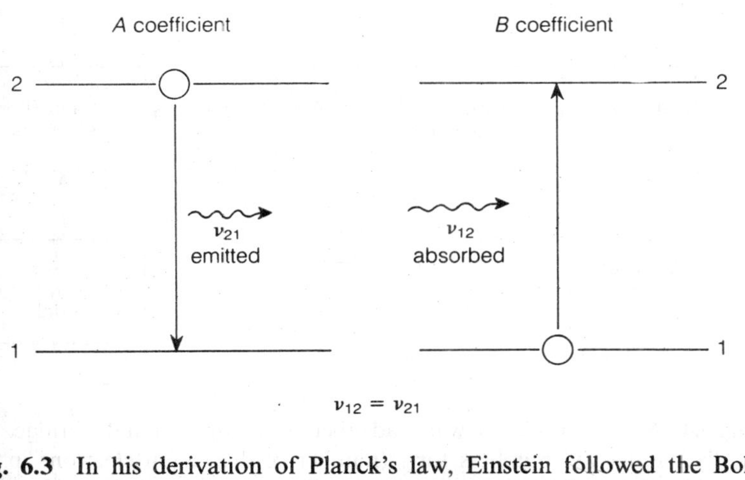

Fig. 6.3 In his derivation of Planck's law, Einstein followed the Bohr model and assumed that emission and absorption of light by atoms occurred via transitions as illustrated here. A and B are transition probabilities associated by him with these processes. He further showed they are related to each other.

$$A = \left(\frac{8\pi^2 e^2 \nu_0^2}{3mc^3}\right) \cdot f \qquad (6.3)$$

where m is the mass of the electron. Observe the following:

1. A comes from the old quantum theory whereas f comes from classical theory.
2. Numerical values of A can be derived from spectroscopic experiments whereas numerical values of f can be derived from dispersion experiments.

Starting with measured values of A from spectroscopy experiments, Ladenberg computed the value of f using formula (6.3). He then independently deduced the value of f from dispersion experiments. When he compared the two sets of f values, there was good agreement. It was now clear beyond doubt that there was indeed something to this radiation oscillator business. I hope you are able to grasp the trend of what I am trying to say; perhaps Fig. 6.4 would make things a little clearer. Bohr is very specific that spectral lines (i.e., the radiation emitted by atoms) must be described in terms of *two* states—an initial state from

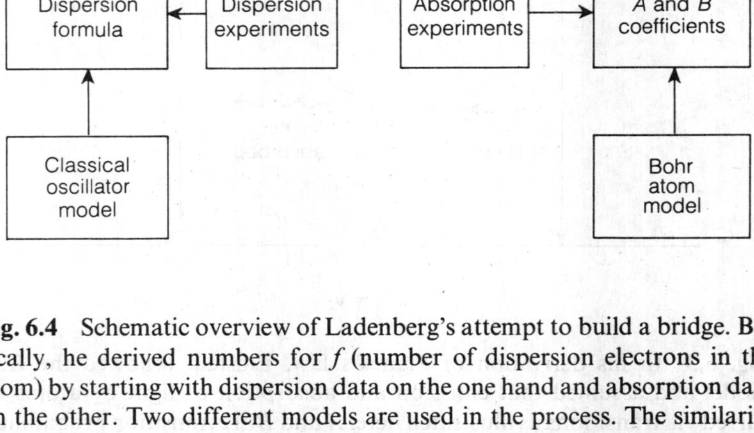

Fig. 6.4 Schematic overview of Ladenberg's attempt to build a bridge. Basically, he derived numbers for f (number of dispersion electrons in the atom) by starting with dispersion data on the one hand and absorption data on the other. Two different models are used in the process. The similarity of the f-values derived by the two methods reinforced the belief that intensities of spectral lines could be discussed using an oscillator model.

where the transition begins and a final state where the transition ends. Classical dispersion theory on the other hand, is able to get away with a picture of radiation linked to an *oscillator*. In particular, only *one* state of the oscillator is involved, i.e., the state in which the oscillator is vibrating with a specified frequency, ν_0 say. Two apparently contradictory facts, and yet there seemed to be some kind of a bridge between them—clearly some funny business going on here!

6.5 The BKS paper

Bohr seized on Ladenberg's discovery and went to town, with his correspondence principle of course. You will recall that according to this principle, the transition between two stationary states can be related to an oscillatory motion, the transition probability being proportional to the amplitude of oscillations. Bohr did this work in collaboration with Kramers and Slater. The Bohr–Kramers–Slater (BKS) paper took off from an idea that Slater had proposed around 1924. Slater said (effectively) the following: It is true atoms emit light as Bohr says. But we also know that something is happening inside the atom which Lorentz earlier had successfully described in terms of an oscillator; and the oscillator idea isn't all that silly as Ladenberg's work now shows. So why not suppose that *while the atom is in a stationary state, it behaves like a virtual Lorentz oscillator*? Further, why not suppose that these virtual oscillators emit radiation which we cannot see or detect but which other atoms can feel and react to? In other words, why not suppose that *virtual atoms communicate with each other by a virtual radiation field*? That would explain the Ladenberg mystery.

Slater was a research scholar from Harvard University on a visit to Bohr Institute. He discussed his idea with Bohr and Kramers and they both liked it very much. They decided to work together and the BKS paper was the result. But when the paper actually came out there were things in it which Slater did not quite agree with. I won't go into those details but I should mention that history showed that whatever Slater had objected to were in fact wrong (e.g., the *statistical* conservation of energy and momentum). Why did not Slater oppose the inclusion of such wrong ideas into the actual paper? He did, but Bohr's prestige was so high that young Slater had no chance; he was overruled! Years later Slater ruefully declared, "Bohr and Kramers opposed ... so vigorously that I saw that the only way to keep peace and get the main part of the suggestion published was to go along with the statistical idea."

The BKS paper is remarkable because although it ran to about 15 pages, there was not a single derivation in it; just one formula namely,

$$h\nu = E_1 - E_2.$$

The paper might have been wrong but it produced a beneficial impact. In particular, there were long discussions about it in the Bohr Institute, and shortly thereafter Kramers and later Kramers and Heisenberg together probed the matter further. And it is this which suddenly led to a breakthrough by Heisenberg.

6.6 Dispersion now with virtual oscillators

The BKS paper was published in *The Philosophical Magazine* in January 1924. Barely a couple of months later, Kramers was at work again, this time trying to derive a formula for the polarisability α using the idea of a virtual radiation field as proposed earlier by BKS. How do we make sure the answer is correct? By using the correspondence principle of course. Kramers did this and found that the traditional formula for α had to be modified to:

$$a = \left(\frac{e^2}{4\pi^2 m}\right)\left[\left(\frac{f_a}{\nu_0^2 - \nu^2}\right) - \left(\frac{f_e}{\nu_0^2 - \nu^2}\right)\right] \tag{6.4}$$

where f_a and f_e are the f-factors associated with absorption and emission respectively. (The actual formula of Kramers is a bit more complicated as it involves several frequencies. I have simplified it here, capturing the essential spirit.) The striking thing about formula (6.4) is that there is a second term which takes account of the fact that an atom can not only absorb but also emit light. Just to remind you again, Kramers was trying to calculate the response of an atom (containing virtual oscillators and emitting virtual radiation linked to a virtual field) to a real applied frequency ν. And he was making sure that his answer was acceptable by subjecting it to the two tests prescribed by Bohr.

6.7 Christening of the baby

The brief paper by Kramers in March 1924 (mentioned above) was followed by a longer one by Kramers and Heisenberg in January 1925. But before that there appeared a few other papers which quickened the pace. Of these, we must take a look at one by Born which appeared in June 1924. Born begins with the remark:

> Since one knows that, in certain circumstances, atoms react to light waves completely "non-mechanically" (i.e., they are excited to quantum jumps), it is not to be expected either that the interaction between the electrons of one and the same atom should comply with the laws of classical mechanics; ... as long as one does not know the laws for the interaction of light with atoms, i.e., the connection of dispersion with atomic structure and quantum jumps, one is left all the more in the dark about the laws of interaction between several electrons of the same atom.

Maybe I should explain what Born means. Recall that the Bohr model did not work for the helium atom. Now the helium atom has two electrons. Naturally they would interact with each other. If one believed the electrons were orbiting, they should, according to classical electromagnetic theory, emit radiation and the radiation emitted by one electron could interact with the second electron. But Bohr had ruled out any emission of radiation when the electron was in a stationary orbit. Perhaps the electrons interacted via the virtual field of BKS and perturbed each other that way. Born thus proceeds as follows:

> What we shall do, is to bring the classical laws for the perturbation of mechanical system, caused by internal couplings or external fields, into one and the same form, which would strongly suggest the formal passage from classical mechanics to a "quantum mechanics".

The last remark is very significant because this was the first occasion when the term *quantum mechanics* was used in scientific literature. Observe that QM had not yet been discovered but the baby had been named (by Born) even before it was born! At the time Max Born wrote this paper, Heisenberg was his assistant (at Gottingen). Born not only discussed his paper with Niels Bohr, he also took Heisenberg's help to do some of the calculations.

Born's work almost brought things to boil, and therefore merits further attention. It is also a good example of how the correspondence principle was flogged those days.

Born was interested in discovering rules for the "formal passage from classical mechanics to a 'quantum mechanics'." His work is rather technical, but in somewhat simplified terms, it can be summarised as follows.

We start with Fig. 6.5. Shown here are two approaches to the radiation frequency, the classical view and the Bohr view. Since classically one deals with an oscillator, one could use all the machinery of the action-angle variables (recall Chapter 3). Thus one could write,

$$\dot{\theta} = \omega = \frac{\partial H}{\partial J} \quad \text{and} \quad \dot{J} = -\frac{\partial H}{\partial \theta}. \tag{6.5}$$

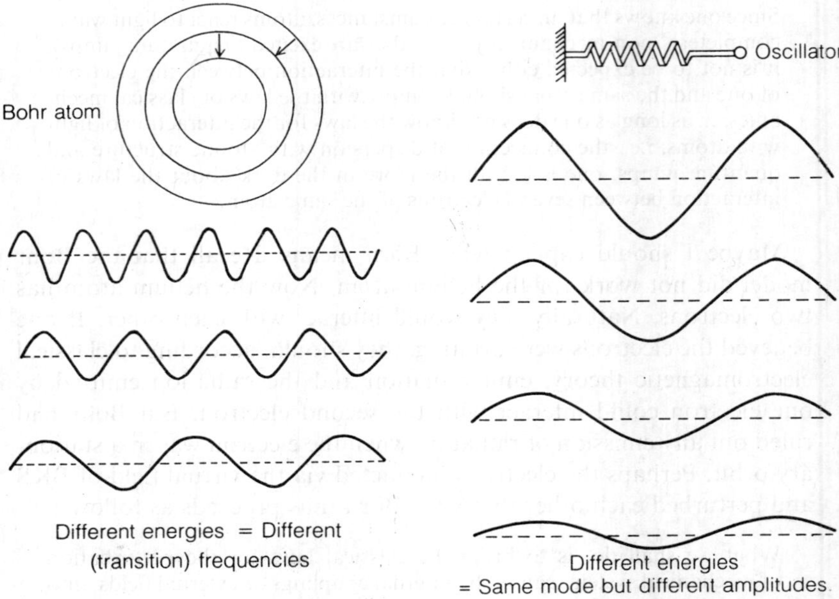

Fig. 6.5 This figure is meant to supplement the discussion underlying equations (6.5) to (6.8). In the Bohr model, the frequency of the emitted radiation is related to the difference between *two* states. On the other hand, in the classical model of radiation emission, radiation is emitted by an oscillator. Like a string clamped at the ends which has many normal modes of vibration, this oscillator could have many states (or modes) of vibration, each state of vibration corresponding to a frequency. Thus, only *one* state is linked to each spectral line. According to the correspondence principle, the intensity of the radiation would depend upon the *amplitude* of vibration.

Here we are interested only in the formula for the frequency. Remember: (i) J is the notation for the so-called action variable, (ii) classically J is a continuously varying quantity, (iii) in quantum theory J can only take the values $J = \alpha\hbar$ where α is an integer.
According to Bohr,

$$\omega(n, n-\alpha) = \frac{E(n) - E(n-\alpha)}{\alpha\hbar}. \tag{6.6}$$

For standardisation of notation, let us write H in place of E. We can then rewrite (6.6) as

$$\omega(n, n-\alpha) = \frac{H(n) - H(n-\alpha)}{J(n) - J(n-\alpha)}. \tag{6.8}$$

In other words, the *transition* frequency of quantum theory has been expressed as a *difference* coefficient. On the other hand, the frequency of periodic motion of a classical system is given by

$$\omega = \frac{\partial H}{\partial J}, \tag{6.8}$$

i.e., by a *differential* coefficient. This led Born to remark:

> We are therefore as good as forced to adopt the rule that we have to replace a classically calculated quantity [obtained via a suitable difference coefficient] by a differential coefficient.

In other words, some kind of a systematic rule for introducing *graininess* or quantum effects into mechanics was being suggested.

6.8 Once more dispersion

In January 1925, Kramers and Heisenberg (KH) decided to take a closer look at the dispersion of radiation by atoms, and extend the earlier work of Kramers (done in March 1924). Although KH used the word dispersion, we would perhaps be more comfortable with the word scattering.

The theoretical study of the scattering of light goes back to the turn of the century when Lord Rayleigh not only explained how light is scattered by atoms and molecules but also the blue colour of the sky. This type of scattering does not involve any *change of frequency*, and is referred to as *Rayleigh scattering*. The application of correspondence principle to light scattering revealed much more. As Kramers and Heisenberg write in their paper,

> When an atom is exposed to external monochromatic radiation of frequency ν, it not only emits secondary monochromatic spherical waves of frequency ν which are coherent with the incident radiation; but the correspondence principle also demands, in general, that spherical waves of other frequencies are emitted as well. These frequencies are all of the form $|\nu \pm \nu^*|$ where $h\nu^*$ denotes the energy difference of the atom in the state under consideration and some other state. The incoherent scattered radiation corresponds in part to certain processes which have recently been discussed by Smekal ...

The incoherent scattering referred to by KH is a story in itself. It is now known as the Raman effect (see Box 6.2). Here we shall stick to the mainstream, i.e., the discovery of QM. In a nutshell, what Kramers and Heisenberg did was to write down a formula for incoherent

Box 6.2 I have described the discovery of the Raman effect in *Raman and his Effect*. Here I shall give a brief summary.

It all started in 1922 when Raman was returning from England after his tour abroad. In those days one had to travel by ship, and when his ship sailed through the Mediterranean sea, Raman was struck by its deep blue colour. Lord Rayleigh who had earlier given an explanation for the blue colour of the sky was of the opinion that the sea appeared blue merely because it was reflecting the sky. Raman was not convinced by this explanation, and straightaway started making simple observations using a grating, polarising filters and a pocket spectroscope which he always carried. In fact when his ship touched Aden, he was able to mail a short paper to the British journal *Nature* describing his observations. And between Aden and Bombay, he had another paper ready!

Back in Calcutta (where he was in those days), he performed exhaustive experiments to establish that molecules of a liquid scattered light exactly the way molecules of air did, and that the blue of the sea also was due to Rayleigh scattering. Soon, the study of light scattering became a favourite topic for Raman and his students, and dozens of papers were published on this subject.

During these investigations, many students, K.R. Ramanathan and K.S. Krishnan in particular, observed a weak type of scattering, quite distinct from the usual Rayleigh scattering. No one could quite make out what it was, and it was dubbed "weak fluorescence". In December 1927, S. Venkateswaran, one of Raman's students, was studying the scattering of light by glycerine. In this case, the so-called weak fluorescence was strong and striking. Raman immediately dropped whatever he was doing and became deeply involved in further experiments to understand this new phenomenon. His collaborator was K.S. Krishnan. There followed a period of hectic experimentation. More experimental results no doubt but they were quite puzzling. And then late one night, Raman burst into Krishnan's room (the latter was sharing a rented room with a few other students of Raman) exclaiming, "I say, what we have been observing is nothing but the Kramers–Heisenberg effect." A few more clinching experiments, and Raman was able to announce his great discovery. This he did on 29 February 1928 (it was a leap year)

Cabannes in France and Landsberg and Mandelstam in Russia were on the same track but Raman had the priority of discovery and eventually won the Nobel Prize. Einstein later recalled that Raman's discovery was received with great enthusiasm because like the Compton effect, it provided clear support for the photon concept.

scattering that was similar to (6.4). Needless to say that it was all done by a generous appeal to the famous correspondence principle.

6.9 At last the breakthrough

And finally in July 1925, a remarkable discovery was made by Heisenberg. About it Born later said, "He cut the Gordian knot by means of a philosophical principle and replaced guess work by a mathematical rule."

In the abstract of his paper Heisenberg said, "The present paper seeks to establish a basis for theoretical quantum mechanics founded exclusively upon relationships between quantities which in principle are observable." What exactly did Heisenberg do? In outline, roughly the following:

What was really bugging people at that time was the inability to calculate the *intensity* of a spectral line of frequency $\nu(nm)$ say. No doubt Bohr had given a formula for the frequency $\nu(nm)$ itself and no doubt Einstein had pointed out that there exists a transition probability $A(n, m)$ which governed the intensity of this line; but how on earth does one actually calculate the intensity? The only way people knew was to start with oscillating charges and then do some skilful gymnastics using the correspondence principle. But this game was getting a bit tiring. One was fed up playing the guessing game, and one wanted instead a *clear cut* set of rules which anybody could use.

Like everyone else, Heisenberg started with the oscillator for describing an atom in the stationary state, say, n (i.e., the principal quantum number is n). Normally when one deals with periodic motion, one starts by assuming a solution of the form

$$x(t) = \sum_{\alpha=-\infty}^{\infty} a_\alpha e^{i\alpha\omega_n t}. \tag{6.9}$$

The above expansion is known as a *Fourier series*. Here ω_n is an angular frequency, being equal to $2\pi\nu_n \cdot \alpha$ is an integer which runs all the way from $-\infty$ to $+\infty$; the sum is over α. The quantity a_α is a Fourier amplitude. To emphasise that one is dealing with the state labelled by n, one writes the expansion as,

$$x(n, t) = \sum_{\alpha} a_\alpha(n) \cdot e^{i\alpha\omega_n t}. \tag{6.10}$$

After assuming a series expansion of the above type, one substitutes the trial solution into the equation of motion and then goes to work.

The focus now shifts to the amplitudes $a_\alpha(n)$ because they hold the key to the intensity of radiation (emitted by the oscillator). Remember that even though Bohr talked of orbiting electrons, when it came to calculating the intensity, one *had to* imagine the electrons were oscillating rather than orbiting. No other method for calculating the intensity was then known. Starting from here one usually went through a tortuous path, making generous use of the correspondence principle on the way.

Heisenberg now wants to try something new. As he says in the opening para of his paper,

> The Einstein–Bohr frequency condition [i.e., the formula $h\nu = E_1 - E_2$] already represents such a complete departure from classical mechanics, that even for the simplest quantum theoretical problems the validity of classical mechanics cannot be maintained. In this situation it seems sensible to discard all hope of observing hitherto unobservable quantities ... Instead it seems more reasonable to try to establish a theoretical quantum mechanics, analogous to classical mechanics, but ***in which only relations between observable quantities occur*** ...

OK, but how does one actually do this? One already had Max Born's rules for replacing classical frequencies by their quantum analogues and a generalisation based on that (namely, the replacement of difference coefficients by differential coefficients). Could one do better? And this is precisely where Heisenberg's genius showed up. He said (in effect): After all, we are trying to use the oscillator model to calculate the intensity of a spectral line emitted during a transition. And we somehow want to pull this intensity out of the amplitude $a_\alpha(n)$. This does not make sense. Why not consider instead the *transition amplitudes* $a(n, n-\alpha)$ to calculate the intensity?

This was a remarkable and bold step and so let us digest it slowly. Recall that in going from the classical to the quantum case, people were used to linking the classical frequency $\alpha\omega_n$ with the *transition frequency* $\omega(n, n-\alpha)$. Heisenberg now said:

1. Replace the *classical frequency* $\alpha\omega_n$ by the *transition frequency* $\omega(n, n-\alpha)$.
2. In addition, replace the *classical amplitude* $a_\alpha(n)$ by the *transition amplitude* $a(n, n-\alpha)$.

In other words, to calculate the intensity, assume that $x(t)$ varies as

$$x(n, n-\alpha;\, t) \sim a(n, n-\alpha)\, e^{i\omega(n,\, n-\alpha)t}. \tag{6.11}$$

Step 1 above was not new but step 2 was.

You might wonder what is remarkable about all this. Well, first recall what happened in the case of frequencies. It was found that they had to be described in terms of an *array* of numbers $\omega(n, m)$. And now Heisenberg was asserting that the *amplitudes too* had to be described by a *two-dimensional* array $a(n, m)$, rather than a *linear* array $a_1(n)$, $a_2(n)$, ...

This was not all. When one considers an anharmonic or damped oscillator as Heisenberg did, one has to deal with $x^2(t)$. Classically this meant dealing with quantities like $a^2(t)$. What happens now? In other words, how does one calculate $[a(n, m)]^2$? Heisenberg had an answer for that. He said that "the simplest and most natural assumption" would be to write

$$[a(n, m)]^2 = a^2(n, m) = \sum_j a(n, j)a(j, m). \tag{6.12}$$

Formula (6.12) is a rule for multiplying arrays, and is another stroke of genius, the reason for which would become evident shortly. Armed with (6.12), Heisenberg was able to write down the replacement recipe for $[x(t)]^m$.

What happens if one has to replace the classical quantity $x(t)y(t)$? Heisenberg notes that a peculiar situation arises here. "Whereas in classical theory $x(t)y(t)$ is always equal to $y(t)x(t)$, this is not necessarily the case in quantum theory. In special instances, e.g., in the expression $x(t)x^2(t)$, this difficulty does not arise." He goes on to add that if one is interested in products of the form $v\dot{v}$, then in quantum theory this product $v\dot{v}$ must be replaced by $(1/2)(v\dot{v} + \dot{v}v)$. In short, physical quantities like position coordinates, velocities, momenta all *had to be represented by arrays and their algebra was quite different from that of numbers. It seemed as if atomic mechanics needed an algebra different from that used in CM.*

One might still wonder what the practical outcome of all this was. As far as Heisenberg was concerned, he was able to completely solve for the first time the problem of the harmonic and the anharmonic oscillators, besides improving the Kramers–Heisenberg dispersion formula.

6.10 Behind the scene

The story of how Heisenberg came to write this paper and the events that immediately preceded it are fascinating. In early June 1925, Heisenberg (he was at that time in the Bohr Institute, thanks to a Rockefeller fellowship) suffered an attack of hay fever. He therefore left for an island called Helgoland in the neighbourhood where grass did not grow. He had been thinking about the anharmonic oscillator problem from 1922 onwards. Here in Helgoland he decided to have a fresh crack at it mainly as a means of amusing himself. On June 21 he returned to Gottingen and not only showed his work to his former boss Max Born but also wrote about it to a few friends, Pauli in particular.

He himself did not think much about what he had done. Years later Born recalled:

> The significance of Heisenberg's idea was at once clear to me and I sent the manuscript to the *Zeitschrift fur Physik*. I could not take my mind off Heisenberg's multiplication rule, and after a week of intensive thought and trial I suddenly remembered an algebraic theory which I had learned from my teacher, Professor Rosanes in Breslau. Such square arrays are well-known to mathematicians and, in conjunction with a specific rule for multiplication, are called matrices. I applied this to Heisenberg's quantum condition and found that this agreed in diagonal terms. It was easy to guess what the remaining quantities must be, namely, zero; and at once there stood before me the peculiar formula
>
> $$pq - qp = (h/2\pi i).$$
>
> This meant that coordinates q and momenta p cannot be represented by figure values but by symbols, the product of which depends upon the order of multiplication ...
>
> I was as excited by this result as a sailor would be who, after a long voyage, sees from afar, the longed-for land, and I felt regret that Heisenberg was not there.

Born now became very active and rapidly began to extend Heisenberg's work. Meanwhile, on July 19, 1925, he took the train to go to Hanover to attend a physics conference. On the train Born met Pauli and about this he recalls:

> I joined him in his compartment, and absorbed by my new discovery, I at once told him about the matrices and my difficulties ... I asked him whether he would like to collaborate with me in this problem. But instead of the expected interest, I got a cold and sarcastic refusal. "Yes I know you are fond of tedious and complicated formalism. You are only going to spoil Heisenberg's beautiful physical ideas by your futile mathematics" ...

Pauli was no doubt a brilliant physicist and colleagues frequently consulted him. The popular belief was that if Pauli approved of something then everything would be OK (see also Box 6.3). But it is remarkable how many times Pauli gave negative comments to really good ideas. In a few instances, the people who came up with radical ideas dropped them altogether because Pauli had disapproved, only to find someone else scooping them later and even winning great honours! In this case, Pauli had refused to collaborate because he had not yet studied Heisenberg's work thoroughly. Also he felt that Heisenberg himself might want to collaborate in which case he [Pauli] would be coming in the way. Anyway, Born then turned to his student Pascual Jordan and thus there appeared in September 1925, a paper by Born and Jordan entitled *On Quantum Mechanics*.

Box 6.3 I cannot help slipping in a few Pauli stories. Pauli was a dynamic person. He was razor sharp and quite strong with his criticism. His presence always made meetings lively. When he lectured, he always walked to and fro, his large frame oscillating slightly. Someone then wrote a poem which Gamow quotes:

When with colleagues he debates
All his body oscillates.
When a thesis he defends
This vibration never ends.
Dazzling theories he unveils,
Bitten from his fingernails!

Pauli is famous for his exclusion principle and for suggesting the *neutrino*. But he was also supposed to be responsible for the "Pauli effect" which Gamow describes as follows:

It is well-known that theoretical physicists cannot handle experimental equipment; it breaks whenever they touch it. Pauli was such a good theoretical physicist that something usually broke in the lab whenever he merely slipped across the threshold. A mysterious event that did not seem at first to be connected with Pauli's presence once occurred in Professor J. Franck's laboratory in Gottingen. Early one afternoon, without apparent cause, a complicated apparatus for the study of atomic phenomena collapsed. Franck wrote humourously about this to Pauli at his Zurich address and, after some delay, received an answer in an envelope with a Danish stamp. Pauli wrote that he had gone to visit Bohr and at the time of the mishap in Franck's laboratory his train was stopped for a few minutes at the Gottingen railroad station!

Pauli established his reputation even as a student with his review article on relativity. During that period, Einstein came to Munich to deliver a lecture. At the end of the lecture, the nineteen-year-old Pauli stood up and said, "You know, what Mr. Einstein said is not so stupid ..." Later when he went to Copenhagen to work with Bohr, he used to have frequent arguments with the latter. Once he told Bohr, "Shut up! You are being an idiot." Bohr protested, "But Pauli ..." Pauli cut short, "No, it is stupidity. I will not listen to another word."

In early 1931 Oppenheimer gave a lecture in America on Dirac's theory of the electron. In the middle of the talk Pauli stood up, walked to the board waving a piece of chalk and said, "All this is wrong anyway ..." Kramers who was in the audience had to persuade Pauli to go back to his seat and let Oppenheimer continue. Pauli was never enthusiastic about Dirac's theory in those days and once he wrote to Dirac about a recent paper of his: "Your comments were—to put it mildly—certainly no masterpiece." In younger days, Pauli often signed his letters, "The Wrath of God".

You should not conclude that Pauli was a neurotic objecting merely for the sake of objection. It is just that he had strong feelings and opinions about how Nature would or rather should (!) behave. Whenever proved wrong, he gracefully yielded.

Pauli was a terror to his students but once when his old teacher Sommerfeld visited him in Zurich, students there were stunned to see Pauli turn docile and reverential!

Before we go on to the Born–Jordan paper, a few words about how Heisenberg himself felt about his great discovery. He says,

> ... one evening I reached the point where I was ready to determine the individual terms in the energy table, or, as we put it today, in the energy matrix, by what would be considered an extremely clumsy series of calculations. When the first terms seemed to accord with the energy principle, I became rather excited, and I began to make countless arithmetical errors. As a result, it was almost three o' clock in the morning before the final result of my computations lay before me. The energy principle had held for all terms, and I could no longer doubt the mathematical consistency and coherence of the kind of quantum mechanics to which my calculations pointed. At first, I was deeply alarmed. I had the feeling that, through the surface of atomic phenomena, I was looking at a strangely beautiful interior, and felt almost giddy at the thought that I now had to probe this wealth of mathematical structure nature had so generously spread out before me. I was far too excited to sleep ...

To his wife Heisenberg said,

> I was lucky enough to look over the good Lord's shoulder while He was at work.

And to his sister he wrote,

> ... the last few weeks were full of excitement for me. And perhaps I can best illustrate what I have experienced through the analogy that I have attempted an as yet unknown ascent to the fundamental peak of atomic theory ... And now, with the peak directly ahead of me, the whole terrain of interrelationships in atomic theory is suddenly and clearly spread out before my eyes. That these interrelationships display, in all their mathematical abstraction, an incredible degree of simplicity, is a gift we can accept only humbly. Not even Plato could have believed them to be so beautiful. For these interrelationships cannot be invented; they have been there since the creation of the world.

We have heard of how the explorer Cortez felt when he first set his eyes on the great Pacific Ocean. And now we know how Heisenberg felt when he discovered one of Nature's greatest secrets.

6.11 The Born–Jordan paper

The Born–Jordan paper not only made many things clear about the new mechanics, but also gave working rules for tackling problems. One might say that it served to lay at rest the work horse of an earlier era namely, the correspondence principle. Among the achievements of this paper were the following:

1. Interpretation of Heisenberg's symbolic multiplication in terms of matrix algebra,
2. a formula for the commutator $[\hat{q}, \hat{p}]$, and
3. some hints about how to quantise the radiation field.

6.12 The wrap up

The Born–Jordan paper was followed in November by another entitled *On Quantum Mechanics, II* by Born, Heisenberg and Jordan. Work on this paper started in September 1925, soon after the Born–Jordan paper was completed. About it Born says:

> There followed [after the Born–Jordan paper] a hectic period of collaboration among the three of us, complicated by Heisenberg's absence. There was a lively exchange of letters ...

The paper went to town about the mathematical apparatus of quantum mechanics, making full use of matrices. Rather interesting that though Heisenberg discovered the utility of matrices in making calculations in the new mechanics, he was not happy (at that time) with it. He thought matrices obscured the physics. Anyway, this paper soon became famous as the "three men's paper".

Barely a week before Born, Heisenberg and Jordan sent their paper, Dirac sent one to the *Proceedings of the Royal Society* entitled *The Fundamental Equations of Quantum Mechanics*, in which many of the ideas of the Born–Jordan paper were rediscovered independently. For Born and others in Gottingen, this was a "dramatic surprise." The history of Dirac's paper is quite interesting. As Dirac himself tells it,

> In July 1925 Heisenberg came to Cambridge and lectured at the Kapitza club [an informal seminar group organised by the famous Soviet physicist Peter Kapitza, then working in Rutherford's lab] but I was not present at the lecture [entitled *Termzoologie und Zeemanbotanik*] and did not know anything about it. The first I heard of Heisenberg's new ideas was in early September, when R.H. Fowler gave me the proof sheets of Heisenberg's paper. At first I could not make much out of it, but after two weeks I saw

> that it provided the key to the problem of quantum mechanics. I proceeded to work it out myself.

An important discovery made in this paper was the connection between the commutator of QM and the Poisson bracket of CM. This was done using the correspondence principle. Later Dirac said:

> At that time I was expecting some kind of connection between the new mechanics and Hamiltonian dynamics (as Hamiltonian dynamics was used so much with Sommerfeld's development of the Bohr theory) and it seemed to me that this connection should show up best with large quantum numbers.

It is worth commenting briefly on what exactly Dirac set out to do and what he achieved. He starts with the remark:

> In a recent paper Heisenberg put forward a new theory which suggests that it is not the equations of classical mechanics that are in any way at fault, but that the mathematical operations by which physical results are deduced from them require modification. *All* the information supplied by the classical theory can thus be made use of in the new thoery.

Dirac then describes how mathematical operations are to be handled in QM, i.e., he lays the foundations for what he calls *quantum algebra*. For example, he defines how derivatives of dynamical variables are to be obtained in QM. This then leads him to the discovery that

> *the difference between the Heisenberg products of two quantum quantities* [we would refer to this quantity as the commutator] *is equal to* $ih/2\pi$ *times their Poisson bracket expression.*

In this way, Dirac not only establishes that the commutator is the "descendant" of the classical Poisson bracket, but also that the quantum mechanical equation of motion has a form similar to its classical counterpart, with the Poisson bracket replaced by the commutator.

Enough machinery had by now been assembled, and it was time to show in some detail that the new mechanics allowed one to do things which could not be done earlier. That step was taken by Pauli in his paper *On the Hydrogen Spectrum from the Standpoint of the New Quantum Mechanics* which he submitted for publication in January 1926. In the abstract, Pauli says:

> It is shown that the Balmer terms of an atom with a single electron are yielded correctly by the new quantum mechanics and that the difficulties which arose in the old theory ... disappear in the new theory ...

Born commented later:

> From this moment onwards there could no longer be any doubt about the correctness of the theory.

Almost simultaneously with Pauli, Dirac submitted a paper containing his own solution to the hydrogen atom problem using the new mechanics. Naturally the essential results of Pauli and of Dirac agreed, though some of the details discussed in the two papers differed. This paper of Dirac is also notable for its introduction of the famous *q*-number. Let Dirac himself explain what it is:

> The fact that the variables used for describing a dynamical system do not satisfy the commutative law means, of course, that they are not numbers in the sense of the word previously used in the mathematics which satisfy the commutative law *c*- numbers ...
>
> At present one can form no picture of what a *q*-number is like. One cannot say that one *q*-number is greater or less than another. All that one knows about *q*-numbers is that if z_1 and z_2 are two *q*-numbers, or one *q*-number and one *c*-number, there exist the numbers $z_1 + z_2$, $z_1 z_2$, $z_2 z_1$, which will in general be *q*-numbers but may be *c*-numbers. One knows nothing of the processes by which the numbers are formed except that they satisfy all the ordinary laws of algebra, excluding the commutative law of multiplication ...

You might feel that this sounds vague and forbidding and wonder what one would do with such strange numbers if faced with the practical problem of comparing them with experimental results. Dirac has the answer:

> In order to be able to get results comparable with experiment from our theory, we must have some way of representing *q*- numbers by *c*-numbers so that we can compare these *c*-numbers with experimental values.

Dirac then shows that when one is dealing with multiple periodic systems, the desired representation is provided by an array of *c*-numbers, i.e., Heisenberg's matrices.

Maybe I should briefly recap the events, stressing what had actually been achieved and what was yet to be.

The Bohr model was a great breakthrough as far as the prediction of spectral frequencies was concerned but it gave no clue about how to calculate the intensities. As Born described it,

> For each transition in the array [$\nu(n, m)$] there must be a corresponding intensity. The question is how to find this through the considerations of correspondence? It meant guessing the unknown from the available information on a known limiting case.

Heisenberg put an end to all this by insisting on dealing with observables and arranging the amplitudes in arrays, even as frequencies were earlier. He went further by discovering the law of symbolic multiplication of these arrays. Born recognized these arrays to be matrices. Soon it was realised that it was no accident that dynamical variables had to be represented in terms of matrices and that q and p did not commute. It all had to do with the uncertainty principle which Heisenberg discovered in March 1927 (see Box 6.4).

In a nutshell, a new mechanics had been discovered, besides which one also knew how to quantise the radiation field. But a *consistent* way of dealing with problems that involved *both* the electron as well as the

Box 6.4 Here is the story of the discovery of the celebrated uncertainty principle. Many teachers and textbooks start QM with the uncertainty principle and I used to think that it was this discovery which triggered the birth of QM. Actually, the uncertainty principle came about a year after the breakthrough by Heisenberg. Perhaps it is not surprising that this discovery too was made by Heisenberg. At that time (late 1926), Heisenberg was a visiting scholar at Bohr's Institute in Copenhagen. In fact he lived in the garret of the Institute buildings and many an evening Bohr would climb up to his room for long discussions which sometimes stretched into the night. Heisenberg recalled:

> Sometimes they would end in complete despair ... Once, after such a discussion, deeply perplexed I went downstairs and outside to take a walk in the fresh air of the Felled Park behind the Institute and to calm down before going to bed. During the stroll under the starry night sky an idea flashed through my mind: Why not postulate that Nature permits the existence of only such experimental situations in which it is impossible to determine the position and the velocity simultaneously?

In February 1927, Bohr left for Norway on a holiday. Heisenberg was now free to think all by himself, and his mind kept going back to a question once asked by a fellow student: "Why can't the orbit of an electron in an atom be observed using rays with very short wavelength, for instance, gamma rays?" And so Heisenberg began thinking about the gamma ray microscope. It is interesting that during his Ph.D. viva voce, he was unable to answer a question about the resolving power of a microscope. His examiner Wien was quite annoyed that the candidate was ignorant about elementary optics. Heisenberg became upset, went to his room, brushed up on optics and faced Wien again (after Sommerfeld pleaded that Heisenberg be given a second chance). That knowledge about resolving power came in handy, and Heisenberg was now able to argue why position and velocity could not be simultaneously measured.

Meanwhile Bohr returned from his holiday and when Heisenberg explained his ideas, again there were innumerable discussions. Finally everyone agreed that Heisenberg's uncertainty principle was a special case of Bohr's complementarity principle (see Chapter 8) a case which could be represented.quantitatively in terms of a simple formula. On 23 March 1927, Heisenberg submitted the paper, *On the Graphic Contents of Quantum-theoretical Kinematics and Mechanics* which contained a statement of his principle. The paper also carried some comments by Bohr.

radiation field was still missing. To that extent, the oscillator mystery continued to remain a mystery, at least in part. How it was eventually sorted out is described in the next chapter.

7 *Act I Scene II*

7.1 Introduction

Heisenberg achieved a breakthrough by relentlessly pursuing the problem of calculating the intensity of spectral lines. Seizing a lead provided by him, Dirac then made independent contributions. Since both Heisenberg and Dirac were quite young at that time, their work was often referred to as *Knabenphysik* or boy physics!

Despite the various discoveries made independently at Gottingen and at Cambridge, many questions still remained unanswered. Examples:

1. Where did de Broglie's idea of the duality of matter fit into the new scheme of things?
2. How was relativity to be integrated with the new mechanics?
3. What about the radiation oscillator business?

The tempo generated by Heisenberg's discovery was such that answers to these and other questions like the above were soon found. We start now on that part of the story.

7.2 Principle of least time

We begin with the law of reflection which was discovered a long time ago, so long ago in fact that we don't even know who the discoverer was. But around 125 BC, Hero of Alexandria proved an important result about reflection. He showed that when a ray of light is reflected by a mirror, the path *actually* followed by light from the object to the mirror and thence to the observer's eye is *shorter than any other possible path*—see Fig. 7.1.

Next we consider refraction. This phenomenon too was known to the ancients but it was only around AD 140, that Claudius Ptolemy made the first detailed measurements on the refraction of a ray of light entering water. Ptolemy built up an impressive table of data, of the angles of incidence θ_i and the corresponding angles of refraction θ_r, but

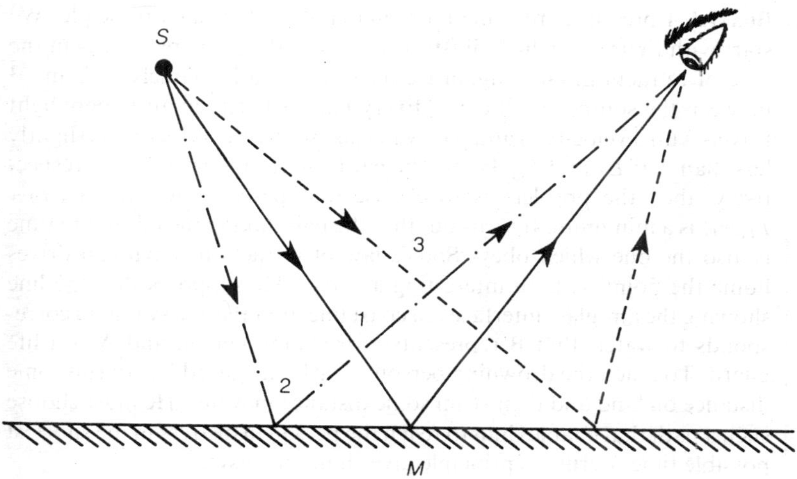

Fig. 7.1 S is a light source and M, a mirror. 1, 2, 3 are three light paths from S to M. Of these, only in the case of path 1 is the angle of incidence θ_i equal to the angle of reflection θ_r, i.e., the law of reflection is obeyed. From geometry it is easy to show path 1 is shorter than any other, like 2 or 3. Fermat stated this idea in terms of minimum time of travel (for the light ray).

he had no formula for relating to the two. Over a thousand years were to pass before Willebrord Snell of Holland showed (in 1621) that the relationship between θ_i and θ_r is given by

$$\sin \theta_i = n \sin \theta_r,$$

where n is the refractive index. This is Snell's law of refraction. Barely quarter of a century later, the next major advance was made which Feynman describes as follows:

> Now in the further development of science, we want more than just a formula. First we have an observation, then we have numbers that we measure, then we have a law which summarises all the numbers. But the real *glory* of science is that *we can find a way of thinking* such that the law is evident.
>
> The first way of thinking that made the law about the behaviour of light evident was discovered by Fermat in about 1650, and it is called the *principle of least time* or *Fermat's principle*. His idea is this: that out of all possible paths that it might take to get from one point to another, light takes the path which requires the *shortest time*. [See also Box 7.1.]

Box 7.1 I present here some more material on Fermat's principle. We start with figure (a) which illustrates the way the principle works in the case of refraction. Once again we have three paths namely 1, 2 and 3 between the source and the eye. Every path is partly in air (where light travels with a velocity c) and partly in glass where the velocity v is slightly less than c. If L_A and L_G denote the path lengths in air and glass respectively, then the problem is to choose that path for which $\{(L_A/c) + L_G/v)\}$ is a minimum. It turns out that the path taking the minimum time is also the one which obeys Snell's law of refraction. Feynman drives home the point with an interesting analogy. He supposes that the line showing the air–glass interface is a coast line, that the glassy region corresponds to water, that B represents a drowning person and A is a life guard. To reach the drowning person, clearly the guard has to run some distance on land and then swim some distance in water. He must choose such a path that enables him to reach the person in distress in the shortest possible time. Fermat's principle gives him the answer!

Suppose a graph is made of the transit times for the various paths in (a). It would appear as in (b). The minimum time corresponds no doubt to the favoured path but the interesting point is that *nearby* paths also correspond to *nearly* the same time. This enables a more precise statement of Fermat's principle.

Suppose we take this business of least time quite seriously. In that case, the path corresponding to the least time in figure (c) would be the direct path AB (dotted line). But clearly we are not talking about that. On the other hand, it is only when we consider the path ACB and others in its neighbourhood that we obtain a graph as in (b). Thus, as Feynman says, "The principle is that light takes a path such that there are many other paths nearby which take almost exactly the *same* time."

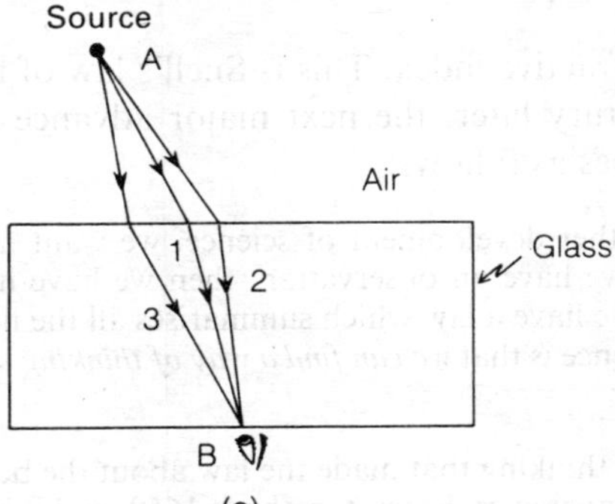

(a)

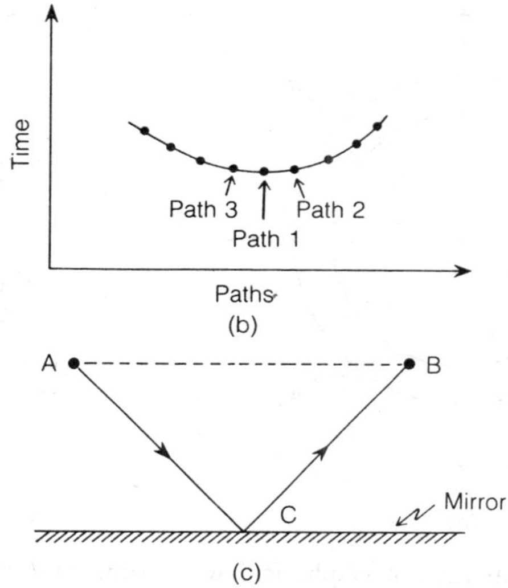

7.3 Rays and waves

Though very elegant, there is a difficulty with Fermat's principle. Now it is a matter of faith that physical phenomena follow a cause-and-effect sequence, e.g., the application of a force results in acceleration; this is the principle of causality. In the case of Fermat's principle, causality faces problems. As Feynman puts it:

> Instead of saying it is a causal thing, that is when we do one thing, something else happens, and so on, it [Fermat's principle] says this: we set up the situation and *light* decides what is the shortest time, or the extreme one, and chooses that path. But *what* does it do, *how* does it find out? Does it *smell* the nearby patterns and check them against each other?

Interestingly, light does seem to "smell" and it does this via waves, which brings us to the wave theory of light and its relationship to geometrical optics.

Strictly speaking, by wave theory of light we should mean Maxwell's electromagnetic theory of light but for our present purposes it is sufficient to consider the older Huygens' theory. Let us say a spherical wave is generated as sketched in Fig. 7.2(a). This would then propagate through the generation of secondary waves as illustrated in Fig. 7.2(b).

In contrast to empty space, the optical properties of a medium could vary with direction and as a result one could have non-spherical waves as shown in Fig. 7.3. The thick lines here are called *orthogonal*

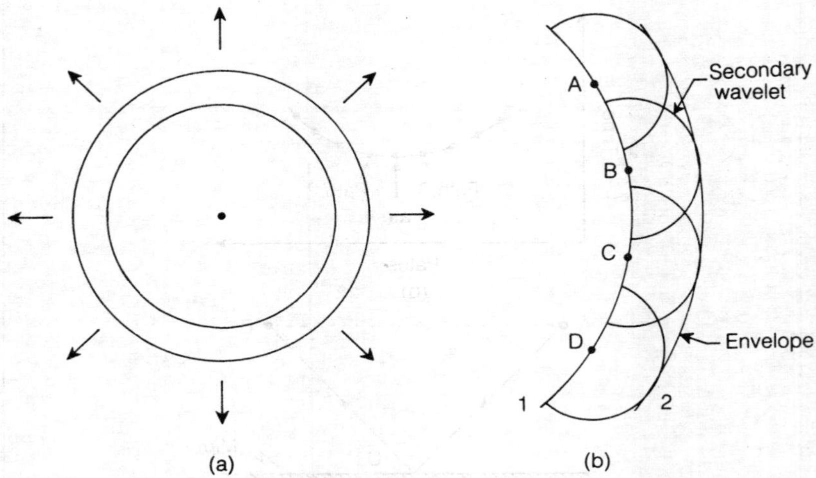

Fig. 7.2 (a) Propagation of a (spherical) wave front. The propagation occurs through the generation of secondary waves as shown in (b). When the wave front is say at 1, secondary wavelets are produced at various points like A, B, C, etc. Their envelope gives the new wave front 2. In this way one can visualise and describe the progress of the wave.

trajectories and are nothing but the rays of geometrical optics. According to the wave theory, light rays are fictitious but given waves and the rules for their propagation, the associated rays can be constructed.

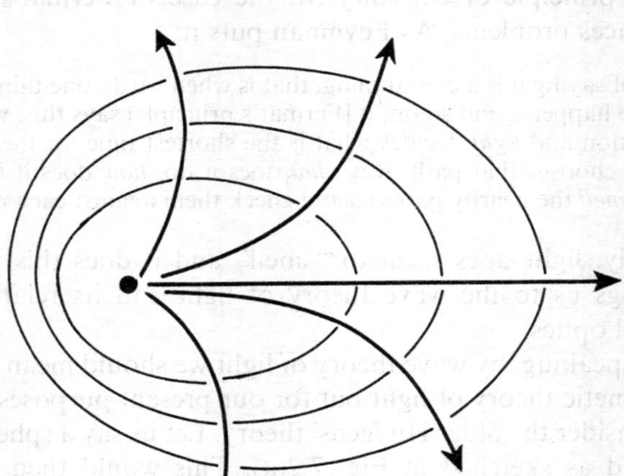

Fig. 7.3 In a non-isotropic medium, one can have non-spherical waves as here. The orthogonal trajectories form the rays. Observe their bending.

Schroedinger neatly summarises all this with the remark, "Fermat's principle appears to be the trivial quintessence of the wave theory".

7.4 Mechanics and optics

Hamilton was the first to notice a strong formal similarity between optics and mechanics. His earlier work was mostly in optics. Starting in 1827, he spent many years developing a mathematical theory of ray optics in which he introduced the famous *Hamilton's characteristic function W*. In his theory, Hamilton studied the progress of rays by considering surfaces perpendicular to them. These were surfaces of constant W — we would call them wave fronts. To determine the path of rays, Hamilton used the principle of least action and in so doing he was struck by the similarity of his action principle to Fermat's principle of least time.

After extensive studies in optics, Hamilton came to the conclusion that many of the mathematical methods he had developed for optics could equally well be applied to mechanics. And from this study came his famous paper *On a General Method in Dynamics*.

Let us now catch a quick glimpse of the connection between optics and mechanics as revealed to us by Hamilton. We start with optics. Consider a plane wave, propagating say along the z-direction. We could represent it as

$$\phi = \phi_0 e^{ik_0(nz - \omega t)} \tag{7.1}$$

Here ϕ_0 is the scalar amplitude, $\omega = 2\pi\nu$ is the angular frequency, n the refractive index and k_0 called the *vacuum wave number* is given by

$$k_0 = (2\pi/\lambda_0) \tag{7.2}$$

where λ_0 is the (vacuum) wavelength. It is related to ν by

$$\nu\lambda_0 = c. \tag{7.3}$$

The quantity nz is called the *optical path length*. It is denoted by the symbol L and given the special name *eikonal*.

Hamilton showed that geometrical optics applies if the refractive index n varies very slowly compared to λ_0. Under these circumstances, the eikonal is determined by the equation

$$[\nabla L(r)]^2 = n^2(r), \tag{7.4}$$

referred to as the *eikonal equation of optics*. Knowing $n(r)$, the spatial variation of the refractive index, equation (7.4) could be solved for $L(r)$. Surfaces of constant L determined by this equation define the wave front. The ray trajectories everywhere are perpendicular to the wave front and are therefore also determined by (7.4).

Hamilton discovered that a similar equation occurs in mechanics, namely,

$$[\nabla W(r)]^2 = 2m[E - V(r)]. \tag{7.5}$$

Here m is the mass of the particle, E its total energy (assumed to be a constant), $V(r)$ the potential energy and $W(r)$ the characteristic function. Hamilton found that particle trajectory is related to the wave front rather in the manner the light ray is related to the wave front—see Fig. 7.4.

Hamilton stopped at this point in drawing parallels between optics and mechanics, and almost a century was to pass before the threads were picked up again.

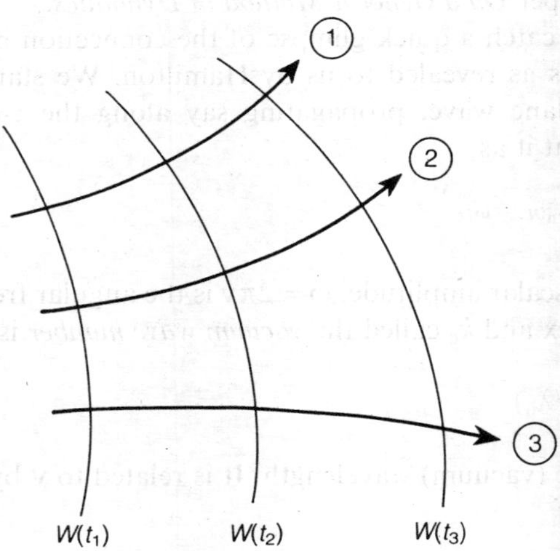

Fig. 7.4 Hamilton's description of particle motions and their relationship to waves. Hamilton did not actually believe that material particles had waves associated with them. He however found it convenient to discuss mechanics via his characteristic function W. In a typical problem, the surfaces of constant W at successive instants might be as sketched here. The lines 1, 2, 3 indicate some of the particle trajectories possible under these circumstances.

7.5 Enter Schroedinger

Schroedinger was somewhat older than Heisenberg and Dirac when he burst forth with five papers on wave mechanics in 1926. All these were written in Zurich where he was a Professor at that time and were published in the *Annalen der Physik*.

Schroedinger begins his first paper with the following remarks:

> In this paper I wish to consider, first, the simple case of the hydrogen atom (non-relativistic and unperturbed), and show that, the customary conditions [Bohr postulates] can be replaced by another postulate, in which the notion of "whole numbers", merely as such, is not introduced. Rather when integralness does appear, it arises in the same natural way as it does in the case of the node-numbers of a vibrating string.

In simple terms, Schroedinger does not impose the quantisation condition

$$J = nh; \tag{7.6}$$

rather, quantisation is allowed to *emerge as a natural consequence of the principle of least action.* Years later Schroedinger explained his thinking in his Nobel lecture:

> On the one hand, Hamilton's principle in particular proved to be the most faithful and reliable guide, which was simply indispensible; on the other hand one had to suffer, to do justice to the facts, the rough interference of entirely new incomprehensible postulates, of the so-called quantum conditions and quantum postulates. Strident disharmony in the symphony of classical mechanics—yet strangely familiar—played as it were on the same instrument. In mathematical terms we can formulate this as follows: whereas the Hamilton principle merely postulates that a given integral must be a minimum, without the numerical value of the minimum being established by this postulate, it is now demanded that the numerical value of the minimum should be restricted to integral multiples of a universal natural constant, Planck's quantum of action. The situation was fairly desparate. Had the old mechanics failed completely, it would not have been so bad. The way should then have been free to the development of a new system of mechanics. As it was, one was faced with the difficult task of saving the *soul* of the old system, whose inspiration clearly held sway in the microcosm, while at the same time flattering it as it were into accepting the quantum conditions as gross interference but as issuing from its own innermost essence.

There was a way out of this impasse which was to recognise the analogy between Hamilton's principle and Fermat's principle. As Schroedinger comments:

> One must attribute to the Hamilton principle, also, the operation of a wave mechanism on which the point-mechanical processes are essentially

> based, just as one had long become accustomed to doing in the case of phenomena relating to light and of the Fermat principle which governs them. Admittedly, the individual path of a mass point loses its proper physical significance and becomes as fictitious as the individual isolated ray of light. The essence of the theory, the minimum principle, however, remains not only intact, but reveals its true and inner meaning only under the wave-like aspect ...

Reduced to brass tacks, what Schroedinger did was the following: He started from the Hamilton–Jacobi equation (recall Chapter 3)

$$H\left(q, \frac{\partial W}{\partial q}\right) = E. \tag{7.7}$$

Next he expressed W in terms of a new unknown function ψ via the relation

$$W = K \log \psi. \tag{7.8}$$

The constant K has the dimension of action. After a bit of algebra Schroedinger obtained (for the hydrogen atom) the equation

$$\nabla^2\psi + \frac{2m}{K^2}\left(E + \frac{e^2}{r}\right)\psi = 0. \tag{7.9}$$

Schroedinger solved this equation to obtain the solutions ψ, keeping in mind the action principle. He then discovered that with E negative, solutions ψ that were "everywhere real, single-valued, finite, and continuously differentiable upto second order" could be obtained only for a discrete set of values of E. In particular Schroedinger found

$$E_n = -\frac{me^4}{2n^2K^2}, \tag{7.10}$$

which is the standard result for the hydrogen atom, provided K is set equal to h. With this value for K, (7.10) assumes the form we are already familiar with (recall (3.4)).

Notice the following:

1. Schroedinger solved the hydrogen atom problem via a differential equation rather than by manipulating matrices.
2. Solutions of the wave equation were obtained rather in the manner one solves for standing waves on a vibrating string clamped at both ends (see also Box 7.2).
3. Quantisation of the hydrogen atom levels emerged as a natural consequence of Hamilton's principle.

Box 7.2 A string clamped at two ends can vibrate only in certain modes. These are called the normal modes of vibration and are illustrated in figure (a). The study of normal modes of vibration is a well-known problem in classical physics. In the case of the string, the equation to be solved is

$$\frac{d^2\phi(x)}{dx^2} + \frac{4\pi^2}{\lambda^2}\phi(x) = 0. \qquad (1)$$

It is easily verified that the solution

$$\phi(x) = A \sin kx \qquad (2)$$

with

$$k = (2\pi n/L), \quad n = 1, 2, 3 \ldots \qquad (3)$$

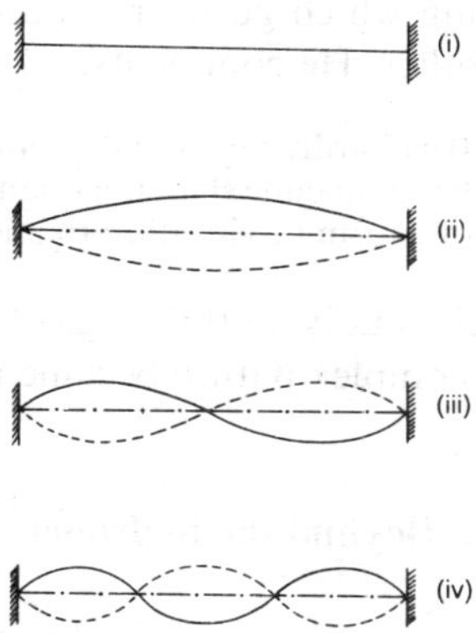

(a)

satisfies equation (1). Solutions corresponding to different n values represent the different normal modes.

In his paper, Schroedinger tackled the hydrogen atom problem very much like the way one tackles the well-known normal-model problem in classical physics. No wonder he felt that wave mechanics did not represent a radical departure from classical physics, contrary to what Born, Heisenberg, Bohr and others of the Gottingen–Copenhagen camp believed.

In short, Schroedinger *dealt with mechanics from a wave theory point of view*, drawing inspiration from de Broglie on the one hand and Hamilton on the other. As he remarked,

> In optics the *old* system of mechanics corresponds to intellectually operating with isolated mutually independent light rays. The new undulatory mechanics corresponds to the wave theory of light.

In optics, the ray theory is not of much use when diffraction effects (i.e., the wave nature of light) become important. CM is like ray optics and according to Schroedinger its failure in the domain of the atom was a clear signal that it was time to develop a wave theory of matter. This is precisely what he did. At the same time he observed:

> The new theory in fact is not *new*; it is a completely organic development, one might almost be tempted to say a more elaborate exposition of the old theory.

What about transitions, spectral lines and all that in the new theory? Schroedinger deals with them by analogy with waves on a vibrating string which go over continuously from one normal mode pattern to another. He comments:

> It is hardly necessary to emphasise how much more congenial it would be to imagine that at a quantum transition the energy changes over from one form of vibration to another, than to think of a jumping electron.

Incidentally, at this stage of the game the wave function ψ was still real; its complex nature became revealed only later.

7.6 Beyond the hydrogen atom

The second paper of Schroedinger was a general enquiry into the "correspondence which exists between the Hamilton–Jacobi differential equation of a mechanical problem and the 'allied' *wave equation*". The success in dealing with the hydrogen atom problem via a wave equation prompts him now to search for a general wave theory of matter. He begins this search by asking where and when CM fails and then adds:

> Perhaps this failure is in strict analogy with the failure of geometrical optics, i.e., "the optics of infinitely small wave lengths", that became evident as soon as the obstacles or apertures are no longer great compared with the real, finite, wave length. Perhaps our classical mechanics is the complete analogy of geometrical optics and as such is wrong and not in agreement with reality; it fails whenever the radii of curvature and dimensions of the path are no longer great compared with a certain wave length, to which, in q-space, a real meaning is attached. Then it becomes a question of searching for an undulatory mechanics, and the most obvious way is the working out of the Hamiltonian analogy on the lines of undulatory optics.

This search for an "undulatory mechanics" was unquestionably inspired by de Broglie's pioneering idea. Despite all the formal analogies drawn earlier by Hamilton between mechanics and optics, nobody had dared to associate a wave-like nature with matter. And when de Broglie suggested such a link, his ideas were frowned upon by many. Lorentz, for example, said, "These young men consider it exceedingly easy to discard old concepts in physics!" Einstein also thought de Broglie was audacious but nevertheless, he commented favourably. To Born he said, "Read it [de Broglie's paper]! Although it seems to have been written by a madman, it has been written soundly". A further favourable comment by Einstein in his paper on Bose condensation attracted the attention of Schroedinger who later said that Einstein gave him "a flick on the nose by pointing out the importance of de Broglie's ideas".

Given the successful results obtained in his first paper and the duality of matter stressed by de Broglie, Schroedinger was now convinced that one should give up "ideas about the 'place of the electron' and 'path' of the electron. If these are not given up, contradictions remain".

The task therefore was to write a general version of (7.9) and Schroedinger approached it roughly as follows: Mechanics gives us two results, namely,

1. $[\nabla W(r)]^2 = 2m[E - V(r)]$
2. $u = E/|\nabla W(r)|$.

We are here considering the motion of a particle of mass m. The first of the above two equations is already familiar to us. The second equation is a result for the wave velocity u. By combining these two we obtain

$$u = \frac{E}{\sqrt{2m(E - V)}}. \tag{7.11}$$

Now

$$T = (E - V) = (1/2)mv^2. \tag{7.12}$$

Hence

$$u = E/(mv). \tag{7.13}$$

On the other hand, from the de Broglie relation we have

$$\lambda = (h/mv).$$

Using (7.11) in the above we obtain

$$\lambda = \frac{h}{\sqrt{2m(E - V)}}. \tag{7.14}$$

In optics we have the scalar wave equation

$$\nabla^2\phi(r) + \frac{4\pi^2}{\lambda^2}\phi(r) = 0 \tag{7.15}$$

where $\phi(r)$ is the (scalar) optical wave amplitude. We look for an analogous equation for the matter wave function $\psi(r)$, remembering (7.14) . This gives

$$\nabla^2\psi(r) + \frac{8\pi^2 m}{h^2}(E - V)\,\psi(r) = 0 \qquad (7.16)$$

which is the Schroedinger equation for a single particle of mass m moving in a potential $V(r)$. Schroedinger also noted that this equation could be generalised for a system of many particles.

With (7.16), the problem of mechanics has been reduced to the problem of solving a partial differential equation. Partial differential equations are "notorious" for the number of solutions they support. Would not (7.16) therefore amount to opening Pandora's box? Not quite, according to Schroedinger, because (7.16) *carries within itself the quantum conditions* which automatically yield the *physically meaningful solutions alone*. In the old quantum theory, one first considered all possible states and then selected some via the quantisation condition. The situation is now changed and Schroedinger declares:

> The definition of the quantum levels *no longer takes place* in two separated stages: (i) Definition of all paths dynamically possible. (ii) *Discarding* of the greater part of those solutions and the selection of a few by special postulations; on the contrary, the quantum levels are *at once* defined as the proper values [eigen values] of equation (18) [our (7.16)], which *carries in itself its natural boundary conditions*.

Schroedinger checks out his equation by thoroughly analysing the problem of the oscillator, the rigid rotator and the diatomic molecule. Does he have any comments on the work of Heisenberg, Born and others? Yes.

> In its *tendency*, Heisenberg's attempt stands very near the present one ... In its method, it is so totally different that I have not yet succeeded in finding the connecting link.

That link was found a few months later. Meanwhile, what did Heisenberg think about Schroedinger's work? He first heard about it in a seminar lecture in Munich in June 1926 and "gave way to absolute despair". Later he wrote to Pauli: "The more I reflect on the physical side of Schroedinger's theory the more dreadful it seems to me".

Arguments about wave mechanics went on and reached a climax in September 1926 when Schroedinger paid a visit to Bohr's institute. Schroedinger was exhausted by the discussions and fell ill but Bohr continued the dialogue at the bedside! Schroedinger did not like quantum jumps while Bohr wouldn't let go of them. Finally in despair Schroedinger exclaimed: "If we are going to stick to those damned quantum jumps, then I regret that I ever had anything to do with the quantum theory". To which Bohr replied, "But the rest of us are much obliged to you for that".

7.7 So near and yet so far

Schroedinger made his discovery essentially by pushing the analogy that Hamilton had first noticed. Could Hamilton himself have made that discovery? After all, he was just a "stone's throw" away. Not quite, because to insist upon a wave theory of matter one had to first *believe* that matter indeed had a wave-like aspect. At least if a discrete energy spectrum as in the case of the hydrogen atom had been known at that time, Hamilton could have made a try, somewhat like in Schroedinger's first paper on wave mechanics. In 1840, there was *absolutely no hint* either about quantisation or the wave aspect of matter. CM had been applied with tremendous success to astronomy, and any attempt to deviate from it would not merely have been frowned upon but even ridiculed. As Schroedinger pointed out, CM fails only when curvatures in particle trajectories become comparable to the wavelength. This is precisely what happens in the case of electrons in atoms, but way back in the days of Hamilton there were no electrons and hardly any physicist believed in the atom.

It does not always pay to be far ahead of the times. If an example is needed, the tragic case of Boltzmann provides one. He was not that far ahead with his kinetic theory of gases and yet it was viciously attacked. So violently in fact, that it drove Boltzmann to despair and made him end his life.

7.8 Waves and particle trajectories

In CM one has a clear cut notion of particle trajectories. Does one have to abandon such notions in wave mechanics? Schroedinger answered that question in a short paper published in *Naturwissenschaften.*

It is well known in wave theory that a wave packet can be constructed by suitably superposing many plane waves. Schroedinger makes the "transition from micro to macro-mechanics" by using such an idea. To illustrate his argument, he considers a one-dimensional harmonic oscillator. The wave functions associated with the five lowest states are sketched in Fig. 7.5. Schroedinger seeks to demonstrate the transition to macroscopic mechanics

> by showing that a *group* of proper vibrations of *high* order-number *n* ("quantum number") and of relatively small order-number differences ("quantum number differences") may represent a "particle" which is executing "motion" expected from the usual mechanics.

Figure 7.6 shows the wave packet constructed by Schroedinger. He comments:

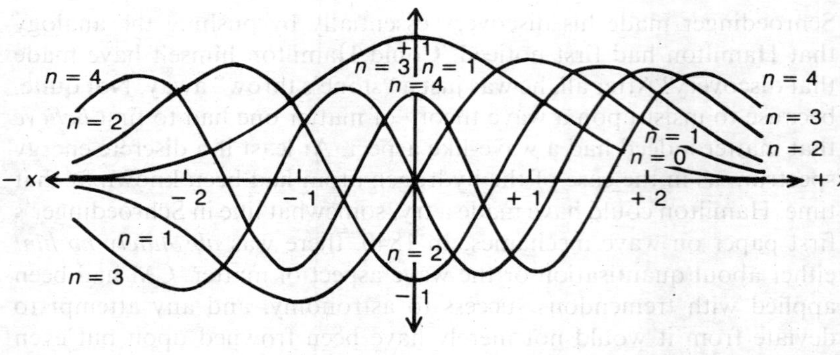

Fig. 7.5 Sketch of the wave functions corresponding to the five lowest states of the harmonic oscillator, as obtained by Schroedinger.

> *Our wave group always remains compact*, and does *not* spread out into larger regions as time goes on, and as we were accustomed to make it do, for example, in optics.

Schroedinger then conjectures that similar wave groups could perhaps be constructed to illustrate motion in three dimensions, including of electrons in atoms.

7.9 Making the two ends meet

Commenting on Schroedinger's work, Max Born later declared:

> Whatever is there more outstanding in theoretical physics? The Schroedinger equation enjoys in modern physics the same place as in classical physics do the equations derived by Newton, Lagrange and Hamilton.

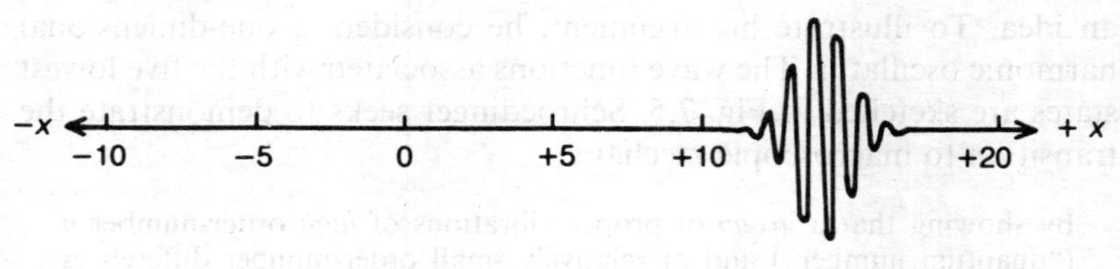

Fig. 7.6 The wave packet constructed by Schroedinger by superposing harmonic oscillator wave functions. The packet is supposed to move periodically back and forth along the x-axis, analogous to the oscillations of the mass point of the classical oscillator.

While this was the retrospective view, in the days immediately following the publication of Schroedinger's first papers, many, especially those of the Gottingen school, viewed wave mechanics with suspicion. According to them QM represented a radical departure from CM. They could therefore not agree with Schroedinger who regarded it (i.e., his wave mechanics) as "a more elaborate exposition of the old theory". On the other hand, Uhlenbeck was quite pleased with Schroedinger's work because "we did not any longer have to learn the strange mathematics of matrices". For his part, Schroedinger was not enthusiastic about Heisenberg's work! In one of his papers he writes:

> I naturally knew about his [Heisenberg's] theory, but was discouraged, if not repelled, by what appeared to me as very difficult methods of transcendental algebra, and by the want of perspicuity.

Nevertheless, Schroedinger was intrigued that both the theories were successful in their own ways and both gave the correct answers for the hydrogen atom, rotator, etc., despite the fact "the departure from classical mechanics in the two theories seem to occur in diametrically opposed directions." Whereas Heisenberg had reduced the problem to one of solving algebraic equations with matrices representing classical variables like coordinate and momentum, Schroedinger relied on solving an appropriate differential equation. Did this mean there was a link between these two seemingly opposite points of view? In March 1926, Schroedinger found the answer; that matrix mechanics and wave mechanics were really two sides of the same coin. The same conclusion was independently arrived at by Carl Eckart in the United States, and by Cornelius Lanczos and Wolfgang Pauli in Germany.

Which of the two versions is better? Schroedinger comments:

> Every discussion of the superiority of the one or the other has only an illusory object ... For they are completely equivalent from the mathematical point of view, and it can only be a question of the subordinate point of convenience of calculation.

He however adds:

> As the natural advocate of one of them, I will not be blamed if I frankly—and perhaps not wholly impartially—bring forward the arguments in its [i.e., wave mechanics] favour.

7.10 What does ψ represent?

In optics, one knew what the wave amplitude ϕ (see equation (7.15)) meant. What did ψ the newly-introduced amplitude for matter waves represent? Schroedinger reflected on this question in his fourth paper on wave mechanics which was submitted for publication in late June 1926. This paper is notable not only for the physical interpretation of ψ which Schroedinger attempted but even more so because Schroedinger now became aware that ψ was actually a complex quantity. He declared that the physically meaningful quantity was not ψ itself but $\psi\psi^*$ the *weight function*. On this basis he asserted that $e\psi(r)\,\psi^*(r)$ for the hydrogen atom represented the *electron charge density* at the point r. We know now that this interpretation is not correct.

The correct interpretation was proposed by Born in a paper submitted barely four days after Schroedinger had communicated his paper containing the interpretation of ψ. Born considered the scattering problem illustrated schematically in Fig. 7.7. In modern notation, the incident and scattered waves would be expressed as:

Incident wave: e^{ikz}

Scattered wave: $f(\theta, \phi)\,\dfrac{e^{ikr}}{r}$.

Here $f(\theta, \phi)$ is the scattering amplitude for scattering in the direction (θ, ϕ). Born denotes it as Φ_{mn} the transition amplitude from the initial plane wave state n to the final state m in which there is a wave in the direction (θ, ϕ). Born now declared:

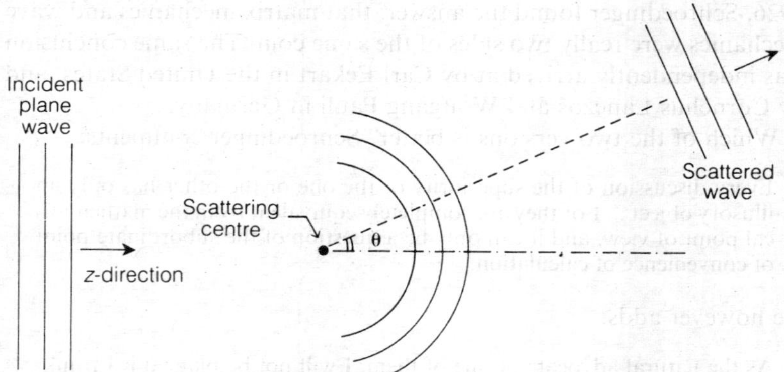

Fig. 7.7 Visualisation of scattering in quantum mechanics. On the left is the incident plane wave. When it encounters the scattering centre, a scattered wave is produced, rather like Huygen's secondary wave. Far away from the scattering centre, the scattered wave again looks like a plane wave. What one usually wants to know is the amplitude for scattering in a particular direction (θ, ϕ).

> Φ_{nm} determines the probability for the scattering of the electron from the z-direction into the direction (θ, ϕ).

Obviously this is not correct, but Born made up by adding the following footnote in the proof:

> A more precise consideration shows that the probability is proportional to the square of Φ_{nm}.

Today of course we would say that probability is proportional to the *absolute* square of the wave function. Born missed the word absolute but perhaps that was an oversight. Around the same time, Dirac and Wigner were also toying with a probabilistic interpretation but they only considered ψ or $|\psi|$. It was Born who realised that neither of these represent the probability and that only $|\psi|^2$ does.

The probabilistic interpretation proposed by Born was a revolutionary break from the past because it meant giving up determinism. As Born himself declared:

> One obtains the answer to the question, *not* "what is the state after the collision" but "how probable is a given effect of the collision" ... I myself tend to give up determinism in the atomic world.

Born accepted Schroedinger's wave mechanics but would not agree with his physical interpretation of material waves, smeared electrons, etc. After all, one could count individual electrons with Geiger counters, and see their tracks in cloud chambers. For his part, Schroedinger made no secret of his dislike for quantum jumps and wanted to return to a classical line of thinking. But Born was insistent and asserted:

> It is necessary to drop completely the physical pictures of Schroedinger which aim at a revitalisation of the classical continuum theory, to retain only the formalism and to fill that with new physical content.

Wave functions, matrices, Schroedinger's equations are all part of the *technology* of QM. Methodology is very important no doubt but from a philosophical point of view, *the introduction of the probabilistic interpretation by Max Born was a clear turning point*. One could no longer apply causality to *individual* events. According to QM, it is only the *probability distribution of events that is determined causally*. And yet, at least at that time, Born's contribution was often ignored. To Niels Bohr, the interpretation of the wave function was "obvious" once Schroedinger had demonstrated the equivalence between wave mechanics and matrix mechanics. "We had never dreamt it could be otherwise," Bohr said. Reflecting on the mood of the times, Sir Neville Mott later observed, "I worked in Copenhagen in 1928 and it was already called the 'Copenhagen interpretation'—I do not think I ever realised that Born was the first to put it forward".

For years Born remained bitter about all this and as late as 1953 he wrote in one of his letters to Einstein, "in those days he [Heisenberg] actually had no idea what a matrix was. It was he who reaped all the rewards of our work together, such as the Nobel Prize". To be fair to Heisenberg, he was not happy when he learnt that Born and Jordan would not share with him the Prize awarded for the discovery of QM. In fact, Born himself acknowledged receiving a "kind letter" from Heisenberg when the Prize was announced. Born felt he was overlooked possibly on account of the resistance to the probabilistic interpretation from many eminent people which included Einstein, Schroedinger, Planck and de Broglie. Lorentz, for example, wrote to Ehrenfest: "I care little for the conception of $\psi\psi^*$ as a probability". Added to this was the "hijacking" of his idea by the "Copenhagen school which lends its name almost everywhere to the line of thinking I [Born] originated". Finally in 1954 Born was honoured with the Nobel Prize "for his fundamental research, especially for his statistical interpretation of the wave function". Later Heisenberg said, "I was so relieved".

7.11 History of spin

As I have indicated earlier, spin (electron) is a quantum mechanical entity although one was led to the idea by first considering an electron that was physically spinning. Prior to the formal discovery of spin, one knew that the electron could have an orbital angular moment $l\hbar$. Depending on the orbit occupied, l would assume a suitable integer value. Associated with l was a magnetic quantum number m_l whose allowed values were $-l, (-l+1), \ldots, -1, 0, 1, \ldots (l-1), l$.

The hydrogen atom is exceptionally simple in that it has only one electron. While analysing the spectra of multi-electron atoms, it was empirically found necessary to have two angular momenta instead of just one. This was explained away by assuming that one of these referred to the "inner" group of electrons or the "core", and the other to the "outer" group of electrons.

Meanwhile Alfred Landé discovered that in the presence of a magnetic field H, the energy E_i of level i of an atom would change by

$$\Delta E_i = mg\mu H \tag{7.17}$$

where

$$\mu = \frac{eh}{4\pi m_e c} \tag{7.18}$$

denotes the *magnetic moment* of the electron, and g is called the *Landé g factor*. One would have thought that the magnetic quantum number m would be an integer but from an analysis of experimental data, Landé found that for alkali atoms it had to be a half-integer. Heisenberg independently got the same idea but did not publish it since his teacher Sommerfeld disapproved. At this stage, Pauli came pretty close to the modern idea of spin. Discussing the anomalous Zeeman effect he observed that it was due to a "peculiar not classically describable two-valuedness of the quantum theoretical properties of the electron". But it was Goudsmit and Uhlenbeck who in October 1925 categorically asserted that the electron actually possessed an *extra degree of freedom* which resulted in an *intrinsic* angular momentum ($\hbar/2$). Shortly thereafter, Bohr went on a trip visiting many centres. At Hamburg Pauli met Bohr and asked him what he [Bohr] thought about spin. Bohr said it was "very very interesting", which was his way of conveying that there was something wrong! Bohr then went to Leiden in Holland where after a long discussion with Ehrenfest he became converted to the idea of spin. This is not surprising because Ehrenfest was something of a father figure to physicists in Holland, and Uhlenbeck and Goudsmit had done their work under Ehrenfest's watchful eye. On his return journey to Copenhagen, Bohr stopped at Gottingen where Heisenberg and Jordan asked him what he thought about spin. This time Bohr replied that it was a great advance. Bohr continued his journey and at Berlin where the train halted for a short while, he was met by Pauli who had specially gone to Berlin from Hamburg to ask Bohr once more what he thought about spin. This time Bohr repeated his comment made to Heisenberg namely, that spin was a great idea whereas Pauli expected Bohr to say "very, very interesting". Annoyed at Bohr's change of attitude Pauli made a sarcastic comment! But soon Pauli accepted spin.

7.12 The Dirac equation, quantum fields and all that

We come to the last part of the great drama enacted during those golden years. The principal actor now is Dirac. I have already narrated how Dirac had independently discovered many of the results obtained by the Gottingen group. But he did not stop there; in fact, his best was yet to come.

In May 1926, Dirac received the Ph.D. degree. Meanwhile, there was the spate of papers from Schroedinger. At first Dirac was cool to them but soon he became more favourably disposed. In August of that year he related the wave function (of a many-particle system) to quantum statistics, and clarified the properties it must have in the case of Bosons on the one hand and Fermions on the other (i.e., the connection between the symmetry properties of the wave function and the statistics of the particles). In September, Dirac went to Copenhagen. Bohr and Dirac had met earlier in 1925 in Cambridge and about this meeting Dirac once recalled:

> People were pretty well spell bound by what Bohr said ... While I was very much impressed by him, his arguments were mainly of a qualitative nature and I was not able to really pinpoint the facts behind them. What I wanted was statements which could be expressed in terms of equations, and Bohr's work very seldom provided such statements.

It was the same story in September 1926. Bohr and Dirac went for long walks during which Bohr did all the talking and Dirac did all the listening! But Dirac was not idle. First he worked out the theory of canonical transformations in QM, now known as transformation theory. A few months later (February, 1927), he published a paper entitled *The Quantum Theory of the Emission and Absorption of Radiation*, laying the foundations of quantum electrodynamics. In the introduction he says:

> The new quantum theory, based on the assumption that the dynamical variables do not obey the commutative law of multiplication, has by now been developed sufficiently to form a fairly complete theory of dynamics. One can treat mathematically the problem of any dynamical system composed of a number of particles with instaneous forces acting between them, provided it is describable by a Hamiltonian function, and one can interpret the mathematics physically by a quite definite general method. On the other hand, hardly anything has been done up to the present on quantum electrodynamics ...

Dirac fills this gap. It was a non-relativistic theory no doubt but for the first time there was a theory which could be used for calculating all the results connected with the emission and absorption of light by atoms, results which were obtained earlier by unreliable arguments. Later this theory would be improved, but already this version of quantum electrodynamics (QED I) was beginning to make waves.

In February 1927, Dirac returned to England and turned his attention to finding the relativistic version of the Schroedinger equation. This was an obvious problem to tackle and many people had a go at it, including Schroedinger himself. When Bohr met Dirac in October 1927 during a conference, he asked the latter what he [Dirac] was working on. Dirac replied that he was trying to construct a relativistic theory of the electron. Bohr then said, "But Klein has already solved that problem". The reference here is to an equation now known as the

Klein–Gordon (KG) equation. Dirac disagreed because the solution of the KG equation did not satisfy the requirements of his transformation theory which to him was his "pet darling". Finally, in early 1928 Dirac presented the world with the now famous Dirac equation. According to Dirac, a great deal of his work was "just playing with equations and seeing what they give". In this case it led him to the jackpot! It should be mentioned that many people had hit upon the KG equation more or less at the same time, and despite its name, Schroedinger discovered it earlier. For a while it (KG equation) was eclipsed by the Dirac equation but later found a niche of its own as it could relativistically describe spin 0 particles.

The Dirac equation was a tremendous achievement because so much was derived from that equation. In fact, Dirac once said that the Dirac equation was more intelligent than its author! But a new mystery arose. In early 1927 Pauli had shown how to handle spin in quantum mechanics via the Pauli matrices and all that. No doubt it was still non-relativistic QM but one could now explain things like the anomalous Zeeman effect. But where did spin come from? That became clear from Dirac's equation for the electron. But here is also where mystery entered the picture. Guided by Pauli, one expected a ψ with two components whereas Dirac offered a wave function with four components. What was the physical meaning of four components?

From Chapter 3 you know the answer—it has to do with the positron. Here let me add a few historical footnotes. In a sense I have to narrate two stories (somewhat in parallel) because the story of the positron is also tied up with the story of various complications in quantum electrodynamics (QED).

We start with Born and Jordan (recall Chapter 6) who made the first attempt to apply QM to radiation. They regarded Maxwell's equations as "matrix equations" and referred to the outcome as "matrix electrodynamics". This was in September 1925.

November 1925: Born, Heisenberg and Jordan (BHJ) take a closer look at radiation. In 1909, Einstein had calculated the energy fluctuations in a cavity filled with electromagnetic radiation in thermal equilibrium. BHJ repeat that old calculation but using their method, i.e., the new matrix mechanics. In the old quantum theory, one visualised an oscillator (of say frequency ν) as being excited to levels with quantum numbers 0, 1, 2, ... n ... BHJ now declare that the quantum number n is equal to the number of quanta with frequency ν. The state of the radiation field is thus specified by them by giving the number of quanta corresponding to the various frequencies. This is the *occupation number representation.* Using this language, they are able to make a direct connection with Bose statistics (as applied to photons).

This change of outlook is important. Whereas earlier one had an oscillator which could be excited to various states, one now had a problem with varying numbers of particles. In other words, there was a jump from a one-body problem to a *n*-body problem, *n* being variable. An even better way of saying it is that there is a jump from a problem with one degree of freedom to a problem with many degrees of freedom, in fact infinite degrees of freedom in the case of radiation. Quantum restrictions had to be imposed *afresh* on this many-body problem and this step is referred to as *second quantisation.*

January 1927: Dirac is in Copenhagen and about to return to England after a stay of several months. He writes his first paper on quantum electrodynamics which Bohr communicates to the Royal Society for publication in its Proceedings. (Reference has already been made to this paper earlier.)

Mid 1927: Jordan and Klein ask: "Earlier Einstein considered a gas of Bose particles, i.e., had studied a gas assuming that atoms obeyed Bose–Einstein [BE] statistics. How does one deal with the quantum mechanics of a collection of such particles?" The answer, they found, lay in replacing the collection of particles by a suitable field $\psi(\mathbf{r}, t)$ rather like in fluid mechanics where continuous fields of density, pressure, etc., are considered in place of discrete atoms. ψ satisfies a Schroedinger equation as usual. Now the Schroedinger equation merely delivers a ψ but this was not enough if this ψ has to represent a *particle field*, i.e., have a *many-body* character. To achieve the latter, an appropriate quantum condition, i.e., suitable commutation conditions must be imposed—see Appendix 1. Once again there is an occupation number representation, i.e., this is second quantisation as applied to a field of Bosons (with finite mass) and automatically leads to BE statistics.

Early 1928: Jordan and Wigner wonder: "Like in the earlier work of Jordan and Klein, is there a second quantisation procedure which leads to FD statistics?" And they answer: "Yes there is; it involves anti-commutators." (see Appendix 1).

Early 1928 again: Commutation relations had been established for mechanical systems and particle fields both of the Bose–Einstein and Fermi–Dirac varieties. But full compatibility with relativity had not yet been proved. Pauli and Heisenberg decide to tackle this problem.

Yet again, early 1928: Dirac announces his famous equation. It is an inspired guess about which Dirac would later say:

> It took me quite a while ... before I realised that there was no need for quantities σ... with just two rows and columns. Why not go for four rows and columns?

The Dirac equation scores many triumphs but there is also an embarassment—the negative energy solutions. Dirac comments:

> One gets over the difficulty in the classical theory by arbitrarily excluding those solutions that have a negative *E*. One cannot do this in the quantum theory ...

He then thinks these unwanted solutions have something to do with positive charge. But his theory is for the electron and a positive charge is therefore an unwelcome intruder. So he declares:

> Half of the solutions must be rejected as referring to the charge $+e$ of the electron.

A few months later, Dirac is not so sure the negative energy solutions can be summarily dismissed. Meanwhile, Heisenberg writes to Pauli:

> The saddest chapter of modern physics is and remains the Dirac theory.

October 1928: Klein and Nishina study Compton scattering (scattering of electron by photon) using the Dirac theory. They find it is necessary to keep the negative energy states since otherwise absurd answers result.
December 1928: Klein who earlier had supported Dirac theory now finds a problem with it. Bohr is totally unhappy.
May 1929: Herman Weyl declares:

> It is possible to anticipate that, of the two pairs of components of the Dirac quantity, one belongs to the electron, one to the proton.

December 1929: Dirac concurs:

> We are led to the assumption that the holes in the distribution of negative energy electrons are protons.

Years later Dirac clarified that at that time people knew only of electrons and protons, which was why he thought of protons (see also Box 7.3).

Dirac also writes a letter to Bohr explaining his ideas and in it he hints at intermediate states, virtual processes and all that—see Fig. 7.8; this is a major step forward, but also portends headaches for the future!
February 1930: Robert Oppenheimer in America has a difficulty. In Dirac's theory, the following process was allowed:

$$\text{proton} + \text{electron} \rightarrow \text{two photons},$$

assuming holes in negative theory solution imply a proton. Now a hydrogen atom consists of a proton and an electron. Thanks to the

Box 7.3 Today, our model of the atom is the following. An atom with atomic number Z and atomic mass number A has

1. Z protons in the nucleus,
2. $(A - Z)$ neutrons in the nucleus, and
3. Z orbiting electrons.

The atom as a whole is electrically neutral.
The neutron was discovered only in 1932. Prior to its discovery, people believed that the atom had

1. A protons in the nucleus,
2. $(A - Z)$ electrons in the nucleus, and
3. Z orbiting electrons.

There are more protons in the nucleus in this model, but some electrons are also put in for charge neutrality! Elementary quantum mechanical arguments show that it is impossible to have electrons in the nucleus. Anyway, after the discovery of the neutrons, there was no longer any need to visualise the existence of electrons inside the nucleus.

above reaction process, the hydrogen atom would annihilate in 10^{-10} seconds which means that there would be no hydrogen atoms in the Universe. Pauli jokes, announcing the Second Pauli Principle, according to which any theory suggested by a theoretician must be immediately applicable to the body of the author of the theory. Thus Dirac is turned into gamma rays before he can tell his idea to anybody!
April 1930: Tamm in USSR also independently concludes matter becomes unstable in Dirac's theory. He regards this as a "fundamental difficulty".
November 1930: Weyl says that according to the theory, the mass of the proton should actually be equal to that of the electron. But in reality, the proton is roughly two thousand times more massive. Clearly something wrong somewhere. Weyl adds:

> I fear that the clouds hanging over this part of the subject will roll together to form a new crisis in quantum physics.

May 1931: Taking note of all the objections to the proton idea, Dirac finally declares:

> A hole, if there were one, would be a new kind of particle, unknown to experimental physics, having the same mass and opposite charge of the electron.

Dirac refers to this particle as the *anti-electron*. Dirac further speculates:

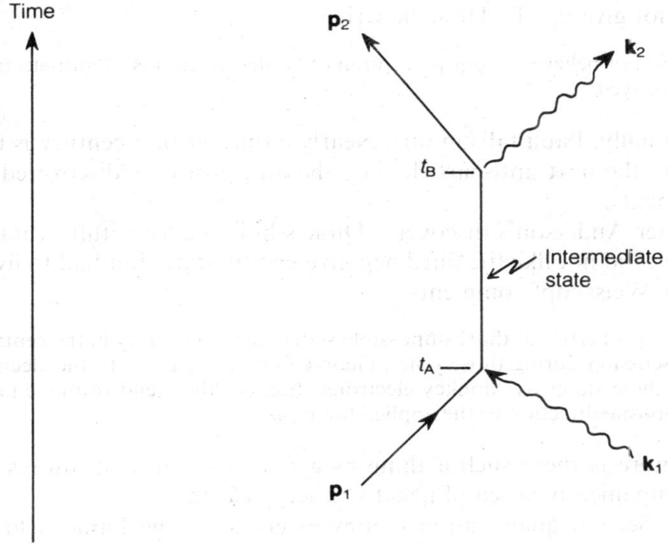

Fig. 7.8 (a) Consider the scattering of an electron by a photon. As a result of the scattering, the system, i.e., electron plus the photon, goes from an initial state ($\mathbf{p}_1$, $\mathbf{k}_1$) to the final state ($\mathbf{p}_2$, $\mathbf{k}_2$). Here $\mathbf{p}_1$ and $\mathbf{p}_2$ denote the momenta of the electron (in the two states) and $\hbar\mathbf{k}_1$ and $\hbar\mathbf{k}_2$ the momenta of the photons before and after scattering. The scattering occurs via an intermediate state in which there is no photon. It is as if the incoming electron has "swallowed" the incoming photon at time t_A, only to emit another photon at time t_B. The Dirac equation allows intermediate states; and with it, Pandora's box was also opened! Diagrams like this are referred to as Feynman diagrams. We will see plenty of them in Part II.

> I think it is probable that negative protons can exist, since as far as the theory is yet definite, there is a complete and perfect symmetry between positive and negative electric charge, and if this symmetry is really fundamental in nature, it must be possible to reverse the charge on any kind of particle. The negative protons would of course be much harder to produce experimentally, since a much larger energy would be needed.

In other words, Dirac now asserts that his hole states actually refers to positrons. He also admits the possibility that like the electron, the proton too could have an anti-particle namely, the anti-proton. Antiparticles thus finally make their entry into physics but Pauli is unhappy, he writes:

> We do not believe that this way [holes and positrons] should be seriously considered.

1932: Carl Anderson detects the positron (see Box 3.3) but Pauli would still not give up! To Dirac he writes,

> I do not believe in your perception of "holes" even if the "anti-electron" is proved.

Eventually, Pauli falls in line. Nearly a quarter of a century is to pass before the next anti-particle, i.e., the anti-proton is discovered in experiments.

After Anderson's discovery, Dirac's hole theory is fully vindicated. People did not like the filled negative-energy states but had to live with them. Weisskopf comments:

> The properties of those impossible states were constantly in the centre of discussion during those years. George Gamow referred to the electrons in these states as "donkey electrons" because they tend to move in the opposite direction to the applied force.

No more is there such a thing as a free electron as it always comes accompanied by a sea of negative energy electrons.
1934: Second quantisation is now extended to the Dirac field and a description is given of the interaction between this field and the quantised electromagnetic field.

In a sense, this last step was the culmination of a journey that started with Kirchhoff almost a century earlier. But unfortunately, things did not quite work out that way. The "new, improved" version of QED (as compared to the earlier 1927 version)—QED II—brought in its wake the "problem of infinites". This prompted Pauli to comment: "Success [presumably Anderson's discovery of the positron] seems to have been on the side of Dirac rather than of logic". The problem of the infinities and how it was tackled is discussed in Part II.

7.13 A rapid overview

I have crowded you with so much information in the last two chapters that maybe I should survey it once over again. This is done in Figs. 7.9 and 7.10. The first of these is essentially a diary of events while the second is a flow sheet indicating the evolution of ideas (see also Appendix 2).

7.14 Mystery resolved

In the last chapter, I made several references to the so-called oscillator mystery. Once Dirac's pioneering paper on QED appeared (in 1927), this mystery vanished. Let me explain how.

We start with Fig. 7.11(a) which shows schematically the energy levels of an atom. Let us say we are interested in the spectral line associated with the transition shown by the arrow. During this transition, the atom emits radiation of frequency $\nu_{32} = (E_3 - E_2)/h$ which then enhances the energy of the radiation field. Now the field is itself quantised as shown in Fig. 7.11(b). Thus the emission of a photon of

1913	Bohr Model
1916–1917	Einstein: A and B coeff.
1921	Landé: Half integer quantum no.
1923	Compton effect de Broglie: duality
1924–Jan	BKS paper
July	Bose statisfics
July	Bose condensation
1925–Jan	Pauli: Exclusion principle
July	Heisenberg: Matrix mechanics
Sept	Born–Jordan paper
Oct	Discovery of spin
Nov	BHJ and Dirac: Quantum algebra
1926–Jan	H atom solved using matrix mechanics Schroedinger's first paper
1926–Feb	Fermi statistics
June	Born: $\lvert\psi\rvert^2$ interpretation
Aug	Dirac: Relation between ψ and spin; wave function symmetry
Oct	Photon named
1927–Jan	Dirac: QED I
March	Pauli matrices Uncertainty principle
Sept	Bohr: complementarity
Oct	Jordan–Klein: Quantisation of Boson field Jordan–Wigner: Quantisation of Fermion field
1928	Dirac equation
1929	Hole theory
1931	Dirac proposes e^+. Positron discovered
1933	QED II

Fig. 7.9 A diary of events connected with the birth of quantum mechanics.

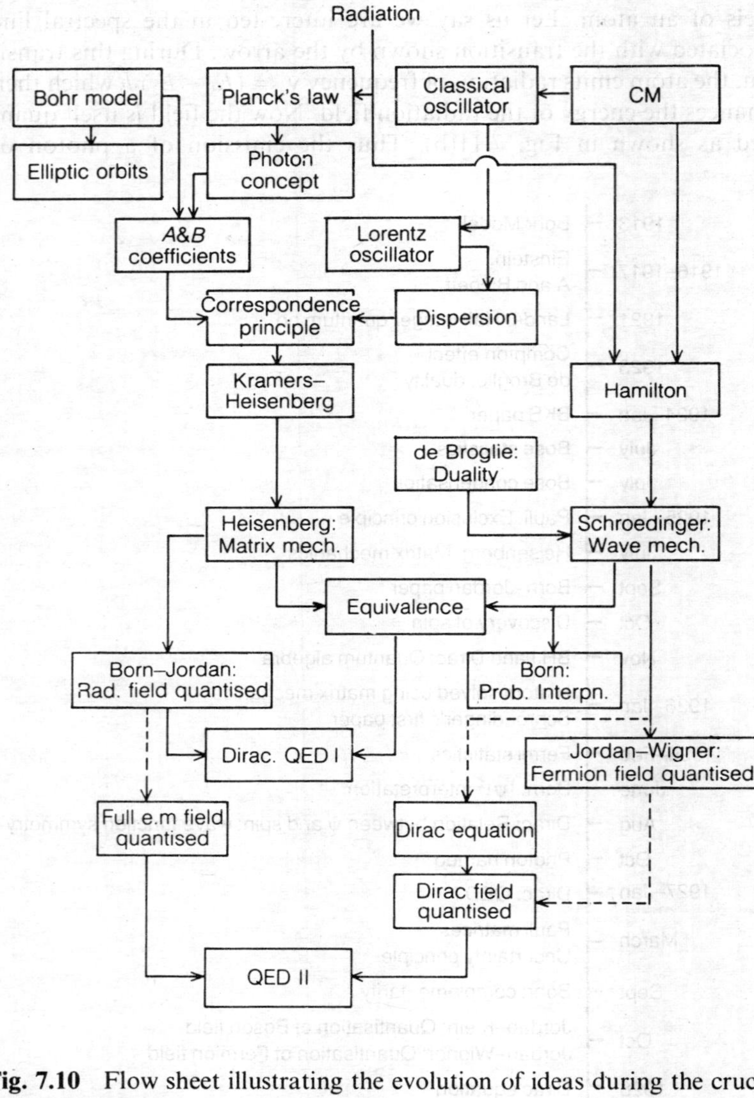

Fig. 7.10 Flow sheet illustrating the evolution of ideas during the crucial period 1925–1934.

frequency ν_{32} can cause various types of transitions in the radiation field some of which are illustrated in Fig. 7.11(c). When many atoms are present, it is likely that several of them simultaneously emit photons of frequency ν_{32}. For example, if two photons are emitted

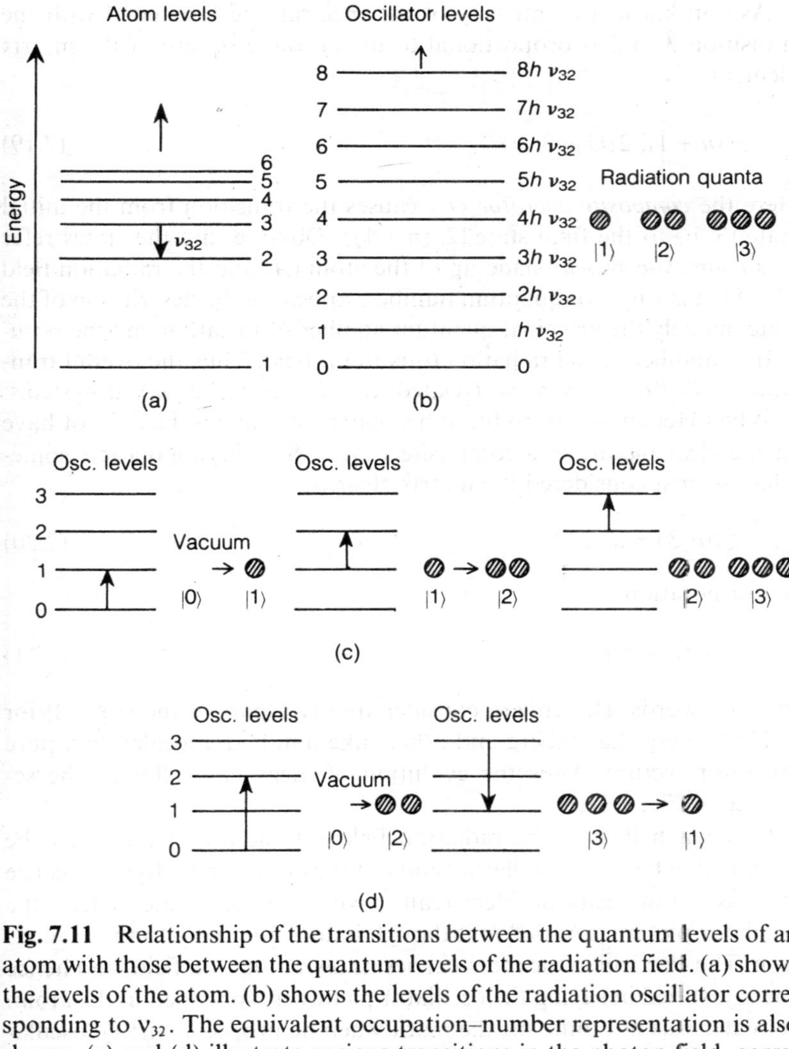

Fig. 7.11 Relationship of the transitions between the quantum levels of an atom with those between the quantum levels of the radiation field. (a) shows the levels of the atom. (b) shows the levels of the radiation oscillator corresponding to ν_{32}. The equivalent occupation–number representation is also shown. (c) and (d) illustrate various transitions in the photon field, corresponding to one and two photon processes respectively (of frequency ν_{32}).

simultaneously, there would be a two-photon transition in the radiation field as in Fig. 7.11(d). We must of course remember, as was first stressed by Born, Heisenberg and Jordan, that a radiation oscillator excited to level n really implies that there are n photons present (occupation–number representation).

As you know, the intensity of the spectral line associated with the transition $3 \to 2$ is proportional to the absolute square of the matrix element

$$\langle (n+1);\, 2 | \hat{O}_{AR} | 3;\, n \rangle \tag{7.19}$$

Here the *composite operator* $\hat{O}_{AR}$ causes the transition from the initial state $|3;\, n\rangle$ to the final state $|2;\, (n+1)\rangle$. Observe that the states refer to a *composite system* made up of the atom (A) and the radiation field (R). That is why two quantum numbers appear in the description of the state, namely the principal quantum number of the atom and the occupation number of the radiation (quantum) field. Thus the overall transition in (7.19) involves two (related) transitions in the two subsystems.

When Heisenberg introduced his matrix mechanics, he did not have such a clear picture of a composite system. Simplifying matters somewhat, he just considered the matrix element

$$\langle 2 | \hat{a} | 3 \rangle = a_{32}\,. \tag{7.20}$$

In our notation,

$$\hat{a} \sim \langle n+1 | \hat{O}_{AR} | n \rangle. \tag{7.21}$$

In other words, Heisenberg considered only a part of the story. Prior to Heisenberg, Ladenberg and others like him had appealed to a pure oscillator picture. Thus the evolution of ideas has followed the sequence in Fig. 7.12.

In a nutshell, it is the radiation field (of the atom) that must be described in terms of oscillators and not the atom itself. However, since the spectral intensity problem really involves a composite system, the oscillator picture is buried in it though it does not apply to the atom as such. The electron in the atom carries its own radiation field, and hence one is justified in saying the oscillator picture is embedded in the atom. So Slater was not quite off the mark when he proposed virtual oscillators and a virtual radiation field (recall Chapter 6).

The story is thus rather like that of the blind men describing the elephant. Here the "elephant" is the composite system. Prior to Dirac, some people like Ladenberg "felt" the oscillator part of the "elephant" while Einstein "felt" the atomic part. By hindsight we are now able to see the entire picture and there is no longer any mystery.

One final remark. According to the 1927 paper of Dirac (QED I), transitions occur due to perturbations caused by the interaction between the atom and the radiation field. Suppose we have an isolated

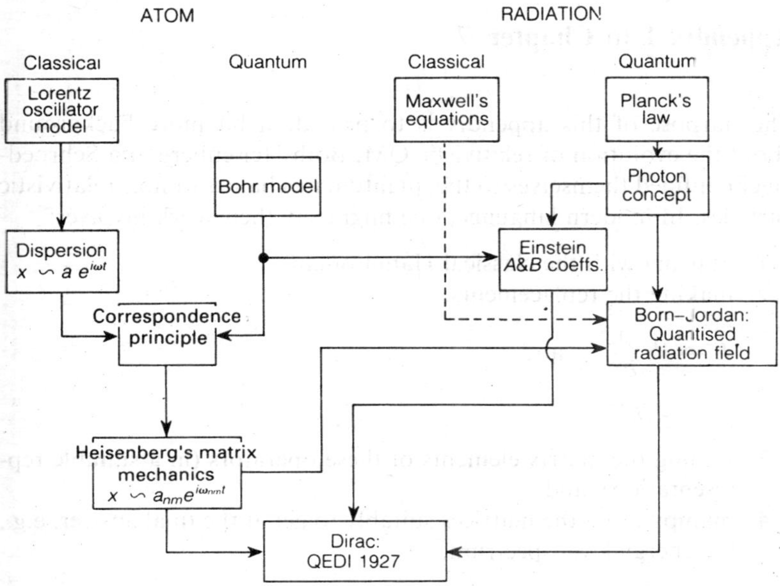

Fig. 7.12 Flow chart showing the evolution of ideas concerning the atom and the emission of radiation by the atom.

atom. How do transitions occur in it? In other words, how do we explain the spontaneous emission of light by atoms in the absence of an *external* radiation field? That also is now clear. As already mentioned, no electron is really isolated since it generates its own radiation field; and the *latter can react back with the atom*, causing transitions.

One would have thought that with all this enlightenment (i.e., QED II–see Fig. 7.10), everybody would have been happy. Not quite because new problems arose in the study of the interaction between the electron and the radiation field. Dirac became so frustrated by these problems that he remarked:

> We have to give up quantum electrodynamics ... we may give it up without regrets—in fact because of its extreme complexity, most physicists will be glad to see the end of it.

Reflecting on the mood of the times Heisenberg later recalled:

> Up till that time [1928] I had the impression that in the quantum theory we had come back into the harbour, into the port. Dirac's paper threw us out into the sea again.

How and when the ship returned again to port is reserved for description in Part II.

Appendix 1 to Chapter 7

The purpose of this appendix is to provide a bit more background about the evolution of relativistic QM. Both Heisenberg and Schroedinger confined themselves to the quantum mechanics of non-relativistic particles. In modern language, one might say their work involves:

1. Starting with the classical Hamiltonian,
2. making the replacements,

   $E \to i\hbar \dfrac{\partial}{\partial t}$ and

   $p \to - i\hbar \nabla$,

3. finding the matrix elements of these operators (in a suitable representation), and
4. manipulating the matrices suitably to get at the final answer, e.g., the energy level spectrum.

This scheme works beautifully provided (i) one does not consider electromagnetic fields and (ii) the particles do not travel at speeds close to *c*. Obviously such simplifying assumptions cannot always be made. What one needs therefore is a mathematical framework wherein

1. relativistic effects are included, and
2. the electromagnetic field is treated in a full-fledged quantum mechanical manner.

But this is not enough. The integrated electromagnetic field cum matter theory must be Lorentz-covariant. Let not these fancy words frighten you! In the companion volume *At the Speed of Light*, I have explained that Einstein's special theory of relativity requires that the laws of physics remain the same as one goes over from one intertial frame say, *S* to another say, *S′* which is moving at a uniform velocity with respect to *S*. In practical terms this implies that there are certain rules called Lorentz transformations which must be obeyed when one relates physical quantities like position, velocity, time, etc., in *S* to the corresponding quantities in *S′*. Producing a Lorentz-covariant quantum mechanical theory of matter *and* radiation has turned out to be a difficult task. An added complication is that the Dirac equation for the electron is really an equation for an infinite number of particles. Therefore, one has to describe this assembly by a particle field, quantise the particle field and then allow this particle field to interact with the quantum electromagnetic field—all in self-consistent and Lorentz-covariant manner. At this point, it becomes a rather tall order! About all these complications Heisenberg once remarked:

> You know, it was not like quantum mechanics. In quantum mechanics—everything came out much simpler and much better than what I expected. Somehow when you touched it and you had a diagreeeable difficulty, at the end you still said "Well, was it that simple?" Here in electrodynamics, it didn't become simple.

There have been many milestones, on the long road to QED. I cannot list all of them but for historical completeness, I should mention the following:

1. ***1925–1926***: Development of non-relativistic QM by Heisenberg and Schroedinger.
2. ***Mid-1926***: Schroedinger extends his equation to the relativistic case. Several others propose the same equation which today is known by the name *Klein–Gordon equation.* But with this equation, there were difficulties in the probabilistic interpretation. The Klein–Gordon equation is temporarily given up. (Later it bounced back in a manner of sorts.)
3. ***January 1927***: Dirac publishes his paper on QED [version I]. Marriage between radiation and QM but with no relativity. It is a kind of hybrid theory but good enough for getting first-order answers to many problems like emission and absorption.
4. ***May 1927***: Pauli modifies Schroedinger equation to tackle the interaction of the electron with an external magnetic field. The interaction arises on account of the magnetic moment of the electron, which in turn is a consequence of the spin. The modified equation is called the *Pauli equation.* The electron wave function now acquires two components, and Pauli matrices are needed to deal with them.
5. ***Late 1927***: Dirac equation discovered. Two components became four components but it is still looked upon as a theory for a single particle.
6. ***1928—1934***: Melting pot. Positron proposed and discovered. One particle theory now becomes an infinite particle theory. There thus emerges a new field, the *Dirac field.*
7. ***1934***: Dirac field quantised. Interaction between matter and radiation now involves interaction between two fields, the Dirac (relativistic Fermion) field and the radiation (Boson) field.
8. There is now a relativistic QED [version II] but ridden with all kinds of problems, i.e., infinities.

As mentioned in the text, the description of the battle against infinities is reserved for Part II.

Appendix 2 to Chapter 7

A few more comments on the commutator business are worth adding. We start with a single particle, for which there is the familiar result

$$[\hat{p}, \hat{q}] = (\hat{p}\hat{q} - \hat{q}\hat{p}) = -i\hbar. \tag{1}$$

When there are many particles, the commutation rules become

$$[\hat{p}_i, \hat{q}_j] = -i\hbar\, \delta_{ij}, \qquad [\hat{p}_i, \hat{p}_j] = 0, \qquad [\hat{q}_i, \hat{q}_j] = 0. \tag{2}$$

Turning next to radiation, let us consider just a single frequency $\omega (= 2\pi\nu)$. The radiation Hamilton can be written as

$$H_{\text{rad}} = \frac{1}{2}(\hat{p}^2 + \omega^2 \hat{q}^2), \quad \text{with } [\hat{p}, \hat{q}] = -i\hbar. \tag{3}$$

Define

$$a = \frac{1}{\sqrt{2h\omega}}(\omega\hat{q} + i\hat{p}), \quad a^\dagger = \frac{1}{\sqrt{2h\omega}}(\omega\hat{q} - i\hat{p}) \tag{4}$$

Then

$$H_{\text{rad}} = \hbar\omega\left(a^\dagger a + \frac{1}{2}\right), \quad [a, a^\dagger] = 1. \tag{5}$$

The quantities a and $a^\dagger$ are referred to as *annihilation* and *creation* operators for photons because they obey the rules

$$a|n\rangle = \sqrt{n}|(n-1)\rangle$$
$$a^\dagger|n\rangle = \sqrt{(n+1)}|(n+1)\rangle, \tag{6}$$

i.e., a decreases the number of photons by one whereas $a^\dagger$ increases it by one. Since the radiation field comprises of all frequencies, the radiation Hamiltonian is really a sum of oscillator terms, i.e.,

$$H_{\text{rad}} = \sum_k \frac{1}{2}(\hat{p}_k^2 + \omega_k^2 \hat{q}_k^2) \tag{7}$$

where $h\omega_k$ is the photon energy corresponding to mode k. As in (4) one can now define the operators a_k, $a_k^\dagger$ which obey the rules:

$$[a, a_k^\dagger] = 1,$$

$$[a_k, a_{k'}] = 0,\ [a_k^\dagger, a_{k'}^\dagger] = 0,\ [a_k, a_{k'}^\dagger] = 0 \quad k \neq k'. \tag{8}$$

To make it simple, I am ignoring the photon polarization.

Suppose that instead of photons, one had an assembly of Bose particles like helium atoms, say. One can now introduce a *field* $\psi(\mathbf{r}, t)$ to describe this collection of particles. The particles constituting the field can have many states k, and one can therefore introduce operators a_k, $a_k^\dagger$, which obey the same rules as in (8).

Jordan and Klein gave the commutation results in terms of ψ itself:

$$[\psi(\mathbf{r}, t), \psi^\dagger(\mathbf{r}', t)] = \delta(\mathbf{r} - \mathbf{r}')$$

$$[\psi(\mathbf{r}, t), \psi(\mathbf{r}', t)] = \psi^\dagger(\mathbf{r}, t), \psi^\dagger(\mathbf{r}', t)] = 0. \tag{9}$$

I suppose the meaning is clear. The only unfamiliar quantity is the Dirac delta function $\delta(\mathbf{r} - \mathbf{r}')$ which is an extension of the discrete Kronecker delta δ_{ij} to the continuous case. In practical terms, all it implies is that the commutator of ψ and $\psi^\dagger$ vanishes unless $\mathbf{r} = \mathbf{r}'$.

What if one has a Fermion field $\psi(\mathbf{r}, t)$ instead of a Boson field as above? Jordan and Wigner gave the answer which is

$$\{\psi(\mathbf{r}, t), \psi^\dagger(\mathbf{r}', t)\} = \delta(\mathbf{r} - \mathbf{r}')$$

$$\{\psi(\mathbf{r}, t), \psi(\mathbf{r}', t)\} = \{\psi^\dagger(\mathbf{r}, t), \psi^\dagger(\mathbf{r}', t)\} = 0 \tag{10}$$

where

$$\{\mathrm{A,B}\} = \{\mathrm{AB} + \mathrm{BA}\} \tag{11}$$

and is referred to as the *anti-commutator*. At this stage, one begins to get deeper and deeper into quantum field theory and so I shall stop! We shall come back to such matters in Part II.

A ticklish issue which has been glossed over is the question of time. Suppose $\mathbf{r}$ and $\mathbf{r}'$ refer to two observers in two different inertial frames in uniform motion with respect to each other. Then, according to special relativity, $t \neq t'$ (see the companion volume *At the Speed of Light*). The commutation relations then have to be written with greater care. This question will come up in Part II. Also, the analogues of (10) have to be written for the Dirac field.

8 *Does God Play Dice?*

> Quantum mechanics is very impressive. But an inner voice tells me that it is not yet the real thing. The theory produces a good deal but hardly brings us closer to the secret of the Old One. I am at all events convinced that *He* does not play dice.
>
> *Einstein*

At last we come to the debate between Bohr and Einstein, two towering personalities of this century who had so much to do with the revolutionary changes that physics has witnessed. Bohr and Einstein knew about each other even before they had personally met and there was also a sense of mutual admiration. As Einstein once wrote to Planck:

> Ehrenfest tells me many details from Niels Bohr's *Gedankenkuche* [thought kitchen]; his must be a first-rate mind, extremely critical and far-seeing, which never loses track of the grand design.

Bohr and Einstein met for the first time in 1920 in Berlin. It was a meeting of giants, each with his own reputation. And it was also the beginning of a life-long friendship that was deep, emotional and firm as the Rock of Gibralter, despite serious differences on matters scientific and philosophical. About this meeting Bohr later commented:

> When I had the great experience of meeting Einstein for the first time during a visit to Berlin in 1920, these fundamental questions [the problems of the old quantum theory] formed the theme of our conversations. The discussions, to which I have often reverted in my thoughts, added to all my admiration for Einstein, a deep impression of his detached attitude.

Soon after this meeting, Einstein wrote to Bohr:

> Not often in life has a human being caused me so much joy by his mere presence as you did.

To this Bohr replied:

> To meet you and to talk to you was one of the greatest experiences I ever had.

Those were years of great scientific harmony between the two. Einstein was simply swept by Bohr as is clear from his letters to his friend Ehrenfest. Soon after his first meeting with Bohr, Einstein wrote to Ehrenfest:

> Bohr was here, and I am as much in love with him as you are. He is like an extremely sensitive child who moves around in this world in a sort of trance.

Later he observed (again to Ehrenfest):

> At present, I am reading a major lecture by Bohr which makes his world of thought wonderfully clear. He is truly a man of genius. It is fortunate to have someone like that ...

People often think that the argument between Bohr and Einstein started after the discovery of quantum mechanics. Not quite, for differences between them surfaced even earlier with the BKS paper to which I have already made a reference in Chapter 6. BKS were interested in the interaction of matter with radiation and took some kind of a hybrid approach, i.e., *free* radiation was treated by the classical electromagnetic theory of Maxwell while that part of the radiation that interacted with atoms was handled in terms of exchange of quanta.

It is interesting that BKS did not wholeheartedly subscribe to the photon idea, despite Compton's discovery during the preceding year. According to them, Compton's experiment did not verify energy–momentum conservation in *individual* collisions (of the photon with the electron). Technically BKS were justified in saying this (although Compton himself used such conservation laws to derive his formula). BKS argued that the wavelength change which Compton actually measured was in fact an *average*. With the hindsight we now possess, we should not jump to the conclusion that BKS were naive. Far from it; at that time, there was in fact NO direct experimental evidence for energy–momentum conservation in individual atomic processes. Indeed, Einstein himself once briefly toyed with the idea of giving up such conservation laws.

To get back to our story, during this period (~ 1924) Bohr and Einstein did not meet; nor did they correspond. However, both Heisenberg and Pauli met Einstein and found that the latter had strong reservations about the BKS paper. In various ways though not in public, Einstein made it clear that he disagreed with BKS; and Bohr was aware that Einstein did not approve. Meanwhile, a crucial experiment by Compton and Simon showed that energy–momentum conservation *did hold* in individual collisions, knocking the bottom out of some of BKS's arguments. Bohr now had to acknowledge he was wrong. He yielded with good grace, declaring that he proposed "to give our [BKS] revolutionary proposals as honourable a funeral as possible."

The differences between Bohr and Einstein over the BKS paper was a mere flutter. Serious argument between them erupted only after the birth of quantum mechanics. As you know, Einstein was merely a bystander but he took keen interest in the rapidly unfolding developments. His views seemed to fluctuate. In December 1925, he was not too sure about Heisenberg's discovery but in March of the following year he distinctly warmed up. As he wrote in a letter,

> The Heisenberg–Born concepts leave us all breathless and have made a deep impression on all theoretically-minded people. Instead of a dull resignation, there is now a singular tension in us sluggish people.

But a little later he was not so sure. Meanwhile, Schroedinger came out with his papers, which Einstein approved.

Trouble really started with Born's interpretation of the wave function. In his very first paper on the subject Born wrote, "I myself am inclined to renounce determinism in the atomic world..." Not everyone agreed with Born, at least at that time, and the dissenters included Einstein. In a letter to Born, Einstein expressed serious doubts, adding the famous words quoted at the beginning of this chapter. Born was deeply upset by this "hard blow" but stuck to his guns. Slowly but surely, all the leading physicists were converted to Born's point of view leaving Einstein severely alone. While Einstein was becoming increasingly restive about the philosophical implications of the new discoveries, Bohr, stimulated by Born's papers, began to polish the interpretation.

In September 1927, there was a meeting in Como, Italy to which leading physicists including Bohr and Einstein were invited. Bohr attended but Einstein did not. It was during this meeting that Bohr unveiled the famous *Complementarity principle*. Dubbed later as the *Copenhagen interpretation* (CI), this became the "official" viewpoint of quantum mechanics—see also Box 8.1. Commenting on this meeting Bohr later wrote:

> The new progress in atomic physics was commented upon from various sides at the International Physical Congress held in September 1927, at Como in commemoration of Volta. In a lecture on that occasion, I advocated a point of view conveniently termed "complementarity", suited to embrace the individuality of quantum phenomena, and at the same time to clarify the peculiar aspects of the observational problem in this field of experience ... At the general discussion in Como, we all missed the presence of Einstein.

Barely a month after the Como meeting, there was again a get together of the bigwigs, this time at Brussels under the umbrella of the

Box 8.1 This is what Heisenberg has to say about Bohr's concept of complementarity.

> The resolution of paradoxes of atomic theory can be accomplished only by further renunciation of old and cherished ideas. Most important of these is the idea that natural phenomena obey exact laws—the principle of causality ... To coordinate a definite cause to a definite effect has sense only when both can be observed without introducing a foreign element disturbing their interrelation ... As a geometric or kinematic description of a process implies observation, it follows that such a description of atomic processes necessarily precludes the exact validity of the law of causality—and conversely.

Heisenberg then goes on to emphasise how Bohr stresses exclusiveness. If we try to describe events using ideas of causality we must not observe whereas if we do, then we violate causality—this is the mystery we encountered in Chapter 1. Heisenberg then paraphrases using the following chart:

CLASSICAL THEORY

Causal relationships of phenomena described in terms of space & time, i.e., causality PLUS space-time

QUANTUM MECHANICS ALTERNATIVES

Space–time description but with uncertainty principle	Causal relationships but no space–time description

Alternatives related statistically

Fifth Solvay Congress. Fireworks were expected but nothing like that happened. The sessions were pretty tame, barring one passing objection by Einstein. Outside the conference room, things were somewhat different. There was constant animated discussion in groups of two's and three's. Bohr recollects:

> Einstein had from the beginning been a most prominent figure, and several of us came to the conference with great anticipation to learn his re-

> action to the latest stage of development which, to our view, went far in clarifying the problems which he had himself from the outset elucidated so ingeniously. During the discussions ... Einstein expressed, however, a deep concern over the extent to which causal account in space and time was abandoned in quantum mechanics.

Einstein came up with many clever thought experiments (*gedanken* experiments) for highlighting the "contradictions" of quantum mechanics. Some like Pauli and Heisenberg who were firmly committed to quantum mechanics hardly paid any attention. But Bohr worried about every objection of Einstein. As he wrote later,

> Einstein's concern and criticism provided a most valuable incentive for us all to reexamine the various aspects of the situation as regards atomic phenomena.

Bohr would ponder over Einstein's arguments and try to come up with suitable answers. So serious was he in making a satisfactory presentation of his counter arguments that he "tried in those days to sketch various apparatus in a pseudo realistic style".

Figure 8.1 shows one of the sketches prepared by Bohr (possibly with some help), and is indicative of the enormous trouble he took in preparing his case. This particular figure was made in order to answer a point raised by Einstein in connection with the famous two-slit experiment. According to Bohr, Nature's rule is: "What you see depends on what you do. If in the two-slit experiment you don't spy on the particles then you will see interference. If, on the other hand, you try to locate the particles and follow their trajectories, then you will see particles

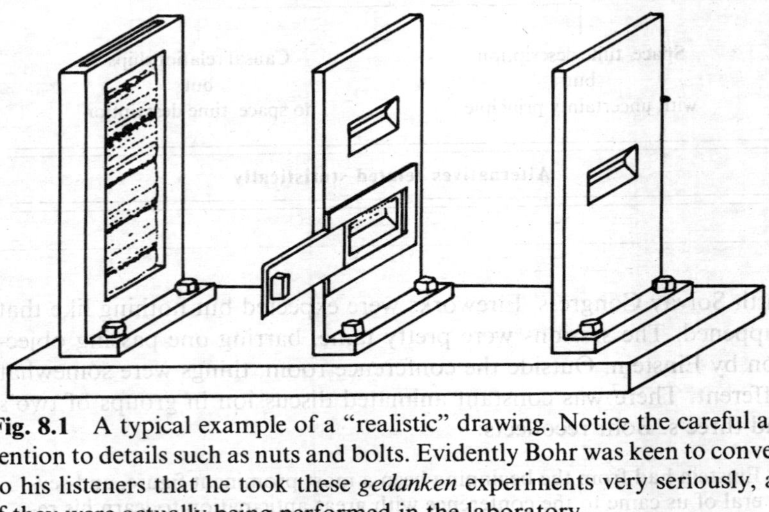

Fig. 8.1 A typical example of a "realistic" drawing. Notice the careful attention to details such as nuts and bolts. Evidently Bohr was keen to convey to his listeners that he took these *gedanken* experiments very seriously, as if they were actually being performed in the laboratory.

for sure but then you should abandon all ideas of seeing wave-like phenomena. This is complementarity or two-faced Nature, as revealed by QM".

Einstein refused to go along with this proposition. He said (in effect): "Shoot the photons (or electrons if you wish) at such a slow rate so that they arrive at the screen in singles. If you look at the screen after a long time, you see a diffraction pattern. So you must agree that the pattern has been built up by photons arriving one by one. Now every time the photon passes through the slits, it must clearly pass through only one of the slits. When it passes through the slit, it would impart a momentum to the slit arrangement. When arriving at a particular point on the target screen or the photographic plate, the momentum transferred to the slit screen would be different for the two slits (see Fig. 8.2). And by measuring the momentum, I know which slit the photon went through. So you cannot tell me that interference is produced only when we don't know anything about how photons go through the slits because here we have interference and I also know which slit the photon came through".

This was indeed a clever argument. After being down for a while Bohr finally answered it by presenting the apparatus in Fig. 8.3. He said (in effect): "Professor Einstein. There is a little problem. Allow me to use the apparatus here to measure the momentum imparted to a slit as the particle passes through it. According to you, the momentum of the slit would give an idea of the deflection of the particle. Granted. I suppose you would measure the momentum of the slit by seeing how much the pointer moves in one second. Therefore, you have to take two pointer readings one second apart. Agree? Fine! You see Professor, this is where the problem arises. When you take a pointer reading, you are looking at the scale and trying to measure a coordinate. But that process would upset the momentum of the scale and therefore also of the slit. In short, the momentum of the slit would be altered to a different value which has no relation to what it was earlier. You are trying to determine the slit through which the photon went from a knowledge of the momentum and you are trying to determine that momentum by taking a pointer reading. However, the very act of taking the pointer reading disturbs the slit and alters whatever momentum it might have acquired when the particle went through. Therefore, you cannot (in the two-slit experiment) ever say what the deflection of the particle is and through which slit it arrived at the screen".

Einstein was floored. In case you are wondering as to what the photon actually does, this is what Dirac has to say:

> Some time before the discovery of quantum mechanics people realised that the connection between light waves and photons must be of a statis-

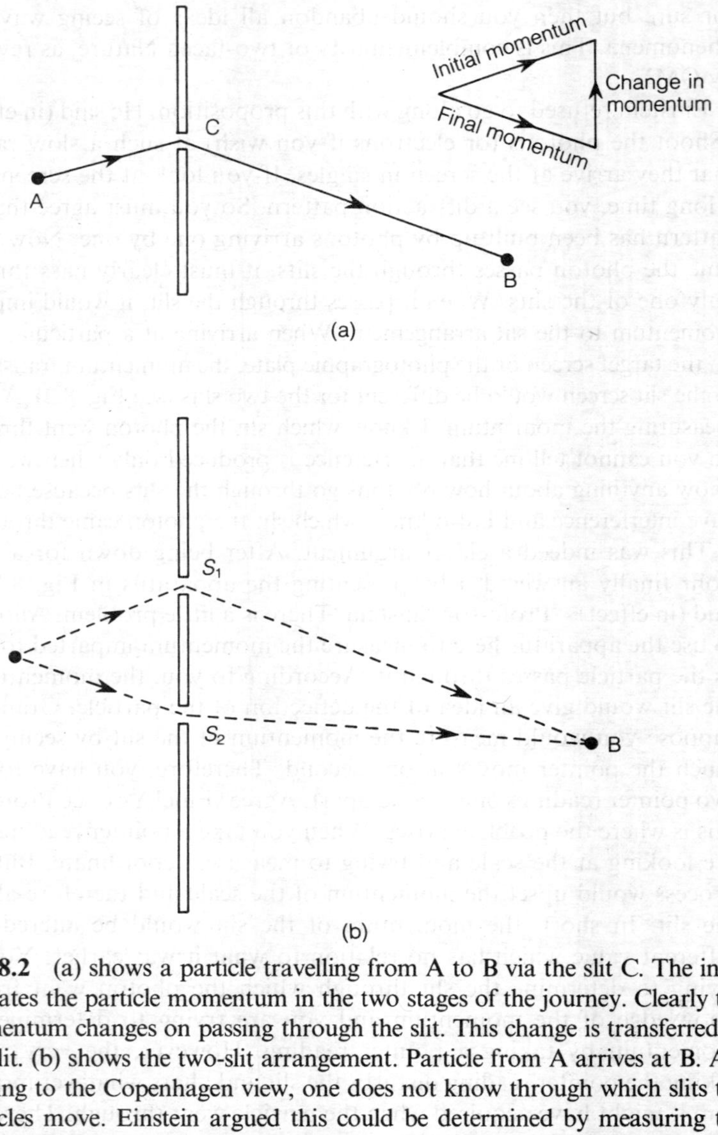

Fig. 8.2 (a) shows a particle travelling from A to B via the slit C. The inset indicates the particle momentum in the two stages of the journey. Clearly the momentum changes on passing through the slit. This change is transferred to the slit. (b) shows the two-slit arrangement. Particle from A arrives at B. According to the Copenhagen view, one does not know through which slits the particles move. Einstein argued this could be determined by measuring the momenta of the slits S_1 and S_2. Thus one gets interference even though one knows through which slit the particle came, in violation of Bohr's thesis.

tical character. What they did not clearly realise, however, was that the wave function gives information about the probability of *one* photon being in a particular place and not the probable number of photons in that place.

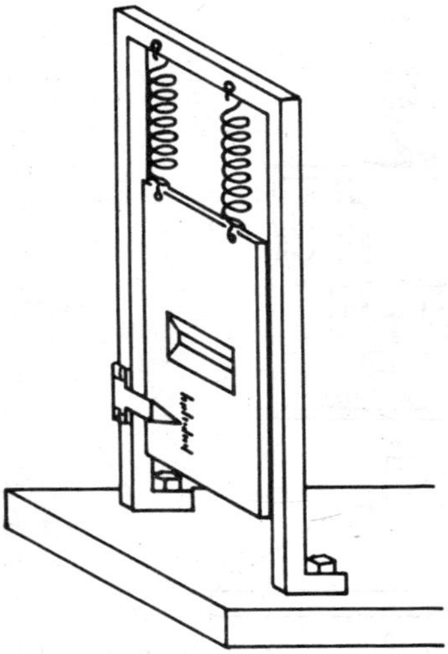

Fig. 8.3 Apparatus devised by Bohr to refute the argument of Einstein discussed in the previous figure. Bohr's counter arguments are given in the text.

Dirac goes on to add that in QM, "Each photon interferes only with itself. Interference between two different photons never occurs." This you must always remember.

To get back to the battle of the titans, it spilt over to the Sixth Solvay Congress held in 1930 because Einstein did not quite give up. His dear friend Ehrenfest chided him:

> Einstein! You are beginning to sound like the critics of your own theories of relativity. Again and again your arguments have been refuted, but instead of applying your own rule that physics must be built on measurable relationships and not on preconceived notions, you continue to invent arguments based on those same preconceived notions.

But Einstein would not give up, and this time he came up with a really clever *gedanken* experiment which had Bohr totally baffled— but only for a while. As Bohr later put it, "our discussions took quite a dramatic turn."

Einstein's argument was directed at the uncertainty rule $\Delta E \, \Delta t \geqslant h$, and may be understood with the help of Fig. 8.4—see also Box 8.2. According to him, since mass and energy are related, energy could be determined from the mass via the formula $E = mc^2$. Let us say we have a box (as in Fig. 8.4) equipped with a shutter and a clock. The box is lined with perfectly reflecting mirrors and contains photons. The clock is very accurate and acts as a timer. Precisely at a certain time t_1, the clock opens the shutter releasing one photon out. The shutter is closed

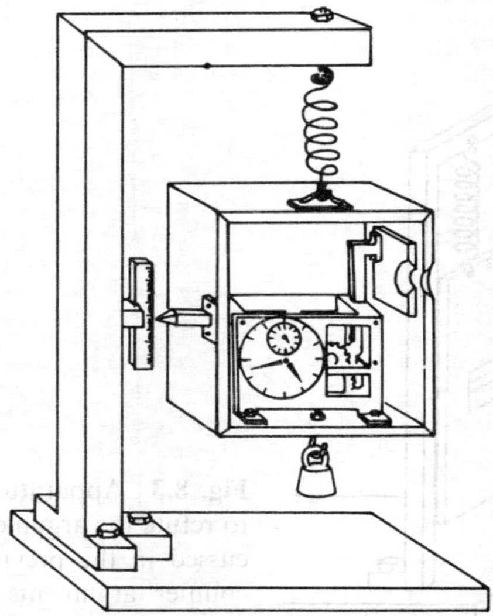

Fig. 8.4 Yet another figure prepared by Bohr. With it, Bohr silenced Einstein's technical arguments for ever. Thereafter, Einstein contested QM purely on philosophical grounds.

at time t_2 (by the clock mechanism). By making the interval $t = t_2 - t_1$ very small, we will know with high accuracy, the time when the photon escaped. In short, the error Δt in t can be made as small as we please.

How much energy went out with the photon? That is easy to determine because all we have to do is to weigh the box after the photon has escaped. From the weight we know the mass and comparing it with the mass of the box before photon escape, one knows accurately the energy of the photon.

Thus, according to Einstein, in his *gedanken* experiment both Δt and ΔE can independently be made practically zero, violating the sacred uncertainty law! Bohr was completely knocked out, at least for the moment. But he came back "fighting".

Commenting on the impact this argument (of Einstein) had on Bohr, Rosenfeld, an eyewitness, wrote:

> It was quite a shock for Bohr ... he did not see the solution at once. During the whole evening he was extremely unhappy, going from one to the other and trying to persuade that it couldn't be true, that it would be the end of physics if Einstein were right; but he couldn't produce any refutation. I shall never forget the vision of the two antagonists leaving the club: Einstein a tall majestic figure, walking quietly, with a somewhat ironic smile, and Bohr trotting near him, very excited ... The next morning came Bohr's triumph.

Box 8.2 The distinguished physicist Sir Rudolph Peierls has this to say about the rule just cited.

> The significance of this rule is not as simple as, for example, that between position and momentum. This is because time is not an observable [in QM]. A measurement of time in itself does not convey any information about any other physical system, and a statement about any other physical quantity usually implies that we are talking about its value at some particular time. In the case of a conserved quantity, such as energy of an isolated system, the result then also gives the energy at any time. Landau was fond of making this point by saying: "There is evidently no such limitation—I can measure the energy, and look at any watch; then I know both energy and time!"
>
> There are, however, a number of meaningful questions, to which the inequality [$\Delta E \Delta t > h$] provides the answer. One of these relates to the transfer of energy from one part of a physical system to another. If ΔE is the error with which we know the transferred amount of energy, and Δt the error in our knowledge of the time when this energy transfer took place, then the inequality is valid.

Bohr later recalled, "This argument amounted to a serious challenge and gave rise to a thorough examination of the problem." And out of this thorough examination came a clever counter argument, supplemented as usual with a "pseudo-realistic style" picture (see Fig. 8.4) and incorporating Einstein's device.

Bohr's argument was clever because in part, it made use of Einstein's general theory of relativity to refute Einstein! The argument went something like this: Intially the pointer is (somehow) adjusted to be at zero reading. When the photon escapes, the spring contracts, but by carefully adding weights, one can make the pointer read zero again; the weight added would then give the mass equivalent of the photon energy (i.e., E/c^2). The accuracy Δm depends on the accuracy Δq of the pointer reading. In other words, if one wants zero error in the photon energy, then one must ensure the pointer reading is exactly zero when the compensating mass is added. Say there is an unavoidable error Δq. According to Heisenberg, this would impart a momentum Δp to the box given by

$$\Delta p \sim \frac{h}{\Delta q}\,. \tag{8.1}$$

On the other hand, let t be the duration of the interval needed for adding extra weights, balancing the box and making the pointer read zero again. During this period the process of adding weights would impart a certain impulse or momentum to the box.

We assume that we measure the momentum gained with an error Δp. Since impule or force equals momentum × time, the above implies that we know the force of gravity on the box with an error of $(\Delta p/t)$, and therefore the mass of the box with an error $(\Delta p/tg)$ where g is the acceleration due to gravity. Using the relation $E = mc^2$, we then get the energy uncertainty as

$$\begin{aligned}\Delta E &= \Delta mc^2 \\ &= (\Delta pc^2/tg).\end{aligned} \tag{8.2}$$

Let us go back to the momentum uncertainty Δp. We have already seen that this implies an uncertainty Δq in the position of the box, Δq being given by

$$\Delta q \sim (h/\Delta p). \tag{8.3}$$

Now comes the crucial point: According to the general theory of relativity, the time measured on a clock is affected by the gravitational potential acting on it. During the weighing, the position of the box and therefore also of the clock inside is unknown to the extent Δq. Our knowledge of the gravitational potential is correspondingly uncertain to the extent $g\Delta q$. This causes an error $(g\Delta q/c^2)$ in the rate of the clock. Thus, at the end of the time t (taken for weighing), the reading of the clock is in error relative to the time of an outside observer by

$$\Delta t = \frac{tg\Delta q}{c^2}. \tag{8.4}$$

Therefore,

$$\begin{aligned}\Delta E{\cdot}\Delta t &\sim \frac{\Delta pc^2}{tg}\cdot\frac{tg\Delta q}{c^2} \\ &= \Delta p\Delta q \\ &\gtrsim h.\end{aligned} \tag{8.5}$$

This is the result which Einstein said did not apply; but in fact it does. In a nutshell, since the position of the clock is uncertain by a small amount because of the "kick", so is the time it measures. Einstein's gedanken experiment did not refute the uncertainty principle but rather confirmed it.

After this refutation by Bohr, Einstein stopped trying to find fault with QM. There followed another Solvay Congress in 1933 but Einstein could not attend that because he was just then in the process of migrating to America. A few months after the Solvay Congress, Bohr and Einstein met each other in America. About this Bohr recalls:

> I had an opportunity to talk with him again about epistemological aspects of atomic physics, but the difference between our ways of approach and expression still presented obstacles to mutual understanding.

Bohr and Einstein continued to meet as friends but their differences about QM were never reconciled. Almost twenty years after their first confrontation, Bohr remarked:

> Although in recent years I have had several occasions of meeting Einstein, the continued discussions, from which I have always received new impulses, have so far not led to a common view ...

And so where QM was concerned, they continued to remain apart.

Einstein no longer argued that quantum mechanics was wrong. He grudgingly conceded that it was a good working prescription. In fact, shortly after his famous confrontation with Bohr, Einstein actually nominated Schroedinger and Heisenberg for the Nobel Prize. At the same time, he steadfastly maintained that QM was incomplete and refused to accept the view that reality was statistical. His objection was thus philosophical and no longer one concerning theoretical physics. As he put it, "I know, this business [QM] is free of contradictions, yet in my view it contains a certain unreasonableness." He firmly believed that a future theory would restore determinism and causality to what he maintained was their righful place. Such was Einstein's prestige and so high was his stature that no one dared to dismiss him as an old crackpot. On the contrary, his philosophical objections were always treated with respect, though not always accepted. Interestingly, while in the thirties Einstein was a loner battling against the CI it seems there are now a few more who are willing to question it. More about all this in Part III.

A few small footnotes before winding up this chapter. Firstly, arguments on matters concerning physics *never* came in the way of friendship between Bohr and Einstein. They were both truly great, rising above differences in their scientific viewpoints. Bohr came to India around 1960, and I vividly recall a lecture he gave to a crowded audience in the Tata Institue of Fundamental Research, Bombay. Bohr was then over seventy, and he spoke about his longstanding debate with

Einstein. He presented slide after slide of the experimental apparatus visualised by Einstein and also himself in their various *gedanken* experiments. Bohr then went on to patiently explain how Einstein was in error. The sound system wasn't good and Bohr's accent wasn't easy to follow. Frankly, I did not understand one word of what Bohr said! And yet I sat there spellbound because Bohr lectured as if the audience did not exist and as if there was Einstein sitting in front of him. In fact, when Bohr came to the end, he did not exult in joy (since his arguments upheld quantum mechanics). Instead he was in tears, unhappy perhaps about having won an argument against his dearest friend.

Abraham Pais who has written biographies of both Bohr and Einstein says that whenever one went to see Bohr, he would start talking about the twenties and the controversies of that period. At first he (Pais) was baffled but soon he began to see the relevance of these remarks of Bohr. Pais observes:

> I began to grasp not only the thread of Bohr's arguments but also their purpose. Just as in many sports a player goes through warming-up exercises before entering the arena, so Bohr would relive the struggles which it took before the content of quantum mechanics was understood and accepted. I can say that in Bohr's mind this struggle started all over every single day... Einstein appeared forever as his leading spiritual partner—even after the latter's death he would argue with him as if Einstein were still alive.

This is precisely what I witnessed in 1960.

I began this chapter with a quote from Einstein, taken from one of his letters to Max Born. Let me end the chapter quoting what Born said in reply:

> If God has made the world a perfect mechanism, He has at least conceded so much to our imperfect intellect that in order to predict little parts of it, we need not solve innumerable differential equations, but can use dice with fair success.

Years later Stephen Hawking remarked:

> God not only plays dice, He also sometimes throws the dice where they cannot be seen!

9 *End Of Act I*

I don't know how you feel about all that you have read so far. Bewildered? Don't worry because that is a natural first reaction. Long ago Bohr said, "Those who are not shocked when they first come across quantum theory cannot possibly have understood it." Therefore take heart; may be you are on the way to understanding the subject!

Perhaps you are wondering what happened after the early thirties by which time the major discoveries had been made. In physics, periods of great triumph are sometimes followed by spells during which there is a feeling that it is all over. After the grand successes of the last century, many leading lights then felt that physics had come to an end. Fortunately for us, and for physics as well, they all were wrong. In the early thirties there were similar forecasts. Max Born declared that physics would be over in a few months while Dirac is reported to have made the famous remark, "The rest is all chemistry." What Dirac meant was that since the tools required for exploring the microscopic world had been assembled, all that remained was to use them. One could use them, for example, to explain the formation of compounds, chemical reactions and their rates, the spectra of molecules, and the like. All very useful no doubt and great addition to human knowledge as well, but none of it required any new and as yet undiscovered principle of physics. Seen this way, it did appear as if one already had everything that was needed to explain Nature.

Many in fact rushed to apply QM to whatever they could lay their hands on. Chemistry opened up in a big way exactly as Dirac had predicted, especially after the appearance of a classic book by Pauling (later to win the Nobel Prize) and Wilson which explained QM to chemists. Max Born went back to his old love lattice dynamics, and rewrote it all in modern quantum language. Eugene Wigner a new star on the horizon not only added an elegant touch by introducing the methods of group theory into QM, but also showed the way for understanding the detailed behaviour of electrons in crystalline solids. That piece of theoretical work later proved immensely useful not only in understanding the transistor, but also in the theory of nuclear reactors.

In spite of all such applications of standard QM, it was not "all chemistry" as Dirac had predicted. In fact right in his own backyard, i.e., Cambridge, new vistas in physics were being opened up by Rutherford and his students. Momentous discoveries were made about the nucleus and about elementary particles, and physics was far from over.

What were the big guns doing in the thirties? Einstein had migrated to America. Comfortably ensconced in the Institute for Advanced Studies in Princeton, he devoted all his time to developing a unified theory of electromagnetism and gravity. Max Born too emigrated, moving to Edinburgh (via Cambridge and Bangalore) where he became engrossed in his theory of lattice dynamics. And Niels Bohr, having made sure that the interpretation of QM was secure, turned his attention to nuclear physics. So did Pauli, Heisenberg and several others, though they were all concerned with different aspects of the subject.

While all this was going on, war clouds began to gather over Europe. Adolf Hitler took charge of Germany and not only converted it into a powerful war machine but also unleashed a reign of terror against Jews. In the midst of all this, Hahn and Strassman discovered *nuclear fission* in 1939. They found that when uranium was bombarded with neutrons, the uranium nucleus split into two large and massive fragments of comparable size. Soon it was noticed that when uranium fissioned, neutrons were emitted during the process. Imagination now began to race. Could the neutron emitted during a fission be used to create another fission? Could the neutron emitted in that be used again in a similar fashion? Could this be made to go on indefinitely, i.e., could one have a *nuclear chain reaction*? Could this chain reaction be controlled? Can the chain reaction also be made to occur suddenly and explosively if required? How exactly did fission occur? What were the values of the nuclear parameters connected with fission?

Physicists in various labs competed with each other to be the first with the answers. But all along, the non-German physicists were also deeply worried. What if Hitler got wind of all this and decided to go for the nuclear bomb? So, soon they imposed a voluntary censorship on themselves and stopped publishing results about fission.

Meanwhile war broke out in Europe and Hitler rapidly ran over most of the Western countries. America was still officially neutral but its sympathy was solely with the Allies (Britain, France and the Soviet Union). The western scientists felt that it was time to alert their governments, and Einstein was roped in for persuading the American government to build the atom bomb (see the companion volume on relativity for that story). Roughly around this time, the Japanese attacked the American naval base in Hawaii, and America now entered the war. Meanwhile the atom bomb project got sanctioned and work picked up in earnest.

In December 1942, Enrico Fermi demonstrated that a controlled nuclear chain reaction was possible; the next step was the bomb itself. To build it, a galaxy of super stars was assembled at Los Alamos in New Mexico under the leadership of J.R. Oppenheimer, a brilliant theoretical physicist and a distinguished scholar. Among those who gathered there were Von Neumann, Stanley Ulam (both top class mathematicians), Enrico Fermi, Rabi, Lawrence, Segre, Bethe, Bohr, Wigner, Feynman ... Some had already won the Nobel Prize while many others were to do so later.

June/July 1945: The bomb had been perfected and tested once. The war in Europe had just ended but that with Japan was dragging on. In early August the atomic bomb was dropped in quick succession, first on Hiroshima and then on Nagasaki, unleashing unimaginable terror. The world was shaken and horrified and Japan quickly surrendered. Every one rejoiced that the war was over but some like Bohr and Einstein were also worried about the advent of weapons of mass destruction.

The war concluded, it was time for the scientists to go back to the campuses. Fermi returned to Chicago, Rabi to Columbia, Bethe to Cornell and so on. The bomb was forgotten and it was back to good old physics. Soon new discoveries were made and new stars appeared on the horizon—Schwinger, Tomonaga and the incomparable Feynman. Their beautiful creation, QED, is the subject of the next part in this three-part series on the quantum revolution.

Suggestions for further reading

1. Born, M. *The Born-Einstein Letters*, MacMillan: London, 1971.
2. Cline, B.L. *The Questioners*, Crowell: New York, 1965.
3. De Broglie, L. *Matter and Light*, Norton: New York, 1939.
4. Heisenberg, W. *Physics and Philosophy*, Harper & Row: New York, 1959.
5. Heisenberg, W. *The Physicist's Conception of Nature*, Greenwood Press, Westport, Conn., 1970.
6. Heisenberg, W. *Physics and Beyond*, Harper and Row: New York, 1971.
7. Hoffman, B. *The Strange Story of the Quantum*, Peter Smith: Magnolia, Mass., 1963.
8. Polkinghorne, J.C. *The Quantum World*, Longman: London, 1984.
9. Schroedinger, E. *Science, Theory and Man*, Dover: New York, 1957.
10. Schroedinger, E. *Letters on Wave Mechanics*, Philosophical Library: New York, 1967.
11. Van der Waarden, B.L. *Sources of Quantum Mechanics*, Dover: New York, 1968.
    This is an advanced book and contains reprints of the original papers (English translations in the case of German papers). There is also an introdution.

Index

Note : Page numbers in brackets refer to illustrations.